THE THREE DIMENSIONS OF LEARNING

2

2

24. 04. 13

05. JUL 13.

D0552720

Knud Illeris

THE THREE DIMENSIONS OF LEARNING
Contemporary Learning Theory in the Tension Field between the Cognitive, the Emotional and the Social

Translated into English by
Dorothy Reader and Margaret Malone

ROSKILDE UNIVERSITY PRESS
AUGUST 2002

Knud Illeris
The Three Dimensions of Learning

1. edition 2002

© **Roskilde University Press 2002**

Typeset by: Vibeke Lihn, Roskilde University
Print: Narayana Press, Gylling, Denmark
Cover: Torben Lundsted

ISBN: 87-7867-121-3

Roskilde University Press
c/o Samfundslitteratur
Rosenoerns Allé 9
DK-1970 Frederiksberg C
Phone: +45 38 15 38 80
Fax: +45 35 35 78 22
slforlag@sl.cbs.dk
www.samfundslitteratur.dk

All rights reserved.
No part of this book may be reproduced or transmitted in any form or by
any means, electronic or mechanical, including photocopying, recording,
or any information storage or retrieval system, without permission in writing from the publisher.

Content

Preface 9

1. Learning, Learning Processes and Learning Dimensions 13
    Learning in modern society 13
    The concept and processes of learning 14
    Learning, development, socialisation, qualification, ... 16
    maturation, and ageing
    The dimensions of learning 18
    The structure of the presentation 21
    Summary 24

2. Cognitive Learning 27
    Piaget as a starting point 27
    Nissen's elaboration of Piaget's theory 32
    Kolb's learning model 37
    Summary 43

3. Reflection, Meta-Learning and Transformative Learning 45
    Learning to learn 45
    Reflection and reflexivity 46
    The cultural historical tradition and the concept of activity ... 48
    Bateson's learning theory 52
    Engeström's theory of learning by expanding 54
    Meta-learning and transformative learning 57
    Summary 60

4. Learning and Emotions 63
    The divided totality 63
    Furth's attempt to bridge the gap 64

Cognitive structures and affective patterns 69
Learning and life fulfilment..74
The resistance potential 80
Summary...84

5. Personal Development and Reflexivity 87
Learning and personal development 87
Personal development as a general qualification....................88
Late modernity and reflexivity 90
Self-experience, reflexivity and biographicity 94
Summary...97

6. When the Intended Learning does not Occur 99
Mislearning and differences 99
Resistance: conflict and potential 101
Defence, rejection, blocking and distortion 104
Everyday consciousness 106
Habits of expectations and sets of assumptions.................. 109
Late modern forms of consciousness 111
Summary... 114

7. Interaction, Social Learning and Socialisation 117
The social dimension of learning 117
Forms of interaction 119
The social embedding of learning 122
The Frankfurt School and the Hanover School 126
Lorenzer's materialistic theory of socialisation 129
Social learning, contradictions and ambivalence 132
Social learning and social responsibility 135
The heritage of the cultural historical tradition 137
Communities of practice as a framework 140
for social learning
Summary... 143

8. Experiential Learning 145
    Learning and experience 145
    Dewey's concept of experience 147
    Negt's concept of experience 150
    Learning by experience 153
    Experiential pedagogy in Denmark 155
    Summary 157

9. Learning Sequences, Learning Jumps, Stages and Models 159
    Circular, spiral and sequential models 159
    Learning jumps 163
    Stage models 165
    Learning and life course 171
    Summary 173

10. Spaces of Learning 175
    The learning situation influences the learning result 175
    Everyday learning, tacit knowledge and informal learning .. 178
    Practice learning and apprenticeship 179
    School learning is institutional learning 184
    Learning at work, organisational learning and "the learning
    organisation" 191
    Collective learning and mass psychology 197
    Summary 201

11. Learning, Motivation and Life Ages 203
    Motivational psychology 203
    Biographical research and life-span psychology 204
    Children want to capture their world 208
    Young people want to construct their own identity 212
    Adults pursue their life goals 216
    Mature adults seek richness and harmony 222
    Lifelong learning 224
    Summary 225

12. Overview 227
    Summary of the developed learning theory........................ 227
    Positions in the tension field 230
    Conclusion and perspective 238

Literature 241

The Author 259

Index of Names 261

Index of Subjects 264

Preface

The book presented here is the English version of my Danish book, "Læring". It has been given the English title "The Three Dimensions of Learning" in order to clearly emphasise the particular message of this book as opposed to the many other books that exist in the English language on the subject of learning.

The basic premise of this book is that human learning is a highly complex matter that always comprises three different dimensions – the cognitive, the emotional and the social – occurring in two processes which, while different, are always integrated: the internal acquisition process and the external interaction process between the learner and the material and social environment.

There do not appear to be any earlier learning theories that fully recognise and deal with this complexity in its entirety. In fact, the behaviourist learning theory conception that has traditionally dominated this field only deals with a very limited part of this complicated subject; other, broader theory structures may aim to capture the entirety but always seem to do so from a particular standpoint, meaning that parts of the whole are highlighted, while others fade into the background. The traditional rivalry between different schools of thought and learning approaches also seems to be very unprofitable – the various sides often talk at cross purposes, and lock themselves into positions that cannot be described as wrong, but rather as definite viewpoints.

In an attempt to break through this game, this book is based on the idea that any learning theory that has achieved a certain amount of recognition and dissemination must have something of potential value to contribute to an understanding of the whole – and therefore the structure of this book will in principle involve taking up a number of existing learning theories and examining them critically to see what contributions they can make. The dimensions previously mentioned form a structural framework for this and create a certain degree of systematism within the process – and the intention is to develop from the range of different contributions a coherent understanding of human learning both generally and in relation to existing societal conditions. I have planned and written this book in such a way as to attempt to bring together three partially differing genres:

Firstly it is a kind of *textbook* in the sense that it attempts to cover the entire breadth of the subject, describing the most important ideas in current learning theory. However, the presentations summarise only the main points of the various contributions, defining briefly the standpoint from which they were written. The main aim is to see what the contribution in question may be used for in the present context.

As well as aiming to be broadly based, the book is at the same time first and foremost presented as an academic *treatise*, in that it concerns a particular problem: that of developing and describing a coherent and comprehensive understanding of learning. For this reason I have striven to link together the various contributions into a particular perspective, and in a number of fields I have gone beyond the existing contributions and added new realisations, based partly on my own and my colleagues' extensive practical and empirical work in the education sector, and partly on the opportunities for transcendent theory developments that arise when a large amount of material is compared. A summary of the book's theoretical construction can be found in chapter 12.

Finally, the book may be defined as a *discussion book* in that it puts forward viewpoints on learning and external/societal and internal/psychological conditions for learning, which I hope will be included in some of the numerous discussions currently taking place on this subject. Last but not least, it is my hope that in setting out the complexities of learning, the book will contribute to the refutation of the many over-simplified approaches to learning that are often the basis for administrative and political decisions taken in connection with the economically-oriented rationalisations that occur in the current educational system and adjacent political areas.

I would like to thank my colleagues Søren Dupont, Birger Steen Nielsen, Lars Ulriksen and Kirsten Weber, for helping me with various sections of the book where they each have specialist knowledge, and Birgitte Simonsen, for reading the entire manuscript and advising me on many improvements. In addition, I have gained much from daily contact and discussion with my colleagues, Ph.D. students and students of educational theory at

Roskilde University. Finally, I would like to mention the great inspiration I have gained from various international contacts, particularly Professor Thomas Leithäuser (Bremen, Germany), Professor Danny Wildemeersch (Nijmegen, Holland and Leuven, Belgium), Professor Robin Usher (Melbourne, Australia), Professor Yrjö Engeström (Helsinki, Finland and San Diego, USA), and the independent writer, researcher and consultant, Dr. Etienne Wenger (N. San Juan, USA).

The Danish edition appeared in August 1999. Norwegian and Swedish editions followed, and it is a great pleasure for me now to be able to present an English edition.

Roskilde, March 2002
Knud Illeris

1. Learning, Learning Processes and Learning Dimensions

Learning in modern society

Education plays a role of growing importance in modern society, and as education is the societal institution taking care of goal-oriented *learning* this concept has also been the object of growing public and political attention. But this does not simply mean that the growing importance of education leads to a growing interest in learning. If one delves a little deeper into the matter, the growing interest in learning would rather seem to relate to rising doubt as to whether the vast resources spent on education are automatically transformed into appropriate and desired learning processes of the pupils and students. Behind this doubt there seems to lie growing uncertainty about what it actually means to learn something and the sort of learning that is suitable to meet the individual and common needs of modern society.

It has been a general and popular understanding that education by and large means that somebody teaches something which the students then learn, more or less. Even though most people to some extent have been aware that these matters may be a little more complicated, such popular understanding has generally been accepted in everyday life as well as in educational planning and thinking, because it is so very convenient to equate what is taught with what is learned. This learning has then been regarded as more or less adequate, and there has been a grading scale to measure the extent to which the desired learning has taken place.

Of course, at some level everybody has known that an understanding of this kind is simplified and untenable. Students do not learn everything that is taught; they will always miss or misunderstand some of it, and at the same time they will very often learn something else on a different level of attitudes and values which may be more or less inadequate or even contradictory in relation to what is intended. Moreover, the grading is uncertain and unjust; schooling and education also serve adjustment, conformity and selection, etc. This is all well known, but nevertheless it has been treated as a sort of acceptable side effect because it has been regarded as secondary in relation to the main issue: i.e. that there is some learning taking place of what is taught.

But along with the growing importance of education – and in recent years also radical changes in the sort of learning which is aimed at – growing uncertainty about all these matters can be traced. Do we actually get the best possible returns from the vast economic and human resources which are devoted to education? Is the learning as adequate and up-to-date as possible? Or are the side effects, after all, the most important? How do students learn such qualities as flexibility, responsibility, independence, initiative and creativity that today are competencies of the same order of necessity as reading and writing? And what about all the learning that takes place outside school and education – what influence does it have, and how does it interfere with institutionalised learning?

The concept and processes of learning

The word *learning* is used broadly and with somewhat different meanings. In general four different main meanings can be discerned, all of which may more or less be included when the word is used without further specification in everyday language:

1. Firstly, the word learning can refer to the *results* of individual learning processes. In this case learning means what is learned.

2. Secondly, the word learning can refer to the individual *psychological processes* that may lead to such alterations or results described as meaning 1. These processes may be called learning processes and learning psychology typically deals with such processes.

3. Thirdly, both learning and learning processes can refer to the *interaction processes* between the individual and his or her material and social environment which are direct or indirect preconditions of the internal

learning processes described as meaning 2 (and leading to the alterations described as meaning 1).

4. Finally, both learning and learning processes, not only in everyday language but also in official and professional connections, are used more or less *identically with the word teaching,* which may be interpreted as the result of a tacit short circuit between what is taught and what is learned as described above.

Whereas meaning 4 evidently is inappropriate, the three first-mentioned meanings may all be adequate. But, of course, it is inconvenient when the same word is used with different meanings and it may be uncertain what precisely is meant. However, this is closely connected to the fact that the matters to which these three meanings refer cannot be separated in practice, but only analytically. The following small example may serve to illustrate this.

A person is involved in an *interaction process* with the environment – for instance, a student in a chemistry lesson. The teacher is giving an account of a specific chemical process, and the student is supposed to be engaged in understanding and "learning" what the teacher says. Thus, the interaction process in this case comprises the teacher speaking and the student listening and perhaps asking some elaborating questions – a quite normal school situation.

At the same time an internal *psychological process* is going on in the student involving the teacher's account being received and somehow fitted into the student's understanding, i.e. it is related to the relevant knowledge and insight that the student has already acquired. Thus, the psychological process comprises reception and incorporation of the teacher's account, and this may take place in various ways comprising the involvement of different feeling. I shall return to this later.

If the situation functions as intended, the result should be that the student has "learnt" what the teacher has explained, that it has become integrated in the student's mental structures or "memory", and under specific conditions it may be "recalled" and reproduced for further elaboration or application.

But the situation does not always function as intended. Errors or distortions of various kinds may occur. Perhaps the interaction process is derailed, maybe because the teacher's account is incoherent or simply too bad, or there may be other sorts of disturbances. In this case the account will only be perceived partially or mistakenly, with a correspondingly negative impact on the learning result. Or perhaps the student's psychological acquisition process is insufficient, maybe due to a lack of concentration, which will also lead to a deterioration of the learning result. Finally, it may be that the knowledge already developed in the student is faulty or absent. In this case the teacher's message cannot be received correctly, and again the learning result will be different from that intended.

To obtain an adequate picture of what is actually happening it is necessary at the same time to relate to the process as a whole and to be able to differentiate between its various aspects analytically. Learning is thus a rather complicated matter, and it has therefore been a constant problem in learning psychology that different approaches and accounts have not caught the total complexity and very often have not even been aware of or made it clear that they have only dealt with a part of a compound totality. Other approaches have aimed at dealing with or claimed to deal with the whole without having really succeeded in covering everything.

In this book learning is fundamentally conceived of as an integrated process consisting of two connected part processes which mutually influence each other:

Firstly, the interaction process between the learner and his or her environment – an interaction which may take place by direct contact or be indirectly brought about through various media (thus it is also regarded as an interaction process to read a book or listen to a tape – cf. chapter 7).

Secondly, the internal psychological acquisitional and elaborative process which leads to a learning result.

Learning, development, socialisation, qualification, maturation, and ageing

Another uncertainty in connection with the definition and conception of learning has to do with the relation between what learning is (and accordingly to be discussed within the discipline of learning psychology) and what development is (and to be discussed within developmental psychology). For instance there is a "classical" conflict on this point between Jean Piaget and Lev Vygotsky, two of the most important figures in learning psychology, the latter claiming that in principle learning precedes and is a basis for development and ascribing the opposite standpoint to the former (cf. Vygotsky 1978, p. 84ff, and 1986, p. 174ff).

This leads on to the question about what is meant by "development" and the part played by genetic-biological maturation in this connection. In addition, since the 1960s this whole problem has been complicated by the concept of "socialisation" coming into the picture, signifying the learning and developmental processes by which the individual adapts to the society to which it belongs. Finally, also the concept of "qualification" enters into this discussion as describing the processes by which the individual develops such capacities as are relevant in relation to his or her societal labour or the labour he or she might undertake.

I shall not here go further into the discussions about definitions and boundaries of these concepts. Learning, development, socialisation and qualification are in my conception more or less identical, or at least overlapping functions, to the extent to which it is derailing to try to treat them as separated processes. The differences between them are mainly about the points of view which are concerned and what the results of the processes are related to. In this book I use the concept of learning to broadly cover all processes that lead to relatively lasting changes of capacity whether it be of a motor, cognitive, emotional, motivational, attitudinal or social character.

Not included in the concept of learning are the processes of maturation and ageing, but they are both of fundamental importance for the learning possibilities. That a baby is not able to solve a quadratic equation is due to both the absence of the necessary learning prerequisites and to the fact that its central nervous system is too undifferentiated. And there are also other genetic-biological conditions of significant relevance for learning, for instance all the genetic differences which have played an important and disputed role in intelligence research. However, such differences will not be considered in this book.

The dimensions of learning

A conception of the character of learning which is fundamental in this book and by which it distinguishes itself from most other writings about the topic is that *all learning comprises three different dimensions* – i.e. that all learning is, so to speak, stretched out between three poles and accordingly may be looked at and analysed from three different approaches.

Firstly, all learning has a content of skill or meaning. The acquisition of this content is primarily a *cognitive process* (the term cognitive comprising both knowledge and motor learning, both of which are controlled by the central nervous system). This is the dimension that traditional learning psychology has concentrated on, whether it be the behaviourist tradition or other important traditions such as those founded by Piaget and Vygotsky. In the following I shall take Piaget's conception as a point of departure in this dimension – a choice which I shall substantiate in detail in chapter 2.

Secondly, all learning is simultaneously an *emotional process,* or what the technical language of psychology more precisely terms a psychodynamic process, i.e. a process involving psychological energy, transmitted by feelings, emotions, attitudes and motivations which both mobilise and, at the same time, are conditions that may be influenced and developed through learning. This learning dimension has only been dealt with peripherally in learning psychology, but much more as part of developmental and personality psychology. A very broad and general basis in this dimension is the psychoanalytical tradition as originally developed by Sigmund Freud and subsequently elaborated in various directions by many others.

Thirdly, learning is also a *social process,* taking place in the interaction between the individual and its surroundings, and thus in the final analysis a process dependent on historical and societal conditions. It is therefore important to realise that this dimension has two connected levels: a directly or indirectly social, interpersonal level of interaction, and an underlying societal level, influencing the character of the interaction as well as the contributions of individuals who are all developed in a societal context. On the interactional level the social dimension is to a certain extent taken up inside group and social psychology, and on the underlying societal level in socialisation theory.

As the background of the social dimension of learning is related to the existing structure of society, in modern capitalist society the understanding of this dimension may appropriately be connected to the fundamental analysis of the basic structures of capitalism which was carried out by Karl Marx. In his sixth thesis on Ludwig Feuerbach, Marx identified human psychological processes by the following brief formulation:

"The human essence is no abstraction inherent in each single individual. In its reality it is the ensemble of the social relations."
(Marx 1845/1969).

Learning is a function of central importance for human nature and thus in the materialist Marxist conception it is decisively characterised by existing societal conditions.

The basic conception of learning in this presentation thus suggests both that learning always consists of two integrated processes of interaction and internalisation, respectively, and that *learning simultaneously comprises a cognitive, an emotional and psychodynamic, and a social and societal dimension.* Or, to put it in a more popular way, that learning and every single learning process is stretched out between three angles or approaches which are typically represented by Piaget, Freud and Marx. Figure 1 is an attempt to illustrate this conception:

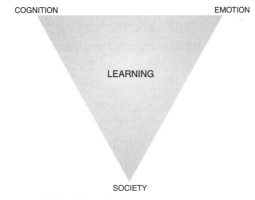

Figure 1: The tension field of learning

The two psychological poles are placed at the top of the tension field so that the psychological process of acquisition is stretched out along the top line between them, and at the bottom point of the triangle the social-societal pole is placed as signifying the underlying conditions that, through the interaction process, are connected with the acquisition – which also in itself has a societal component as the learner always is a societally developed individual. Thus, it is possible also to relate the two part processes of learning to the figure (cf. chapter 7). But primarily the figure shows the three-pole field in which learning is situated and inside which it may be understood and analysed from different positions that to a different extent accentuate or tone down the learning dimensions. I shall return to this in the final chapter of the book (cf. chapter 12).

In connection with the figure, it is important to stress that all three dimensions are always integrated parts of the learning process and in practice do not exist as separate functions, although there may be a need to separate them analytically in order to obtain a more differentiated picture. Accordingly, such separation must only be carried out with the underlying understanding that the dimensions are always integrated in reality.

If we return to the example of the chemistry lesson, the immediate focus in this situation is on the cognitive content dimension: it is intended that the students develop knowledge and understanding of the chemical process in question.

But for each of the students it is in this connection of decisive importance how the emotional dimension functions, i.e. how the situation is experienced, which emotions and motivations are attached to the process, and thus what psychological energy is mobilised. The character of the learning result with respect to usefulness and durability, i.e. in which situation it may be recalled and how long it may be remembered by the learner, will be closely connected with how the emotional dimension has been functioning as part of the entire process. It is this dimension that, so to speak, determines the internal psychological conditions of the learning process.

Moreover, both the cognitive and the emotional dimensions and the interplay between them are decisively dependent on the function of the social dimension. If for each student the interaction situation in the chemistry lesson has not been of an acceptable character as to content and emotions, the learning will be distorted, or perhaps no learning at all will take place, or something quite different will be learned: maybe a negative impression of the teacher, of some other students, of the subject, or of the school situation in general.

And, in addition, there are always societal conditions influencing the learning situation and process. More directly, it could be the consciousness of grading or examination, and in general the fact that the life situation and the societal conditions of each student may constitute a more or less rejecting or indifferent attitude. Conversely, it may exert a positive influence on the situation and the learning if, for instance, the qualification demands – in this case the understanding of chemical processes – are experienced as important and relevant. Thus, the social and societal situations constitute the external conditions of learning.

For the individual learner all these circumstances function, as already stressed, in an integrated manner, constituting an indivisible totality. But analytically the totality may be separated into the three dimensions that I have pointed out. In the following I shall do so in order to go deeper into the nature and conditions of learning – and then, at the end of the book, to try to reach an overall understanding.

The structure of the presentation

The purpose of this book is to present a generally accessible, coherent understanding of human learning – an understanding which I can answer for, which is in my opinion the best that can be achieved today, and which attempts to cover the whole subject area in accordance with current knowledge in this field. But the field is ambiguous; there are many different and in some cases even opposing views and approaches, and accordingly the presentation can in no way claim to constitute the only correct and proper way of understanding. Like all other learning psychology, it is in the nature of a construction based on a series of assumptions or hypothesises that can be argued for but never definitively "proved". Of course, some assumptions may seem more probable than others, but there is certainly no general agreement on that. On the contrary, there is a multitude of opinions in the field which may be more or less related, overlapping, disconnected or even conflicting.

What I am going to present is thus an understanding of learning which in the course of many years of occupation with the subject I have aimed at making plausible, coherent and comprehensive in order to make it as adequate as possible, especially from the perspective that it should form applicable input in relation to current educational planning and practice, even though the educational perspectives in this presentation will only be taken up peripherally. There is, of course, an experiential foundation which can support such applicability, but to imagine any sort of certainty in this connection would definitely be to greatly overshoot the mark. The value of my presentation must accordingly be judged by the reader in relation to the likelihood and the applicability he or she ascribes to my assumptions.

Specifically, I shall deal with the vast complexity of my subject by starting with the cognitive dimension in chapters 2 and 3. In chapters 4 and 5 I shall continue by including and integrating the emotional dimension in order to develop a coherent understanding of the internal psychological process of acquisition which then, in chapter 6, will be related to various circumstances that may restrict, hamper, block or "derail" the intended learning. In doing this I shall already be touching on the interaction process which will be treated more specifically in chapter 7. In chapter 8 I shall then try to launch a comprehensive conception of my subject, and in chapter 9 I shall take up various models that try to picture learning processes in different ways. Finally, in chapters 10 and 11 I deal with various external and internal conditions of learning, and in chapter 12 I conclude with some reflections.

In my presentation I have thus chosen a procedure which takes its point of departure at a certain place in the complicated field, namely in the character of the cognitive processes of acquisition. This is not because I in any way regard this dimension as being more important or fundamental than the other two, but because it seems most straightforward in relation to both the understanding and the presentation to start where learning psychology usually starts. From this point I shall then gradually disseminate the presentation to cover the whole field that is relevant for learning.

I have chosen this gradual procedure because it implies a relatively clear structure, and not least because it is my experience that those approaches which choose a more holistic form of presentation tend never to truly get the whole field sufficiently into the picture.

Thus Piaget, whom I take up first, has clearly limited himself from dealing in depth with anything but the cognitive dimension of learning – a delimitation which on the one hand enabled him to deal very thoroughly with this dimension, but on the other hand has implied some limitations in the applicability of his theories, e.g. in relation to teaching and education.

The Russian cultural historical approach, represented by Vygotsky, among others (cf. chapter 3), has by some been preferred in opposition to the Piagetian approach because it combines cognitive understanding with a societal perspective. But here again the emotional dimension is more or less omitted. And in the critical theory of the Frankfurt School (cf. chapter 7), the emotional and social-societal dimensions are combined, but then the cognitive dimension is by and large neglected.

I shall return to all this later, but it is important for me to emphasise these overriding considerations already here to give the reader an impression of the basis of my presentation. The structure that I have chosen has the advantage of starting with some fundamental and relatively simple areas and from here gradually takes up increasingly complicated circumstances until the whole complexity is involved. It should thus be fairly manageable for the reader to follow the procedure, although it has the obvious disadvantage that the totality is only gradually established.

At first the reader may reasonably raise a multitude of important objections about conditions which are not taken into account. How about the emotional side of learning? What if the learner is not motivated or maybe even shows resistance to the learning? What about the social context of the learning situation? And what about societal conditions and their influence on the learning? All these perspectives are only gradually incorporated, for instance by a problematisation or complication of earlier parts of the presentation.

Thus it may be demanding and sometimes irritating to follow these continuing complications. But on the other hand I regard it impossible to present the complicated totality all at once, and the chosen procedure conforms to a certain extent to the learning process that I myself have been through over a number of years. The dedicated reader may experience the process as a kind of detection or uncovering in the same way as I have experienced it - and then at the end may ask him- or herself if I did actually get through. I am sure there will be something to go on with.

Finally, it should be mentioned here that my presentation aims to be at a general level, i.e. that it relates to such conditions as are generally at work in connection with human learning. But when it comes to the social and societal conditions there will be increasing focus on the learning which is possible in society as it exists today and not least in institutionalised educational processes in Denmark and similar countries today.

However, this does not in any way imply that learning by education is better or more important than other learning. On the contrary, a lot of fundamental and indispensable learning obviously takes place before and outside schooling and education, in private life, in working life and, for instance, also in the public social and health sectors. But in modern society the education sector is the centre of precisely *institutionalised learning,* i.e. the learning that society in a goal-directed way aims to generate in its members, and therefore this learning is of special interest. It is in schools and other educational institutions that learning efforts are consciously and systematically carried out in order to fulfil specific political and societal purposes.

Summary

In this introductory chapter the following fundamentals with respect to learning and its conditions have primarily been presented:

1. In this book learning is conceived of and discussed broadly as any process that leads to psychological changes of a relatively lasting nature and which are not due to genetic-biological conditions such as maturation or ageing. Thus, learning includes psychological development, socialisation, and qualification.

2. Learning is a holistic process which includes, as two integrated part processes, a direct or indirect social interaction process and an internal psychological acquisition process.

3. All learning includes three simultaneous and integrated dimensions: a cognitive content dimension, an emotional, psychodynamic, attitudinal and motivational dimension, and a social and societal dimension.

4. Analytically it is possible to deal with the part processes and dimensions mentioned separately, but only as elements of a holistic totality.

2. Cognitive Learning

Piaget as a starting point

As stated previously, I will begin my presentation with the learning theory developed by the Swiss biologist, psychologist and epistemologist Jean Piaget.

My reason for choosing Piaget's theory over many others is not that I regard it as more "correct" than other learning theories. As already stated, there are many approaches to learning, all of which have something to contribute that can have different significance for different contexts, as well as all being based, in the final analysis, on certain fundamental assumptions that cannot be proven in any scientific sense (cf. Wenger 1998, p. 4).

My grounds for preferring Piaget in this case are that his theory is in fact an appropriate choice on the basis of the method utilised here, in which I will begin with the cognitive dimension of learning and gradually develop a broader perspective. Later I will include contributions from many other researchers and theorists – but it must be stated at this point that taking Piaget as a starting point means rejecting from the beginning the whole of the traditional behaviouristic type of learning theory that has strongly dominated the field throughout the history of psychology, particularly in the USA, and which has only in recent years begun to be seriously challenged by other approaches.

Piaget was almost exclusively concerned with the cognitive aspect of learning. However, his methods were extremely painstaking and convincing (closer examinations of Piaget's theory can be found in the works of Flavell 1963 and Furth 1981, among others), so that today he is generally acknowledged to be one of the founding fathers of psychology – as the English sociologist Anthony Giddens writes:

"...the influence of Jean Piaget's work has been not far short of that of Freud." (Giddens 1993, p. 72).

In the present context there are both a number of fundamental factors concerning Piaget's approach and some central features to his theory, that in my view make it highly appropriate to choose this particular theory as a *starting point* – even though there are also, in my opinion, a number of problematic factors and limitations, which I will return to later.

Quite basically I consider it a vital strength that Piaget, who originally trained as a biologist, constructs his theory on a *genetic-biological* basis, which is to say that he views the human ability to learn as a characteristic that has developed phylogenetically through the struggle for survival of the various species, in line with other species-specific characteristics. This view Piaget shares with many others, including Vygotsky, the Russian learning theorist mentioned previously, and other representatives of the Russian cultural historical school (cf. chapter 3).

Another fundamental strength, which has come to the fore particularly in the years following Piaget's death in 1980, is the *constructivist* approach, which holds that a person constructs his or her own comprehension of the surrounding world through learning and knowledge – which excludes any form of learning approach as a filling process, in which someone, a teacher, for example, transfers knowledge and skills to others, for example, pupils (an approach which many other learning theorists have also dissociated themselves from, the most well known perhaps being the Brazilian Paulo Freire with his rejection of all that he calls "banking education" - Freire 1970, p. 58ff).

Besides these two very central basic factors are a number of important factors in the very construction of the theory to which I also ascribe vital significance:

Firstly, Piaget differentiates between the *dynamic* and the *structural* aspects of learning – somewhat analogous to the differentiation between the emotional and the cognitive dimensions in this presentation. The dynamic aspect is concerned with what drives learning, where the motive comes from, and the "why?" of learning, and Piaget specifically emphasises that he does not deal with this aspect of learning. The structural aspect is concerned with the content and nature of learning, the "how?" of learning. It is this aspect of learning that Piaget's theory is concerned with, and in which he has involved himself in such detail.

To this are added Piaget's view and analysis of developmental stages. Piaget's *stage theory* was previously viewed as central to his work and has always been highly controversial. This holds that cognitive development from birth to puberty runs through a number of developmental stages which Piaget perceives as essential and unavoidable, and that come in a particular order according to age. The ages may vary slightly, but not significantly.

The extensive criticism of the stage theory has partly been aimed at the definition and age determination of individual stages, but there has also been a more general criticism that the process is less clear-cut than Piaget describes it, and that the stages can set in at different times for different spheres within the same individual, depending on influence and interests (cf. Donaldson 1986). However it is my opinion that the four main stages in Piaget's construction – i.e. the sensory-motor period in roughly the first two years of life, the preoperational period up to around school age, the concrete operational period up to around puberty, and the formal operational period after that – stand largely unchallenged by such criticism. In any case, the stage theory is of minor importance for the structural aspect of the learning theory.

Finally, it is extremely important in the present context that what I might call Piaget's actual learning theory is centred on the concept of learning as a *process of equilibration.* The individual strives to maintain a steady equilibrium in his or her interactions with the surrounding world by means of a continuing *adaptation,* i.e. an active adjustment process by which the individual adapts himself or herself to his or her environment as well as attempting to adapt the environment to meet his or her own needs. This adaptation takes place in a continuing interaction between two types of processes that are occurring in parallel and are continually balancing each other out.

The individual's adaptation of his or her environment occurs through *assimilation,* i.e. the taking in of impressions from the environment into previously developed psychological structures. By means of this assimilation, sensory impressions from the environment are taken in and adopted as additions and extensions to existing *cognitive schemes* or knowledge structures. In the context of assimilation one could talk of *learning by addition.*

The chemistry lesson situation outlined in chapter 1 can be taken as a typical example of this. This situation presupposes that the pupil has already acquired a certain knowledge of chemistry, i.e. that a cognitive scheme has been developed to hold and structure the acquired chemistry knowledge. The way it is supposed to work is that when the teacher explains a chemical process that has not previously been dealt with in class, the pupil acquires the new knowledge by means of an assimilative extension of the pupil's chemistry scheme.

The adaptation of the individual to the environment takes place via *accommodation*, i.e. a changing of the structures already developed in relation to new conditions in the environment, cf. the accommodation of the eye to altered light conditions. Accommodation, which takes place when impressions from the environment cannot fit into the existing schemes, consists of dissociation and reconstruction, by which means the schemes are altered so that the impressions can be taken in. Accommodation thus implies a going beyond, or a transcendence of, the readiness already developed, and can be characterised as *transcendent learning*. When the necessary preconditions are present, the accommodative processes can be short and sudden: the learner understands immediately how something works. But it can also be a lengthy process, in which the learner struggles with a problem or a difficult relationship and gradually, or step by step, develops a new comprehension or a solution.

At any rate, knowledge schemes that assimilation and accommodation occur in relation to are various individual formations that will be full of particular forms of comprehension, and even in relation to the clearest structures in, for example, the field of mathematics and logic, there will be individual ways of perceiving the subjects. Piaget declared that individuation – the differences that make us develop into separate and distinct individuals even under uniform external conditions – lies in the diversity of accommodations:

"There is a great diversity in structures. - Accommodation gives rise to unlimited differentiations. The fact that a number is the same for everyone, and the series of whole numbers is the same for everyone, doesn't prevent mathematicians, taken one by one, from being unique as individuals. There is such diversification of structures..." (Piaget 1980, quoted from Furth 1987, p. 4).

However, the individuation of accommodation also leads to individuations in the assimilative processes. For when the schemes are individuated by means of accommodation they will of necessity take on an individual stamp, and when assimilation to individualised schemes takes place, the assimilations must necessarily be different, even though the influences are the same for several individuals. (Therefore there will always be differences in even the most educated logicians' or mathematicians' knowledge schemes: even if they apparently "know" the same thing, they do so in different ways, which may lead to differences in when this knowledge is recalled and what likelihood there is for it to be transcended).

As a whole Piaget's theory thus implies a process conception in which developed structures are constantly elaborated and remodelled in an interaction with impressions from the environment – a continuing construction and reconstruction in which it is fundamental that all learning takes place in an interaction between the existing structures (what is already there) and the new impressions obtained from the environment (what is added from outside). The American learning theorist David Ausubel has, with reference to teaching, briefly formulated this idea, as follows:

"The most important single factor influencing learning is what the learner already knows." (Ausubel 1968, p. vi).

It is thus equally important for a teacher to be interested in what the pupils already know as in what he or she wants them to learn. At the same time this approach makes it clear why pupils very often learn different things even though they have all received the same teaching: each pupil has unique and individually developed cognitive structures, and when the meeting between specific impressions and these different structures brings about learning, the results will in principle be different.

I will proceed no further with Piaget's learning theory at this point, but will leave it as sketched out above, to return to with modifications and extensions in the following sections.

Nissen's elaboration of Piaget's theory

Naturally, many researchers have worked on elaborations or adaptations of Piaget's theory, both major and minor. First I will look at some elaborations described by the Danish psychologist Thomas Nissen in a small book entitled "Learning and Pedagogy" (Nissen 1970), which, even in Denmark, is not very well known and somewhat inaccessible. Nissen's work is interesting in the present context among other things because it has the direct aim of making learning psychology more applicable to actual teaching.

On the fundamental level I am concerned with here, Nissen's elaboration consists of two parts: he makes an actual distinction between assimilative and accommodative learning processes; and he also operates with a third basic type of learning process, which he calls *cumulative processes.*

Cumulative learning occurs in situations where the learner does not possess any developed scheme to which specific impressions from the environment can be related, i.e. when the first element in a new scheme is established. Nissen presumably found it necessary to take this situation into consideration because he was concerned with basic forms of learning such as those that occur in a number of animal experiments, on which American traditional behaviourist learning psychology has largely focussed.

Cumulative processes in humans are, by their very nature, of particular importance in the earliest years of life, but situations also occur later in which it may be necessary to learn something that is in no way connected with anything of which one has any previous knowledge. A good example of this is the practical task of learning telephone numbers off by heart. The first few numbers usually refer to a geographical area, and this makes them easier to remember: there is something to connect them with. But the last numbers are random and have no systematic connection with anything; these must either be learnt off by heart, or one must "invent" a connection to something one knows, a kind of mnemonic. If you learn them off by heart, that is cumulative learning – which may also be termed *mechanical learning.* If you make up a mnemonic, what is happening is that you are linking them to something already known, a scheme previously established, and that is therefore assimilation. However, cumulation may also be regarded as a particular kind of assimilation which occurs under particular conditions.

When it comes to the relationship between the assimilative and the accommodative processes, it is a matter for discussion how great is the distance between Piaget's and Nissen's conceptions. Piaget's position is perhaps best expressed in the following summary by Flavell:

"However necessary it may be to describe assimilation and accommodation separately and sequentially, they should be thought of as simultaneous and indissociable as they operate in a living cognition. Adaptation is a unitary event, and assimilation and accommodation are merely abstractions from this unitary reality. – Some cognitive acts show a relative preponderance of the assimilative component; others seem heavily weighted towards accommodation. However, 'pure' assimilation and 'pure' accommodation nowhere obtain in cognitive life; intellectual acts always presuppose each in some measure." (Flavell 1963, p. 48-49).

In spite of this basic opinion there are nevertheless countless places in Piaget's work where the two processes are treated separately, and conversely Nissen takes his starting point in separation, while he makes a general reservation:

"In the following, three forms of learning are postulated: cumulative, assimilative and accommodative learning. – They are less 'pure' than they appear, but examination of them may ...be treated as an attempt to construct search models that can perhaps point out important points in learning." (Nissen 1970, p. 43).

From this point the separation that Nissen makes leads to some pedagogically fruitful work in identifying on the one hand the conditions in which the three types of learning process can occur, and on the other hand the nature of the learning products that are thus developed. Thus, despite all reservations, Nissen operates with three basic and essentially different forms of learning:

Cumulative learning can be described as processes

"in which the individual acquires situation-specific skills, which can only be applied and recalled under the learning conditions, i.e. in that situation or that environment where the learning occurred. Outside the learning environment what is learnt is 'forgotten' and not subject to the individual's 'will'. The learning product is thus extremely vulnerable. This can only be justified if the aim is for the subject learnt to be applied under constant conditions, or if one can anticipate its later application by arranging a less situation-dependent learning process. Cumulative learning may occur as part of several strongly programmed learning processes, in which control is so intense that the individual has no choice, and where it takes the nature of traditional conditioning." (Bjerg 1972, p.17-18).

In the context of education, cumulative processes typically relate to the old-fashioned learning by rote of hymns, lists of kings and vocabulary, but cumulation also occurs in the acquisition of the first hesitant motor skills in, for example, riding a bicycle or skating. To summarise, it may be said that cumulative learning is first and foremost characterised by rigidity. In its purest form it is the concept of training as used in the training of animals or simple conditioning.

In assimilative learning, the learner adapts and incorporates impressions from his or her surroundings as an extension and differentiation of previously established cognitive structures. The learning products are typically knowledge, skills and experiential opportunities that can be activated in a broad spectrum of situations with certain specific common characteristics (e.g. that they are seen to relate to a specific subject), and thus that the products can to a certain extent be adapted to altered situations with new learning. In its "pure" form, assimilative learning is characterised by a steady and stable progressive development in which the learning products are constructed, integrated and stabilised. This category can include the majority of knowledge and skills learning that is traditionally aimed at in our education system, where systematic attempts are made within the various subjects to comprehensively extend the knowledge and skills structures that exist. In more popular terms, assimilative learning is comparable with "ordinary school learning".

In accommodative learning, previously established cognitive structures are altered through dissociation and reconstruction, as learning elements acquired earlier are released from their original context to subsequently form part of new structures. The individual changes and adapts him- or herself in line with impressions from the environment, but this adapting should not be perceived in a passive sense. On the contrary, the existing readiness is inadequate for this situation, and the learner transcends previous limitations by dissociation and reorganisation of the structures:

> "Accommodative processes provide the individual with opportunities for action, for use in various situations, whatever the context. Here we are dealing with the basis for openness, sensitivity, creativity, flexibility and so on." (Bjerg 1972, p. 19).

In more popular terms, accommodative learning thus relates to the concept of consciousness-raising. Like other learning categories, it is linked to the cognitive sphere, but it is interesting to note here that the well-known American humanistic psychologist Carl R. Rogers, in the development of so-called client-centred therapy and student-centred teaching, works with the concept of *significant learning*, which broadly relates to personal development (cf. chapter 5), but is also completely parallel to accommodative learning. Significant learning involves "a change in the organization of the self"(Rogers 1951, p.390), as it involves "the whole person, both his emotions and the cognitive aspects are involved in the learning" (Rogers 1969, p.5). The concept is probably best defined in the following statement:

> "By significant learning I mean learning which is more than an accumulation of facts. It is learning which makes a difference - in the individual's behavior, in the course of action he chooses in the future, in his attitudes and in his personality. It is a pervasive learning which is not just an accretion of knowledge, but which interpenetrates with every portion of his existence." (Rogers 1961, p. 280).

My inclusion of this concept at this point is partly in order to draw attention to the fact that although Piaget's and Nissen's work is closely tied to cognitive development, their learning categories can also be understood in a broader sense (I shall return to this in more detail in Chapter 4), and partly because this concept indicates an extremely important relationship, to which both Nissen and Rogers draw attention, concerning accommodative learning and significant learning respectively. Time and time again Rogers points out that

> "any significant learning involves a certain amount of pain, either pain connected with the learning itself or distress connected with giving up certain previous learnings" – "learning which involves a change in self organization – in the perception of oneself – is threatening and tends to be resisted" – "all significant learning is to some degree painful and involves turbulence, within the individual and within the system." (Rogers 1969, p. 157-8, 159, 339).

This differs only in nuance from Nissen's statement:

> "The actual accommodative learning process is a strain for the individual, characterised by anxiety, bewilderment and confusion, and requires a certain amount of strength." (Nissen 1970, p. 68).

Accommodative learning therefore presupposes, firstly, that relevant structures that can be reconstructed are already in place (e.g. presuppositions regarding a subject, attitudes or social relations), secondly, that the individual needs or is keen to mobilise energy for a reconstruction of that type, and thirdly – as Rogers emphasises – that the individual in that situation perceives sufficient permissiveness and safety to "dare" to let go of the knowledge already established. These three kinds of preconditions for accommodative learning are not separately absolute in nature, but occur in a reciprocal interactive relationship, such that strong motivation for advancement, for example, can reduce the need for preconditions and security – or vice versa.

As accommodation is the form of learning that advances the individual's development most markedly, it can naturally come to be viewed as "better" learning than that which occurs with assimilation or cumulation. Such a view is, however, mistaken, for two reasons: accommodation requires that there already be established (through cumulation and assimilation) relevant structures that allow accommodation to take place; and an exaggerated focussing on accommodative processes might lead to disorganisation and confusion.

A suitable development process, therefore, consists in an interaction between the three learning forms that is reasonably balanced according to the given context – in the education process it is typically an inter-process exchange that predominantly sets the stage for assimilative and accommodative processes respectively.

Kolb's learning model

Finally, as a continuation of Piaget's learning theory, I would like to include the concept of learning developed by the American psychologist David Kolb in his book "Experiential Learning" (Kolb 1984).

As the title suggests, Kolb himself regards his theory as being on experiential learning (which I will deal with in greater detail in Chapter 8). Nevertheless he begins by developing a learning theory in a general manner, and through a number of discussions reaches a common definition of learning as "the process by which experience is transformed into knowledge" (Kolb 1984, p. 38). In a footnote he states that on the basis of this definition all learning is essentially experiential learning, and that consequently, that is what his book is about. However, he does not go into detail on how he distinguishes between learning generally and experiential learning. As it is also clear that Kolb is only concerned with what I understand as the cognitive dimension of learning, I have decided to deal with his theory in this chapter on cognitive learning – since I view it as crucially important that the concepts "experience" and "experiential learning" span all three dimensions of learning: cognitive, psychodynamic and societal.

On the whole I regard Kolb's theory as somewhat problematic in places, with some quite uncertain conclusions on a basis that is not always clearly developed (for a more detailed examination and criticism in Danish of Kolb's book see Illeris 1995) – but it also contains some important elaborations of Piaget's concept, including a transcending of the limitations that result from Piaget's restricted interest in learning in formal logic spheres, where it is clear what is right and what is wrong.

There is, however, a vast distance from the certainty of formal logic to the numerous structuring possibilities that exist in other spheres, e.g. in the acknowledgement of the chaotic mass of conditions and impressions that characterise everyday life in a modern society. In concentrating on logical structures, Piaget attempted to get to what he viewed as the core of knowledge, and was thereby able to uncover some fundamental features in the nature of knowledge. At the same time, though, other features that have far more importance in ordinary life were pushed out onto the periphery or even right out of sight. Kolb's work can provide a partial remedy to that, and therefore I will here concern myself with Kolb's theory and concentrate on what I find of significance in order to reach his treatment of the question of the ambiguity and unambiguity of learning.

Kolb starts by referring to Piaget together with the American philosopher and educational theorist John Dewey (cf. chapter 9) and the German-American gestalt psychologist Kurt Lewin. By transforming the essence of these three learning approaches into three somewhat crude models, Kolb finds that they all understand learning as a process with four stages or adaptive learning modes, which can be inscribed in a *learning cycle* from concrete experience through reflective observation and abstract conceptualisation to active experimentation, and then back to a new concrete experience (Kolb 1984, pp. 30 and 32-33).

Kolb uses very different elements in the three theory formations to compare and put into a common model. He refers to the practical process in Lewin's model for action research and laboratory training (Kolb 1984, p. 21). From Dewey he refers to a very general description of "how learning transforms the impulses, feelings, and desires of concrete experience into higher-order purposeful action" (p. 22). And from Piaget he takes the order of the characteristic learning patterns in the four main stages from newborn to adult from the stage theory mentioned earlier (pp. 24-25) – and thus not at all the single learning process.

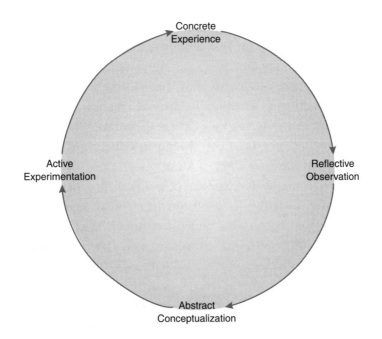

Figure 2: Kolb's learning cycle
(cf. Kolb 1984, p. 33)

From one viewpoint it is not obvious that these three very different elements in the three theories may be taken to express the central themes in the three learning concepts, and Kolb does not discuss this problem at all. However, it can also be seen as an important innovation in Kolb's work that he was able to spot a parallel not immediately apparent because of the very great differences between the three theorists' approaches.

At any rate, Kolb's learning cycle constitutes a systematisation of the learning processes which could perhaps in some contexts be a valid analytical blueprint, but which also involves a vigorous rationalisation of the diversity of reality. In that way it makes one think of differing scientific methodological models that produce systematised interpretations of research processes. But neither learning nor research take place in the real world, according to that kind of logical systematism. In both cases it is more that one starts off with what one knows and regards as important or striking, whether it is a question of experiences, observations, knowledge, understanding, conjectures or problems, and from there one attempts to make progress in a combined acquisition and clarification process. This is documented by, among others, another American psychologist and learning theorist, Donald Schön, who has studied how "reflective practitioners" cope with different situations by drawing on and combining in parallel the relevant elements that they have at their disposal (Schön 1983, cf. chapter 10 – there is a brief corresponding criticism of this element in Kolb's theory in Mezirow 1991, p. 103).

The next step in the development of Kolb's theory that I wish to cover here is that after a lengthy discussion on the nature of learning, he reaches the conclusion that there are two dimensions present in all learning, a grasping, or to use Kolb's own term, *"prehension"*, and a *transformation,* in which that which has been grasped is embedded as an element of the learner's psychological structures.

Kolb here refers to a number of earlier researchers, from William James (1890) onward, who have identified this dualism in learning in various ways (Kolb 1984, p. 44ff). However, comprehension of this dualism is inherent in the language for speakers of German or the Scandinavian languages, as the English word "experience" may be translated in two ways, viz., "Erlebnis" for the immediate perception and "Erfahrung" for the trace deposited in the consciousness. What Kolb regards as an important discovery is more of an ordinary awareness for these language speakers and this may be why what English speakers express as "experiential learning" often appears to us more like experiential events than the German "Erfahrungslernen" and the Scandinavian "erfaringspædagogik" ("experiential pedagogy" – cf. Webb & Nielsen 1996), in which cognitive acquisition typically takes a central position – I shall return to this subject in chapter 8.

The most innovative aspect of Kolb's work in my view thus lies not in his learning dimensions as such, but in his further analysis of them, for he finds that they each stretch between two dialectically opposed adaptive orientations that together are identical to the four stages in the learning cycle. The prehension dimension stretches as a vertical axis in the learning cycle between an immediate *apprehension* that points towards concrete experience, and an adapted or reflective *comprehension* that points towards abstract conceptualisation. And correspondingly the transformation dimension stretches as a horizontal axis in the learning cycle between *intention,* pointing out towards reflective observation, and *extension,* pointing out towards active experimentation. According to Kolb, the structural basis of the learning process lies in the interaction between these four orientations (Kolb 1984, p.41).

Thus Kolb develops a learning model that can provide an inspiring picture of the structure of the internal learning processes:

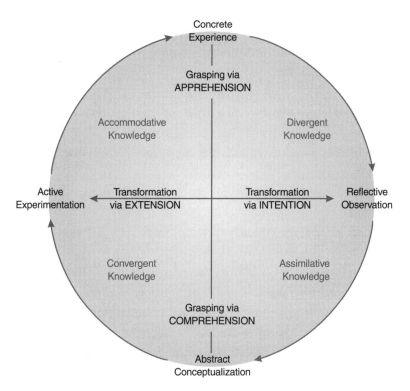

Figure 3: Kolb's learning model (Kolb 1984, p. 42)

The two interacting dimensions mark out four spaces or fields within the learning cycle that are filled by four adaptive orientations or basic forms of knowledge. In his further work, Kolb drops the problematic succession in the learning cycle and instead concentrates on these forms of knowledge, and it is in this that I regard him as having transcended Piaget.

This emerges clearly from the naming of the forms of knowledge as assimilative, convergent, accommodative and divergent knowledge, respectively – the assimilative and accommodative concepts are clearly taken from Piaget, while the convergent and divergent concepts come from John P. Guilford, the researcher into intelligence and creativity. Convergent (unambiguous) knowledge concerns concentration on a specific output from a given input, i.e. what we typically call inference or deduction, while divergent (ambiguous) knowledge means the development of various potential outputs from the same input, i.e. what we typically understand by creativity and diversity (cf. Guilford 1967, p.213ff).

In addition the model indicates the typical conditions for each of the forms of knowledge thus:

- assimilative knowledge typically develops from comprehension and intention
- convergent knowledge typically develops from comprehension and extension
- accommodative knowledge typically develops from apprehension and extension
- divergent knowledge typically develops from apprehension and intention.

In comparison with Piaget, it could be considered problematic that the four forms of knowledge in the model are of equal standing. This is not immediately in accordance with Piaget's theory of equilibrium. But it is still possible to conceive of assimilation and accommodation as the two basic types of processes, and then, on the basis of Kolb's work, make the important addition that both these types of process can have a nature that to some extent favours the direction of the convergent or the divergent. Thus a very important differentiation from Piaget's concept emerges, as many relationships in life cannot be interpreted with certainty and with clear criteria for what is right and what is wrong. In addition Kolb's model to a certain extent – although only on a more theoretical level than in Nissen's description – indicates which situations tend to advance the various forms of knowledge. I have previously looked more deeply into this area and found evidence for the idea that subject-oriented teaching predominantly provides for convergent knowledge, while problem-oriented activities are more likely to encourage divergent knowledge (Illeris 1995).

Summary

The interpretation of the cognitive dimension of learning which has been outlined in the previous section can be briefly summarised in the following points:

1. The human ability to learn developed together with the other characteristics of our species in the struggle for survival of the various species, and this can be understood as one of several tools for the continued struggle.

2. The internal psychological aspect of learning consists of the individual's development of psychological structures or schemes through a continuing process of construction and reconstruction, as new impressions are related to previously developed structures. This interaction takes the nature of an adjustment process for the individual, which can be described as an active adaptation. In this continuing adaptation, three types of processes can be identified:

3. *Cumulative learning* can take place when impressions from the environment cannot be related to previously established structures. This learning is mechanical in nature, and the learning products can only be recalled in situations that are almost identical to the learning situation.

4. *Assimilative learning* consists of the adaptation and incorporation of new impressions into previously established structures, which are thus extended and stabilised. The learning is additive in nature, and the learning products can be activated in a broad spectrum of situations that the individual perceives as related to the learning situation or otherwise relevant to it in some way.

5. *Accommodative learning* consists of the reconstruction of established structures through dissociation, liberation and reorganisation. The learning is transcendent in nature, and in principle the learning products can be activated regardless of the nature of the situation. Accommodative learning involves a relinquishing of acquired structures and the establishing of new, and is thus typically perceived as a demanding process and a strain. Accommodative processes presuppose the existence of, firstly, relevant structures that can be reconstructed, secondly, individual motivation to undertake such a demanding reconstruction, and thirdly, a perception of safety and permissiveness in the situation. These three types of preconditions are present in a mutual interaction, and can partially compensate for each other.

6. Both assimilative and accommodative processes can be predominantly convergent (unambiguous) or divergent (ambiguous) in nature.

7. A profitable development process involves an interaction between assimilative and accommodative (and perhaps also cumulative) processes, balanced in relation to the context.

3. Reflection, Meta-Learning and Transformative Learning

Learning to learn

In recent years concepts such as reflection, meta-learning or "learning to learn" have played an increasing part in both political and academic debate on the subject of learning, even to the extent that this kind of function has come to be seen as an important general goal for education and socialisation.

The popular phrase "learning to learn" is a modern catchphrase that, when viewed from an academic perspective, can be traced back to the observation within learning psychology that if an individual constantly applies him- or herself to learning within a given field, there will typically occur a gradual increase of learning speed (presumably because one gradually has more and more relevant presuppositions at one's disposal, a closer net of structures is woven, or however one may like to put it – cf. Bateson 1972, p. 166ff). However, this original meaning seems to have been lost, and the modern catchphrase seems more like a mystification, as if one has to be trained to be able to learn something.

It must therefore be maintained, as has already been pointed out several times in this book, that the ability to learn is one of mankind's innate skills – and moreover, in the next chapter it will emerge that this also fundamentally includes the desire to learn: learning is basically libidinal. When the catchphrase appears time and time again in debate, however, there must naturally be a response to it – and part of that response surely lies in the fact that institutionalised learning in schools and institutions can tend to undermine the desire to learn, at least in certain contexts and under certain forms (cf. chapter 10). But at the same time there is no doubt that the catchphrase also expresses a societal need for a new form of learning, which the concepts of reflection and meta-learning can sum up more precisely.

Reflection and reflexivity

The word "reflection" can encompass two different main meanings, both in everyday language and that of academic study. One concerns *afterthought:* one reflects on or gives further thought to something, perhaps an event or a problem. The other can best be characterised as *mirroring* – in line with the word's original optical meaning: an experience or comprehension of something is mirrored in the self of the learner, i.e. its significance for the self is in focus and the experience is evaluated with the personal identity as a yardstick – which is why the word *self-reflection* is also used in this sense.

It is particularly the ability for or inclination to this form of reflection that is today often defined as *reflexivity,* although it must be said an accurate vocabulary does not always occur in this sphere. Reflexivity in this sense has in recent years become a central concept in a number of current sociological, cultural theory and socialisation theory approaches – e.g. from theorists such as Anthony Giddens, Ulrich Beck, Niklas Luhmann and Thomas Ziehe. I will deal with this in greater detail in chapter 5.

In this chapter, for the time being, I will concentrate on reflection in the cognitive sense of afterthought and, most importantly, I will attempt to clarify how this concept can be defined and understood in relation to the more general theory of cognitive learning that was dealt with in the previous chapter, starting with Piaget.

What seems to characterise this kind of reflection is that new impulses arising from interaction with the environment do not occur directly – the words *after*thought and *re*flection contain this element of time lag. Of course, the process is sparked off by interaction with the environment, and it is also quite possible that some immediate learning from this interaction has taken place. However, something remains unfinished, the impulses have not been completed, there is an element of cognitive dissonance (Festinger 1957), and when a suitable situation appears, perhaps a quiet moment, the afterthought makes itself felt. As the American adult educational theorist Jack Mezirow has pointed out, reflection also occurs when what has been learnt is to be used in a later context or an examination or justification of acquired comprehension (Mezirow 1990, 1991).

In psychology this situation was first considered by the German psychologist Karl Duncker (1935), who was one of the first to systematically research the psychology of problem solving – and it is characteristic that afterthought takes the nature of problem solving. The original interaction has left behind something uncertain or unsolved, some problems, which must be put into place by means of elaboration later. As a learning process, reflection can therefore be characterised as accommodative learning that does not occur immediately in connection with the trigger impulses, but after a time lag implying a further elaboration of the impulses.

Reflection is thus basically of the same nature as other accommodative learning processes, but it includes a further elaboration process. Therefore reflection will also require more psychological energy, and at the same time involves a potential for further elaboration in relation to the immediate accommodation (I shall return to this point below in this chapter). This is certainly the case regarding what the English adult educator Stephen Brookfield (1986, p. 16ff) and the American adult educator Jack Mezirow (1990, 1991) define as *critical reflection,* which also involves an assessment of the validity of the presuppositions for acquired knowledge.

Conversely it should be noted that – particularly in organisational psychology – the popular concept of *reflection-in-action,* developed by the aforementioned American psychologist, Donald Schön (1983, cf. chapter 10), does not fall within this concept of reflection as a particular form of learning. For Schön, reflection-in-action is a process in which one immediately reacts to a problem or a situation by finding new potential solutions, drawing on one's familiarity with the field in question – and if there is no element of examination or new thinking, then it is a typical example of what I have dealt with in the previous chapter, as have also Piaget and Nissen, as an "ordinary" accommodation, i.e. a direct learning reaction to impulses in an interaction with the surrounding world (cf. Mezirow 1990, p. 112ff).

Rather more complex to deal with is the concept of meta-learning – or *meta-cognition* as it is also called, using a slightly broader term (Engeström 1987, p. 128, Mezirow 1991, p. 6). The concept involves the notion that there exists a superior kind of learning in some form or other that is general in nature and spans the individual learning processes, a form of learning that puts other learning processes in a comprehensive overall perspective.

In order to go more deeply into this problem, I will deal with the theory on *learning by expanding* or expansive learning, developed by the Finnish learning and organisational psychologist Yrjö Engeström (1987). Engeström's theory, however, is constructed partly on perceptions from the Russian cultural historical tradition, and partly on a learning theory developed by the English scientist Gregory Bateson. Therefore I will start by sketching out these two basic theories and then return to Engeström's work below in this chapter.

The cultural historical tradition and the concept of activity

The cultural historical tradition in the field of psychology was originally developed in Russia between the two world wars by a number of psychologists, including Lev Vygotsky, Aleksei Leontjev and Aleksander Luria. Since the end of the Second World War, this tradition has become more prevalent in Denmark, Germany, the USA and elsewhere.

The definition "cultural historical" refers to the basic view that mankind's phylogenetic development, and that which separates humans from animals, centres on the human development of culture, and that mankind's fundamental psychological structures have developed in interaction with the development of culture. Leontjev (1981) was among the most important contributors to have thoroughly elaborated this view, and in addition Luria tested and confirmed this approach through an investigation of changes in the knowledge processes of farmers in Uzbekistan, who experienced an abrupt change in the early 1930s from a primitive feudal farming society to a modern communist farming collective (Luria 1976).

The central point in the approach of this tradition is that psychological factors can only be understood in a historical perspective and based on interaction with the cultural environment. This interaction takes the nature of what Leontjev terms as *object reflection*:

"The organisms' adaptation, which is always ... a kind of reflection of properties of the environment by them ... acquires the form ... of reflection of affective properties of the environment in their objective connections and relations. This is also a specific form of reflection for the psyche, object reflection." (Leontjev 1981, p. 45).

This concept of object reflection is to a certain extent in accordance with Piaget's constructivist approach, for both concepts involve an active development of psychological structures based on an interaction between the individual and his or her environment. But in the cultural historical approach, the psychological structures are developed from a reciprocal mirroring process, while Piaget deals with a construction that to a great extent can involve interpretations and deviations from the conditions of the environment.

In the cultural historical approach, mankind's interaction with the environment is characterised by the key concept of *activity*. Through activity, the individual acquires the cultural conditions that he or she is a part of, and at the same time he or she influences cultural development within the society:

> "What is the concrete link between the psychological features of man's individual consciousness and his social being? – The answer to that stems from the basic psychological fact that the structure of man's consciousness is linked in a regular way with the structure of his activity. – Man's activity then can only have a structure that is created by given social conditions and the relations between people engendered by them." (Leontjev 1981, p. 231).

It must be emphasised that activity is defined as *goal-directed* endeavours. It can only be considered activity when the individual pursues definite aims through his endeavours. Activity is seen as different actions that can again be divided up into different operations, and it is characteristic that in his or her activity, a person can make use of different *tools,* which are not simply material instruments and devices, but can also include language, social conventions, theories and so on.

There are many kinds of activity, but the most important – which activity theorists return to time after time – are *play, learning* and *labour,* which are the predominant forms of activity in the pre-school, school-age and adult stages respectively. The Danish learning theorist Mads Hermansen finds, however, that in this connection learning is better characterised as a result of activity, and that the prevailing form of activity in the school-age years should probably be called school activity (Hermansen 1996, p. 63ff).

Thus we enter the sphere of the more specific learning approach of the cultural historical tradition, as developed by Vygotsky in particular in connection with his central work on thought and language – and at this point it seems to me characteristic that while object reflection and activity are the general comprehension categories, Vygotsky deals with learning as something more specific that occurs in school and other "educational" situations. I think it is no coincidence that Vygotsky perceives learning as a particular form of activity on a level with play and work, for the concept is related to contexts in which the very fact that someone is to learn something is vitally important to the situation, and the underlying thought pattern seems to involve an interaction between one person who is more capable, and others (one or more) who are less so – one who represents the evolved culture, and others who are to acquire it.

This is particularly the case regarding two concepts that play a central role every time there is an attempt to set Vygotsky's learning concept into pedagogical theories, instructions or practice, viz., the concept of the *zone of proximal development* (Vygotsky 1978, p. 84ff, 1986, p. 187ff) and the concept of *scientific concepts* (Vygotsky 1986, p. 146ff). Vygotsky defined the zone of proximal development as

> "the distance between the actual developmental level as determined by independent problem solving and the level of potential development as determined through problem solving under adult guidance or in collaboration with more capable peers." (Vygotsky 1978, p. 86).

Scientific concepts are concepts that are real and genuine, i.e. they must be precise and defined in a systematic context.

I have always been somewhat sceptical of these two key concepts in the cultural historical tradition because it is so clearly adults and those in power who are able to decide both what the specific zones of proximal development are for children or participants in education, and what concepts can be characterised as scientific. Therefore, applying Vygotsky's learning concepts, teaching easily becomes a predominantly teacher-directed form of encounter, which in turn can easily result in the nearest zone of proximal development being conceived of in the perspective of academic systematism, e.g. the next chapter in the textbook (whereby logical and psychological arrangement become confused, which Dewey so strongly warned against – Dewey 1902). Hence, scientific concepts will become synonymous with the concepts of those in power.

Though it was hardly Vygotsky's intention, it appears that his learning conception and account may easily lead to a form of goal-directed activity in which it is the teacher or the adults that control the process to a very great extent. In Denmark in the late 70s and early 80s we saw what this can lead to in practice, when Vygotsky-inspired so-called "structured learning", which was very much pedagogically controlled, was a widespread ideal in Danish childcare institutions (Brostrøm 1977). But there have been other experiments in Denmark, also based on Vygotsky's learning concept, without that same dogmatic kind of teacher control, and in which more emphasis has been placed on the pupils' own contributions to the concept development (Hedegaard & Hansen 1992, Hedegaard 1998).

As I see it, the cultural historical tradition has first and foremost used the historic-genetic approach to build up an important basis for the understanding of the biological, historical and societal anchoring of psychological processes. But perhaps because the tradition was developed within the ideal of a contradiction-free communist society, it lacks an understanding of societal conflicts and their fundamental structural importance – and in extension of this there is an idea that transfer of cultural and societal matters to a particular individual can take place as a more or less frictionless process. This implies a simplification of the understanding of the learning conception and may, in practice, cause a number of problems with respect to authority.

Bateson's learning theory

The second important source of inspiration for Yrjö Engeström's theory on learning by expanding was Gregory Bateson, English-born zoologist, ethnographer, epistemologist, cyberneticist and philosopher, who with his interdisciplinary approach in the period from the mid-30s to the end of the 70s, was an extremely creative and sometimes controversial figure across a wide academic field, particularly in research into communication and consciousness (cf. Lipset 1980).

On a system theoretical basis, Bateson developed a learning theory that embraces five types or levels of learning in a hierarchical order, with each superordinate level transcending the conditions that regulate learning on the closest subordinate level (the theory was set out in a 1964 article which was later reproduced in Bateson 1972, p. 279-308). Bateson summarises the individual levels as follows:

"*Zero learning* is characterized by *specificity of response*, which – right or wrong – is not subject to correction.

Learning I is *change in specificity of response* by correction of errors of choice within a set of alternatives.

Learning II is *change in the process of Learning I, e.g.*, a corrective change in the set of alternatives from which choice is made, or it is a change in how the sequence of experience is punctuated.

Learning III is *change in the process of Learning II, e.g.*, a corrective change in the system of sets of alternatives from which choice is made. (We shall see later that to demand this level of performance of some men and some mammals is sometimes pathogenic).

Learning IV would be *change in Learning III*, but probably does not occur in any adult living organism on this earth. Evolutionary process has, however, created organisms whose ontogeny brings them to Level III. The combination of phylogenesis with ontogenesis, in fact, achieves Level IV." (Bateson 1972, p. 293).

However, I am not going to concentrate on this cybernetically oriented model as a whole entity. Levels 0 and I are so simple that they are only relevant to human learning at a very early stage and in particular situations – Hermansen characterises them as the "amoeba stage" (Hermansen 1996, p. 144) – and Level IV is a non-existent, hypothetical level. On the other hand, almost all ordinary human learning occurs on Level II, including processes that Piaget was concerned with, such as assimilation and accommodation. For this reason, both Engeström and Hermansen appear to have difficulties in elucidating this level, and Engeström divides it up into a IIa-level and a IIb-level in order to better understand it (Engeström 1987, p. 148). Level III is thus the superordinate level which human learning can reach in particular conditions, and which provides the opportunity for detachment from the ties that regulate learning on Level II.

The basic idea in Bateson's learning theory is that in order to reach a higher level of learning, one needs to use feedback to transcend the fundamental conditions that apply on the current level. So in order to get from Level II to Level III, one has to transcend the set of alternatives that one can operate with on Level II. In Hermansen's interpretation the movement from Engeström's Level IIa to IIb appears to be much the same as the transcendence of acquired structures found in the form of accommodation described by Piaget (Hermansen 1996, p. 144ff).

But what then about Level III? This concerns the transcendence of conditions of what is known in order to acquire something that is new in the sense that it is fundamentally or structurally different, or on a different level, from what was hitherto known. In connection with this, Engeström refers to Bateson's own concept of *double bind*, which was first introduced in 1956 in connection with a theory on schizophrenia, but which Bateson himself did not take into account when he put forward his learning theory (the article on double bind was reproduced in Bateson 1972, p. 201-227). The Danish researcher Bent Ølgaard has summarised Bateson's characterisation of a double bind situation thus:

"It concerns two or more people, and refers to repeated experience of the same kind of situation, whereby Bateson expressly dissociates himself from the hypothesis of a single traumatic experience (author's note: as a cause of schizophrenia). Following this are three kinds of commands or prohibitions: firstly *a primary negative command*, e.g: 'If you do not do such-and-such a thing, I will punish you.' Next there is *a secondary command, which conflicts with the first on a more abstract level* and is enforced by punishment or signals threatening punishment, e.g.: 'You should not see this as a punishment', 'You should not see me as the one doing the punishing', 'You should not comply with my prohibition'. *And thirdly, a tertiary negative command, preventing the person caught in the double bind from leaving the field.* – Finally, Bateson adds as a last characteristic of double bind situations that the entire set of ingredients is unnecessary once the 'victim' has learnt to view his world according to a double bind model." (Ølgaard 1977, p. 250).

More generally, a "classic" double bind situation can thus be characterised as a recurrent communication model involving conflicting commands or messages from a person or instance on whom or on which the person concerned is dependent and cannot escape from. A situation like this is ultimately intolerable, and the person concerned therefore reacts by developing schizophrenia, i.e. escapes by not being present mentally.

Engeström's theory of learning by expanding

The Finn Yrjö Engeström's academic work is from the sphere of the cultural historical tradition, but in connection with the development of the theory of learning by expanding, in my opinion he takes a decisive step ahead by connecting his work with Bateson's learning theory and the concept of double bind (Engeström 1987).

The most important element from the cultural historical tradition that Engeström has adopted is Vygotsky's concept of the zone of proximal development – but he has not done so without criticism. On the contrary, he makes the same criticism I put forward above in this chapter, i.e. that Vygotsky's version of the concept can very easily lead to a teacher-controlled and more or less authoritarian form of teaching – and after a lengthy discussion of this, he ends by endorsing the following reformulation of Vygotsky's definition of the zone of proximal development, proposed by the Americans Peg Griffin and Michael Cole:

"Adult wisdom does not provide teleology for child development. Social organization and leading activities provide a gap within which the child can develop novel creative analyses... – a Zo-ped (author's note: zone of proximal development) is a dialogue between the child and his future; it is not a dialogue between the child and an adult's past." (Griffin & Cole 1984, p. 62).

But Engeström does not stop at this reformulation. Such a radical alteration of the definition of the concept must have further consequences. A dialogue between the child and his future in the form of new analyses clearly indicates creative processes, and therefore the reformulation involves an understanding of the zone of proximal development as a space for creativity. This is a clear expansion of Vygotsky's comprehension, and in Engeström's opinion it is a necessary one: we must stop talking about the acquisition of what has already been developed, and understand that what is important are creative processes (cf. Engeström 1987, p. 169ff). This is also an indirect connection to a constructivist learning concept.

This is where the combination of Engeström's two approaches comes in: if learning in the zone of proximal development is understood as transcendent, innovative, creative processes, it must be what Bateson defines as Learning III. Even though Engeström's arguments take a different course and therefore do not reach the following conclusion in a very clear manner, the reinterpretation of Vygotsky's definition opens up the possibility of perceiving the zone of proximal development and Learning III as two different expressions of the same thing. A process involving a creative innovation that is important for the development of the individual and that transcends the limitations of what has previously been developed, must be the same as a process that goes beyond the set of alternatives that previously regulated comprehension in the sphere in question; in any case, when it concerns school-age children, young persons or adults, it must be a transition from Level II to Level III or a process of learning through expansion.

However, the precondition for such a process taking place is that the individual must have a pressing problem or conflict of interests that cannot be solved within the existing set of alternatives. And this is where

Engeström introduces the concept of the double bind, though in a slightly different sense from that of the original in Bateson's schizophrenia article, for here there is a potential for a positive solution in the form of a transcendence of the situation's basic conditions. Bateson has himself also widely used the double bind concept in a similar way, as illustrated by the following quote:

> "In the Eastern religion, Zen Buddhism, the goal is to achieve enlightenment. The Zen master attempts to bring about enlightenment in his pupil in various ways. One of the things he does is to hold a stick over the pupil's head and say fiercely, 'If you say this stick is real, I will strike you with it. If you say this stick is not real, I will strike you with it. If you don't say anything, I will strike you with it.'" (Bateson 1972, p. 208).

This is a clear double bind situation because all the proposed solutions are ruled out, yet it can be solved without schizophrenia or flight, if the pupil manages to take the stick from the master and thus transcend the constituent conditions of the situation.

On the basis of Vygotsky's and Bateson's theories, Engeström thus finds that humans have the potential for a particular kind of learning through expansion that is characterised by the transcendence of the constituent conditions of earlier learning, and concerns an insight into and thus a detachment from these very conditions. Learning of this nature can typically occur when the learner in a problem situation asks him- or herself questions such as:

> "What is the meaning and sense of this problem in the first place? Why should I try to solve it? How did it emerge? Who designed it, for what purpose and for whose benefit? As Bateson notes, this kind of behavior is easily coined as disruptive." (Engeström 1987, p. 151).

With reference to the philosopher Marx Wartofsky, Engeström also finds that the situation is characterised by processes such as "non-practical or 'free' play or game activity ... so called 'disinterested' perception or aesthetic perception, or sheer contemplation" (Wartofsky 1979, p. 208), and Engeström sums it up thus:

"In Learning III, the subject becomes conscious and gains an imaginative and thus potentially also a practical mastery of whole systems of activity in terms of the past, the present and the future. Individual manifestations of Learning III are commonly called 'personal crises', 'breaking away', 'turning points' or 'moments of revelation'." (Engeström 1987, p. 153).

Engeström also feels able to distinguish between two different types of Learning III, viz. "development as personal crises and explosions, and development as tacit, invisible contributions" (Engeström 1987, p. 161). Moreover, he stresses the significance of the social or collective dimension in such learning processes, and he himself uses learning theory primarily in the development of public and private organisations. I will return to this matter in chapter 8.

Meta-learning and transformative learning

In the previous section I have set out a possible interpretation of Engeström's theory of learning by expanding. I have not followed his own argument directly, but have attempted to present a concise description of what I consider to be the central points in the present context. I may have over-interpreted some points; and there is certainly much I have left out. I have, however, made room for Vygotsky's concept of the zone of proximal development even though I do not consider it absolutely essential for Engeström's construction, other than that it anchors his theory in his own cultural historical basis. But it *should* be possible, as far as I can see, to carry the argument through simply on Bateson's concepts of double bind and the learning levels.

My question is now: how does that which is described as Learning III or learning by expanding in the previous section relate to the theoretical basis I dealt with in the previous chapter, particularly the Piagetian basic concepts of assimilation and accommodation?

It is immediately obvious that Learning III, like reflection, is related to accommodation. Learning III involves a thorough restructuring of earlier structures, so extensive that it even includes the former basis of the structures. As far as I can see, it involves structures from several schemes being brought together or placed in connection with each other in a new way, so that an overall understanding is created that transcends earlier distinctions – and that is precisely what we find in the concept of *meta-learning* as described above in chapter 3.

Meta-learning can occur whenever there is a significant conflict of interests and there is the potential for a transcendent adaptation. The learning process may take the form of coming through a crisis, in which the learner struggles for a certain length of time with a problem which is of urgent subjective importance – this is both reflection and meta-learning. But meta-learning can also occur as a shorter and more intense process, even like a kind of explosion in the most concentrated cases.

In modern creativity theory, precisely this kind of conflict-filled and chaotic situation can be seen as a typical background for creative transcendence (e.g. Joas 1996), and the Swede Feiwel Kupferberg has noted that project work can form a pedagogical framework that contains possibilities of this kind (Kupferberg 1996). A more general pedagogical observation is that there must be *challenges* that the learner feels obliged to deal with, and that there must be the potential for, and input to, a relevant *processing* of such challenges if learning of this kind is to take place.

In terms of learning theory, it is important for the further development of Bateson's and Engeström's theories that the challenges are on the one hand such that they not only require a transcendence of the previously developed comprehension, but also of the fundamental premises of this comprehension – and on the other hand that they are perceived as imperative, i.e. that there is an unavoidable motivation, anchored either in a strong personal interest or in a perceived obligation to do something about conditions that are deemed unacceptable (i.e. a form of social responsibility, cf. chapter 7).

A similar view is to be found in the concept of *transformative learning* developed by the American adult educator mentioned earlier, Jack Mezirow (1990, 1991), that is seen as a central perspective in adult education. This concerns changes in the basic perceptions of context and meaning complexes that are deeply incorporated from childhood, and which are often unconsciously the basis for the individual's opinions and forms of comprehension – what Mezirow defines as meaning schemes and meaning perspectives. It also concerns altered action patterns as an extension of this, i.e. an attitude to parts of the life basis one previously acted on.

Typical examples Mezirow gives of this kind of learning include the re-evaluation of identity, self-image, values and opinions, as undertaken by many women in the 1960s and 70s in connection with gender role debates and consciousness-raising groups in the feminist movement, and the education initiatives for poor agricultural workers that Paulo Freire started at the same time in South America, and which he has written about in his book "Pedagogy of the Oppressed" (Mezirow 1990, p. 3 and 14, Freire 1970).

Although the examples illustrate which profound learning processes are being referred to, at the same time they show the gap between the immediate comprehension of cognitive learning as acquisition of knowledge and skills and the thorough processes that can also be involved in cognitive learning.

Thus, in addition to the three types or levels of learning processes described in chapter 2, there would seem to be a fourth level that occurs only in connection with crisis-like situations in which a solution must be found by transcending the premises of the situation and where the learner has an urgent motivation and can summon psychological resources to learn. Structurally this type of learning may be characterised as a complex accommodation involving the simultaneous restructuring of several cognitive as well as emotional schemes. Functionally, it changes the learner's self, thereby providing the learner with qualitatively new understandings and patterns of action.

Following the terminology of Jack Mezirow, I suggest that the terms "transformation" or "transformative learning" be used for this type of learning, as from a language point of view this term is in line with the Piagetian terms of assimilation and accommodation. But it is worth mentioning that this is basically the same process that Engeström has described as expansive learning, whereas Rogers' concept of significant learning as described in chapter 2 seems to cover both accommodation and transformation. I have here omitted the term of meta-learning as it is generally used very imprecisely or in connection with the idea of "learning to learn", from which I dissociated myself early in this chapter.

In relation to Bateson's learning types as elaborated by Engeström, a certain parallelism can be seen where

- Learning I is parallel to cumulative learning,
- Learning IIa is parallel to assimilative learning
- Learning IIb is parallel to accommodative learning
- Learning III is parallel to transformative learning

In this connection I have deliberately used the term "parallel to" as the levels are defined in very different ways and it is by no means possible to speak of identity or the like.

Summary

The most important points in this chapter can be summarised as follows:

1. A particular form of accommodation exists when a transcendence of previously developed psychological structures is established by means of a time-displaced *reflection*, unconnected directly with new impulses from the environment. Reflection requires even more psychological energy than other forms of accommodation.

2. A particular and very demanding form of reflection is *critical reflection*, which involves an assessment of the validity of the presuppositions for previously acquired understandings.

3. One special and very demanding type of learning may be termed as transformation or *transformative learning*. This type of learning occurs in crisis-like situations that can only be solved by transcending the premises of a problem or situation. It may take place through long and often painful adaptation or through shorter, intense processes. In both

cases very strong motivation and the ability to raise considerable psychological resources is required.

4. Structurally, transformative learning involves the simultaneous restructuring of several cognitive as well as emotional schemes. Functionally, it changes the learner's self and thereby provides the learner with qualitatively new understandings and patterns of action.

4. Learning and Emotions

The divided totality

The previous chapters dealt mainly with learning as the acquisition and development of cognitive structures – although it has become increasingly clear that motivational and emotional factors have great significance for learning.

This limitation is in accordance with the traditional approach of learning psychology and with the approach that has predominantly underpinned the theory developments I have considered up to this point. Thus, up to now I have continued with the classical distinction between the cognitive and the affective or emotional that exists both in psychology as an academic discipline and more generally in our culture and language, and which can be traced back as far as the ancient Greek distinction between logos and psyche.

Two central disciplines of psychology are learning psychology and personality psychology. Learning psychology, as a part of cognitive psychology, is concerned with knowledge and epistemology, popularly expressed as *how we learn something*, while personality psychology, closely connected to parts of developmental psychology and clinical psychology, is concerned with the development and structure of the personality, or *how we become who we are.* One can also refer to the purely linguistic distinction between learning *something* and developing *oneself.*

It is typical that learning psychology has drawn the limit at emotional matters – as in the following characteristic quotations from two prominent representatives of American learning psychology, Robert M. Gagné and Jerome S. Bruner:

"In the most comprehensive sense of the word 'learning', motivations and attitudes must surely be considered to be learned. But the present treatment (author's note: Gagné: The Conditions of Learning) does not attempt to deal with such learnings, except in a tangential sense. Its scope is restricted to what may be termed the intellectual, or subject matter content that leads to improvement in human performances having ultimate usefulness in the pursuit of the individual's vocation or profession." (Gagné 1970, p. 25).

"A theory of instruction is prescriptive in the sense that it sets forth rules concerning the most effective way of achieving knowledge or skills." (Bruner 1966, p.40).

Against this is a personality and developmental psychology that is typically broadly concerned with human psychological development and structures, but seldom takes any interest in the acquisition of concrete knowledge, skills or competence – cf. the definition of significant learning in chapter 2, in which Rogers as humanistic psychologist clearly draws the limits at ordinary acquisition of knowledge, even though he has written several books on the subject of learning and formulated the concept of student-centered teaching. Rogers is only concerned with learning processes that result in actual personal development – and thus the acquisition of subject matter knowledge and skills, which constitute a considerable part of almost all educational processes, is for the most part beyond his attention.

A comprehensive learning theory thus has to transcend the classical division and concern itself with the person as a whole, both the cognitive and affective aspects, and not least the interaction between them. In the terminology of this book, this is about the interaction between the cognitive and emotional dimensions of learning, and it is this relationship I want to take up in this chapter and the next.

Furth's attempt to bridge the gap

This division of the whole person is not a new problem, and attempts have often been made to bridge the gap. The most fundamental and the most interesting of these attempts are concerned with a bridging of the two theories that are regarded as the most comprehensive and the most widespread, each on its own side of the divide, viz. Piaget's theory of cognitive development and Freud's theory of personality development – because based on these two development-oriented theoretical constructions, the basis of the division itself in human development will come to be central.

Attempts of this kind with a predominantly psychoanalytical basis have been made by Peter Wolff (1960) and Stanley Greenspan (1979). But although these were comprehensive and serious attempts, there does not seem to have been wider interest, in either the cognitive or the psychoanalytically-oriented contexts, to move forward in this direction – everyone seems to have had enough problems of their own to solve.

The following section is based on what I consider to be the most thorough attempt to bridge the gap between Piaget's and Freud's theory bases, a book by the American Piaget specialist Hans Furth, entitled *Knowledge As Desire* (Furth 1987). The title suggests that the acquisition of knowledge and skills is essentially libidinal and thus also includes something positively emotional – that ultimately in mankind's genetically evolved nature there lies a capacity for acquiring knowledge and skills, and a fundamentally limitless desire to do so, (in line with the development of other human libidinal and life maintaining functions).

In his introduction, Furth stresses that not only did Piaget and Freud develop the best known and most comprehensive theories in the cognitive and personality spheres respectively, but that they also – despite the apparently huge difference in their theories – share some important fundamental features: they were both trained in biology, and they both anchored their theories in the biological development of the child, which they had studied empirically in detail. Naturally there are significant differences, for

"Freud's theories speak to the interest of those trying to understand the less conscious and less controlled components of human actions, and the linkage of development and emotions is a key component of this understanding. In a similar way, I think, Piaget's theory appeals to many on account of his linking development and knowledge." (Furth 1987, p. 3).

However there are also grounds for emphasising the crucial similarity that makes the two theoretical constructions comparable:

"We can firmly hold that the developmental theories of Piaget or of Freud describe a general (if you like, universal) progression of logical and psychosexual maturity without having to deny either an innate directional disposition or the autonomy of the individual agent." (Furth 1987, p. 60).

With regard to the relationship between emotions and epistemology, however, there is a considerable difference. For Freud the two spheres were in clear contradiction to one another, which is perhaps most clearly expressed in the conflict between the pleasure principle and the reality principle. For Piaget, however, it is a positive interaction; but his research concentrates on the development of knowledge and only refers to emotional issues on rare occasions – I will return to this at a later point.

Furth's interpretation is that in spite of obvious differences there is a clear link between Freud's and Piaget's development theories in their conceptions of symbol formation, i.e. the capacity to engage in and deal with matters that are not physically present, which the child begins to develop at the age of two on the basis of his or her experiences.

The precondition for being able to form symbols is the ability to form objects, and here is another important point where there is agreement between Freud's and Piaget's approaches: objects in a psychological sense are not the objects or persons that exist in the surrounding world, but are instead the psychological representation or the "inner picture" formed by the individual of the objects or persons in question, and which can be "obsessed" with positive or negative emotions.

From object formation, symbol formation can occur, which may be expressed in language, numbers and figures, in ideas, fantasies or dreams, or in imitation and play. But Piaget finds that there is a common psychological background for any symbol formation:

Gradually as the young child begins to notice his or her environment and orient him- or herself within it, he or she also begins to deal actively with external conditions, in a diffuse and uncertain way at first, but later with elements of repetition and control. In this way, the objects and persons in the surrounding world take on the nature of objects-of-actions, i.e. internal ideas to act in relation to. Slowly, set action patterns form for particular external conditions, but the child makes no distinction between the action and the object. Later, the objects-of-actions become objects-of-knowledge; i.e. there is knowledge of the object beyond the action. And from this a symbol formation can occur, involving the crucial capacity for the psychological management of non-present conditions.

For Piaget it is important to emphasise that all of this fundamental development is libidinal in nature, and it can thus be related to the fundamental and innate pleasure principle and to the life or Eros drive described by Freud (whereas the common translation into English of the German word "Trieb" as used by Freud is usually "instinct", Furth deliberately prefers the more correct translation "drive" – and I shall follow him in this respect). Every normal healthy child will go through this development. There is no division between the libidinal life fulfilment and the formation of these first cognitive structures: desire and learning coincide. This is also very much in line with the approach of the psychoanalytically-oriented socialisation theorist Alfred Lorenzer, who, starting with earliest childhood, interprets learning as the internalisation or in-socialisation of forms of interaction that are experienced and converted into symbolically-organised meaning structures or personality structures (Lorenzer 1972, cf. chapter 7). These structures, like the interactions, must necessarily have both a cognitive and an affective content.

Between the ages of approximately two and six, symbol formation is developed and consolidated, and there occurs more and more of what we normally understand as thinking, though it is still of an intuitive and un-connected nature, without the coherent trains of thought Piaget refers to as operations. In the same period the child comes through the whole emotional and interactional process that Freud describes as the oedipal drama, and which in Freudian theory results in the separation of the three elements of the personality, the id, the ego and the superego. In Furth's approach, this drama has the nature of

"a slow, gradual and expanding process of symbol formation that eventually becomes stabilized in internal images or fantasies."
(Furth 1987, p. 59).

At first this process establishes the newly acquired capacity as a kind of uninhibited wishful thinking, but ends up in the Freudian model with the fundamental oppression that represses forbidden or non-feasible wishes to the unconscious, and balances out the uninhibited pleasure principle with a reality principle that allows a more realistic relationship with the surrounding world. At much the same time the child seems to have developed through his or her experiences the cognitive capacity that allows what Piaget calls "concrete-operational" thinking, characterised by coherent and stable thought patterns, systematic in nature.

Between the ages of about two to six, knowledge and emotions gradually develop in step with each other, symbol formation brings both wishful thinking and intense development in interpersonal relationships, and both lead to a rounding off that at around school age amounts to relative independence and the cognitive capacity to acquire knowledge and skills from school in an organised fashion. Children have at this point made *"sense of themselves as persons in relation to the proximate world in which they live."* (Furth 1987, p. 59). The formation of identity has begun.

This stabilisation concludes Furth's comparison of the development of the child in the models of Piaget and Freud respectively. The most important aspect of them in the present context is the assertion that knowledge and emotions are things that do not exist as independent spheres from the start of life, but gradually form during the individual's active acquisition of his or her environment. At the age of six the two spheres have to a certain extent become independent, but they are still always two sides of the same thing, two aspects that are involved in every act of learning and in every action, and which have been researched separately by both Piaget and Freud:

> "While Piaget explained the how of actions and symbols, their internal organization and logical cohesiveness, Freud explored the why behind these acts and the dynamic economy within the household of personal impulses and drives. – There is an implicit sexual drive component and an implicit logical reason component in any action, but no human action is (or can be) merely one or the other." (Furth 1987, p. 11 and 12).

Cognitive structures and affective patterns

Structuralistic not much concerned with emotional aspect [handwritten margin note]

The question now is how the cognitive and the affective interact with each other after the partial independence that appears to have developed around the age of six. Even though Piaget was not much concerned with the emotional aspect, there are some indications in his extensive work, e.g. the following:

> "All schemes, whatever they are, are at the same time affective and cognitive." (Piaget 1946, p. 222, quoted from Furth 1987, p. 127).

> "Affective life, like intellectual life, is a continual adaptation, and the two are not only parallel but interdependent, since feelings express the interest and the value given to actions of which intelligence provides the structure. Since affective life is adaptation, it also implies continual assimilation of present situations to earlier ones – assimilation which gives rise to affective schemes or relatively stable modes of feeling or reacting – and continual accommodation of these schemas to the present situation." (Piaget 1951, p. 205-206).

> "Obviously for intelligence to function, it must be motivated by an affective power. A person won't ever solve a problem if the problem doesn't interest him. The impetus for everything lies in interest, affective motivation. – If the problem at hand is the construction of structures, affectivity is essential as a motivation, of course, but it doesn't explain the structures." (Piaget 1980, quoted from Furth 1987, p. 3 and 4).

These three quotations were formulated over a period of 35 years, and it is therefore no surprise that they are not immediately consistent. The first quotation concerns schemes that are both affective and cognitive at one and the same time. The second refers to affective schemes, that can, however, be characterised as "relatively stable ways to feel and react", i.e. they are not of the same nature as the cognitive schemes that Piaget usually characterises as structures. In the third quotation, affectivity lies outside of the structures, but is necessary as motivation. How can these differences be explained and elucidated?

In examining this question I will go first to an approach developed in German "critical psychology" (cf. chapter 7), in which Ute Holzkamp-Osterkamp in particular has concerned herself with the same problem:

> "As we have been able to show with a thorough functional-historical analysis of the conditions for the differentiation of emotionality from the life process... the emotions consist of evaluations of environmental conditions perceived cognitively with their subjective meanings and the individual action potential as a standard. The emotions are thus a significant defining element for actions concerning cognitively perceived circumstances and events. These emotional evaluations of the surrounding conditions form the basis for every life activity. They are not conscious on an organismic level, but result from the immediate matching of the individual behaviour with the concrete surrounding conditions, and control the organismic adjustment to the current circumstances as a general behaviour regulator." (Holzkamp-Osterkamp 1978, p.15).

For Holzkamp-Osterkamp, the cognitive and the affective are clearly perceived as two distinct spheres, functioning in close interaction in a particular way. This perception appears to parallel closely the last of the Piaget quotations, which concerned cognitive structures motivated by an affective power. But Holzkamp-Osterkamp continues:

> "The response concerning the evaluation of the adjustment of the individual behaviour reflects the individual organism not separately for each level in the environmental conditions, but as a 'compound quality', i.e. as a compound emotional mood that automatically sums up all single evaluations into a compound action direction, and only that can make goal-directed action possible." (Holzkamp-Osterkamp 1978, p.15).

The influence of affectivity on the cognitive is thus perceived as an overall function, characterised by converting a differentiated influence from the surroundings into one overall impression. Although this summarising is described rather categorically by Holzkamp-Osterkamp – after all, one can easily experience both differentiated and contradictory emotions in a given situation – there is a certain parallel to Piaget's approach in that it concerns "relatively stable modes of feeling and reacting". In both cases there is a form of mediation of the diversity of the emotional possibilities, but no fixed structure, as in the cognitive sphere. Or to put it another way: where as a rule it is clear what one knows and does not know, what one understands and how one understands it, on the emotional level it is more a case of gradual transitions which for the individual at any rate follow a certain pattern that can change over time – and these changes occur according to Piaget's approach in the second of the three quotations by assimilation and accommodation in the same way as for the cognitive structures. Where the individual builds up structures and schemes in the cognitive sphere, in the affective sphere it could be a case of developing emotional *patterns*.

However, Holzkamp-Osterkamp continues with another observation that is of interest in the present context:

> "Normally such emotional evaluations come forward only when there are 'disturbances' of the customary and 'automated' consequences of action and when there are actual threats to the ability to act, or in 'new' situations, requiring increased 'attention'. Thus they are characteristic for phases in which the organism 're-orients' relations with the surrounding world." (Holzkamp-Osterkamp 1978, p.15-16).

If this is translated into the Piagetian and Freudian terminology used here, it can be seen that Holzkamp-Osterkamp perceives the emotions as more or less unconscious in assimilative processes, while in accommodation they come more to the forefront, and become conscious. If, for example, you work at actually acquiring the principles and history of social legislation, you are typically not very conscious of the emotions you attach to the matters being discussed, but if in that work you begin to grasp what some of these matters mean for people you actually know, the emotional aspect of the case can become conscious and very insistent.

Using Piaget's sporadic declarations as a basis, and with Holzkamp-Osterkamp's approach as a filter, I am able to summarise the structural relationship between the cognitive and the affective after the relative separation that occurs around the age of six years as follows:

In learning, one can distinguish between the cognitive or epistemological aspect, which is concerned with the content of learning, and the emotional, affective, motivational and psychodynamic aspect, which is concerned with the dynamics of learning. Through the cognitive processes, knowledge structures and schemes are developed, while affective experience develops emotional patterns of a relatively stable nature. Both the cognitive structures and the emotional patterns change and develop through an interaction of assimilative (additive, consolidating) and accommodative (transcendent, restructuring) processes. In assimilation the emotional aspect typically functions unconsciously for the most part, while in accommodation it typically becomes more conscious.

However, the cognitive and the emotional develop from a common totality and always function in close interaction. So the next question has to be: what is this interaction like, and what is its function? Here I would like to come back to another of Furth's many Piaget quotations:

> "Take, for instance, two boys and their arithmetic lessons. One boy likes them and forges ahead; the other ... feels inferior and has all the typical complexes of people who are weak in math. The first boy will learn more quickly, the second more slowly. But for both, two and two are four. Affectivity doesn't modify the acquired structure at all." (Piaget 1980, quoted from Furth 1987, p. 3-4).

The example is clear, plausible and unquestionably correct – and yet it does not tell the whole story, and it suffers from a weakness in Piaget's approach that was noted earlier: it only concerns a learning situation in which what is right and what is wrong can be clearly distinguished, i.e. convergent knowledge.

But what if it concerns divergent knowledge, in which the learning situation is ambiguous and there can be many equally "correct" learning results? Do the emotions in that case still not have any significance for what is being learnt? And although in terms of content, both boys learn the same thing, have the emotions or the motivation no significance for the nature of the learning result, e.g. how well it is remembered, how inclined one is to use it in new contexts (transfer potential), or how it is at one's disposal as an element in connection with new learning?

If one moves just a little beyond Piaget's very straightforward example, it is easy to see that learning motivation will have a significance for the learning results, even if what is being learned is apparently the same. The well-motivated boy will as a rule be better at remembering his maths, even if the less-motivated boy slaves over it and eventually learns the same. The well-motivated boy will be inclined to use his maths skills in all relevant contexts, while the less-motivated one will tend to avoid such contexts, or avoid seeing them from a mathematical point of view – and this in turn will also make him more likely to forget it.

More generally, the emotional aspect of learning will always affect the cognitive learning result, even if it does not influence the epistemological content itself. To use an expression from Freudian terminology, we can say that cognitive learning is always affectively "*obsessed*": there are always emotional tones or imprints attached to the knowledge being developed. And generally it will be the case that the stronger the emotions that are present in the learning situation, the stronger the emotional obsession will be – just think of the powerful tensions that characterise the oedipal drama as described by Freud, and how this influences the individual for the rest of his or her life.

However, the interaction works in both directions. The emotions are also influenced by knowledge:

"In the study of feelings, when you find structures, they are structures of knowledge. For example, in feelings of mutual affection there's an element of comprehension and an element of perception. That's all cognitive." (Piaget 1980, quoted from Furth 1987, p. 4).

Comprehension and perception, knowledge and insight all also influence the emotional patterns. But since these patterns differ in nature from the cognitive structures and have a less manifest nature, the interaction is also different. It cannot be stated that particular emotional features are "obsessed" by a particular comprehension. The emotional patterns have the nature, as Piaget expresses it, of "relatively stable modes of feeling and reacting", and precisely this "*relatively* stable" means that the patterns typically shift gradually through processes of assimilative nature under the influence of impulses from the individual's constant interaction with the environment, including the building up of new knowledge.

However, strong cognitive accommodation can also be accompanied by strong accommodative restructurings in the emotional patterns. If a sudden event or the kind of cognitive processes that have earlier been referred to as reflection, meta-learning or transformative learning cause a radical reconstruction of the individual's comprehension of certain set conditions and contexts, there may also be a correspondingly radical shift in the emotional patterns, not as obsessions, but more what could be described as a *toning*: the nature of particular parts of the emotional patterns shift generally in strength and direction. For example, if, on the basis of various experiences and influences, one reaches a point of eliminating one's prejudice concerning the opposite sex or other ethnic groups, it will probably also bring about general shifts in the emotions concerning these groups.

Learning and life fulfilment

Previously I have concerned myself with that part of the interaction between the cognitive and the emotional dimensions in learning that concerns the structural nature and interaction of the two dimensions. However, the emotional dimension also has a completely different function that clearly emerges from the earlier quotations from Piaget, Furth and Holzkamp-Osterkamp: the dynamic in the learning processes emanates from the affective, emotional and motivational patterns – these provide the psychological energy for learning.

Furth is very much interested in this question of where the energy for learning comes from, and so I will once more use his work as my base, even though I can only go along with him so far.

As I have explained previously, Furth starts from the premise that the capacity to learn is part of man's biologically evolved capacity for survival and life fulfilment, and that the learning function is therefore also fundamentally of a libidinal nature: *Learning As Desire*. In this there is an immediate link with Freud's concept of a basic *life or Eros drive,* which, together with the death or Tantalos drive, is the source of all psychological energy. Freud linked the life drive with sexuality to a great extent, but Furth (and many others) stress that it can be more broadly understood in the direction of life fulfilment and note that Freud has more generally described the life drive as a need "to unify and connect" and "to bring together biological elements into ever-widening units" (Furth 1987, p.70).

These statements make it easy to see the parallel with Piaget's concept of assimilation, and Furth makes much of explaining and maintaining Piaget's perception of assimilation as the active and constructive process whereby the cognitive knowledge schemes are built up:

> "To 'understand' an object means to assimilate it to an increasingly complex and logically and hierarchically ordered network of schemes. – The co-ordination of schemes gives the objects meaning and a certain degree of permanent substance. Note that schemes are instruments of assimilation, nothing else; the phrase assimilatory schemes is really redundant, there are no other sort of schemes." (Furth 1987, p. 26).

Against this, accommodation in Furth's approach is reactive in nature and somewhat negative for the individual. Accommodation presupposes resistance or obstacles in the environment that disturb the individual's current equilibrium and must therefore be actively countered by reconstructing the schemes in order to maintain equilibrium.

The basis for Furth's emphasis on the primacy of assimilation in relation to accommodation lies in the tendency that has evolved to focus on accommodation, particularly when there are attempts to use Piaget's theory in educational contexts:

> "Piaget's most crucial concept of his theory of knowledge is assimilation. It is a biological notion, almost equivalent to life itself. To respond to a particular situation by assimilation characterizes the action as alive since assimilation presupposes the existence of a living unit with its

obligatory instruments of assimilation. – Accommodation alone is not a living response, but a mechanical reaction. – Piaget insisted on assimilation, not in order to belittle the role of accommodation, but because too many scholars had exclusively focused on accommodation as the source of learning and knowledge, quite oblivious to the fact that it is schemes of assimilation that a person accommodates to objects of action or thinking." (Furth 1987, p. 67).

"Accommodation by itself is the negative imprint on the action from a resisting force, while assimilation is the positive imprint of the acting organism on a given situation." (Furth 1987, p. 69).

"Piaget's is primarily a theory of development, and schemes of knowledge are precisely what develop. In Piaget's terse language, 'the logic of development is the development of logic'." (Furth 1987, p. 69).

Furth thus finds here too a certain fundamental agreement between Freud and Piaget: they have both – due to their scientific backgrounds – a basic acceptance of an innate tendency or drive towards life fulfilment. Piaget's contribution was to include knowledge in the sphere of life fulfilment and research it as such, while Freud focused predominantly on the sexual sphere in a broad sense.

But what about Freud's death drive? Furth deliberates a great deal over this question, rejecting the notion of a corresponding parallel between the death drive and accommodation, and coming at last to the conclusion that the death drive corresponds to another aspect of assimilation: the death drive cannot reasonably be understood as an active drive towards death (as many critics of Freud have maintained), but according to Furth it can be explained as a tendency towards conservation and consolidation, of which the most extreme consequence will be death, as organisms can only survive through activity. Yet conservation and consolidation are also part of assimilation; it is, after all, in the assimilative schemes that acquired knowledge is maintained.

Furth therefore finds that a distinction can be made between a *constructive* aspect of assimilation, that corresponds to Freud's life drive, and a *restrictive* aspect corresponding to the death drive (Furth 1987, p.80). The development of knowledge takes place in a constant interplay between these two forms of assimilation, between expansion and conservation, and the two aspects of assimilation go hand in hand:

> "In expanding the assimilable universe, the child at the same time conserves the self as a logic thinker." (Furth 1987, p. 77).

Against this, accommodation must be understood as a balancing process that is required whenever assimilation in the surrounding world meets with obstacles and disturbances. Accommodation is essential for development, for it is through reconstructions that important gains are made, but it does not itself take part in the actual building up of knowledge in the assimilative schemes.

The general pattern for learning and development, which also applies beyond the temporary stabilisation that occurs around the age of six, is thus based on a biologically founded life fulfilment drive and typically happens through assimilative *expansion* towards the environment, *disturbance* from conditions in the environment, accommodative *compensation* or balancing, assimilative *reconstruction, conservation* and consolidation, new assimilative *expansion* and so on. (cf. Furth 1987, p.78 – cf. both similarities and differences in relation to Kolb's learning cycle, chapter 2).

And this pattern is not in principle restricted to the cognitive aspect of development. Although Piaget was not much concerned with this, there is no doubt that he regards his basic theories as covering the entirety of human development, including the affective sphere.

Furth is therefore connected primarily to Piaget, but notes that Piaget's theory explicitly leaves a space for the motivational or dynamic dimension in learning, which Piaget then does not concern himself further with. In this space he puts Freud, and therefore it is not surprisingly Freud's theory of drives (or instincts) he relates to, while the personality theory and the development theory are only touched on in passing.

However, it is important at this point to note that Freud altered his theory of drives several times, and that it is one of the most problematic and controversial parts of his comprehensive theory complex. In addition to this, Furth's work clearly shows his thorough knowledge of and familiarity with Piaget's thinking, while his attitude to Freud displays less empathy and can rather be likened to his searching for the right pieces amongst a vast number in order to get his jigsaw puzzle to fall into place.

When this is compared with a more empathic Freud interpretation, it becomes obvious that Furth tends to over-interpret Freud's concepts of the life drive and particularly of the death drive. The central position of aggression goes right out of the picture in favour of a tendency towards conservation and consolidation – which can be a very reasonable interpretation of Freud and, for example, puts the life and death drives in a line with a dialectic between progression and regression that can be found in the works of a modern psychoanalytically-based theorist like the German development and youth researcher Thomas Ziehe (Ziehe & Stubenrauch 1982, p. 107ff); nevertheless it is undeniably very far away from Freud's own definitions of the concepts.

In the present context it might have been more profitable for Furth to deal more with the previous stage in the development of Freud's theory of drives, in which he focused on the conflict between the sexual drives, concerned with the preservation of the species, and the ego drives, or self-preservation drives, concerned with the preservation of the individual – the two drives that were later condensed into the life drive. In the ego or self-preservation drives the libidinal drive applies itself quite naturally to use common sense and learn something, which is what Furth is primarily concerned with. In a thorough Danish interpretation of Freud the authors state that the ego drives "serve the ego with their aptitude for logical thought ..." (Olsen & Køppe 1981, p. 335).

In this way Furth could have held on to the fundamentally libidinal nature of knowledge with a direct anchoring in Freud, and traced it back to its basis in a more Darwinist treatment of its significance for the struggle for survival of both the species and the individual.

At the same time, there would have been the opportunity for a direct link to Freud's energy concept as a starting point for the idea that the life drive can constitute the dynamic basis for the knowledge processes, since the importance of including Freud should be to clarify this dynamic basis, which is not developed in Piaget's theory, which limits itself to the structures of knowledge.

However, Furth gets no further than a dividing of assimilation into a constructive aspect, which is connected to the life drive, and a restrictive aspect, which is connected to the death drive. This split can in itself be very reasonable; at any rate, it indicates two different assimilative functions and the significance of consolidation; however, the connection to Freud's rather problematic concept of the death drive does not contribute any new and decisive matter, but seems rather mystifying.

By instead making a connection with the ego- or self-preservation drive, both accommodation and the two forms of assimilation could be positioned where they naturally belong, i.e. within the life drive. And that could have led to what I particularly feel is lacking, i.e. some Freud-based energy deliberations in relation to Piaget's concepts.

However Freud's energy considerations are not especially detailed. They are based on the notion that the total psychological energy is constant, just as energy is constant in physics, and particularly concern the idea that when a need is repressed, the energy that is connected to bringing it about gets transferred to other spheres:

"The energy of the nervous system appeared to Freud like steam in a steam engine. It pushes and presses to get out, and in so doing, makes the wheels go round." (Olsen & Køppe 1981, p. 329).

In relation to the psychological processes inherent in the Piagetian theoretical construction, it is however possible to compare the Freudian considerations on energy with the relationship between the assimilative and the accommodative processes discussed in chapter 2, i.e. that the accommodative processes require a particular motivation or a particular psychological reserve of energy. The outcome of this is the very important consideration in pedagogical terms that if it is not possible for the individual to mobilise the energy necessary for the kind of effort that can further his or her development, i.e. if there is not sufficient motivation, the individual can be "tempted" to pull back or to seek to deal with the situation by means of a less demanding assimilation, that then on the other hand will be distorted because there is no reconstruction of the cognitive structure – I will return to this in chapter 6.

The resistance potential

Here I will go one step further in my criticism of Furth's selective and inadequate use of the qualities in the Freudian theory: in more or less limiting himself to the structural elements of Freud's theory of drives, Furth overlooks what this theory of drives is actually used for by Freud when it is brought into play with his personality and development theory.

Furth is not interested in the striking difference that lies in the fact that while Piaget's cognitive development theory describes a process of equilibration, in which imbalances are rather unproblematically adjusted so that the process gains a positive nature that leads to ever-expanding knowledge, Freud's theory describes human development as a dramatic battleground, where the different layers of the personality engage in fierce conflicts both with each other and externally with other people and societal realities, with results that can be developing and progressive but can just as easily lead to psychological breakdown and perversity.

On a line with Piaget, Furth more or less holds to the assertion that learning is a positive and progressive process, with both a cognitive and an affective component, and that both spheres evolve in a constant interaction between assimilation and accommodation. Admittedly, the affective sphere distinguishes itself by being connected to drives whilst also transmitting the necessary psychological energy for the processes, but what that means in practice is not dealt with.

But in everyone's life course and development there are obstacles and resistance that cannot just be overcome and accommodated, but which on the contrary seem to act as a brake on development and life fulfilment. In cognitive terms, it could be conditions that seem incomprehensible and unreasonable; in affective terms, it might be frustrations or relational conditions that in some cases can assume dimensions as dramatic as the violent emotional processes involved in the oedipal situation described by Freud.

Limitation of life fulfilment is thus an existential condition that no-one escapes. In early childhood the limits are typically imposed by parents and/ or other close carers, but later it increasingly becomes a case of societally-organised regulation through institutions and structures that limit or directly repress opportunities for life fulfilment that the society in question does not find acceptable.

In terms of learning and development, what happens is that when a small child comes up against an insurmountable obstacle that limits his or her life fulfilment, he or she reacts with a form of psychological resistance that manifests itself as anger, fury and aggression. The potential for life fulfilment always also contains the potential for resistance to conditions that limit that life fulfilment – and throughout the pre-school years, there can be seen as well as the relative separation of the cognitive and the affective, a relative independence of the respective potentials for life fulfilment and for resistance.

Freud's oedipal drama can be seen as a particular variant of this process, characterised by the fact that limitations on life fulfilment in bourgeois society in Freud's day were strongly concentrated on the sexual sphere, which therefore came to take a central position in the process. The oedipal drama can also serve as an example of how the resistance potential can fail against the realities of the surrounding world, and how that can bring submission, repression and so on that can lead to psychological problems and illness.

Generally speaking, the resistance potential is ultimately biologically embedded in humans as part of the human equipment in the struggle for survival (cf. Illeris 1981, p. 63ff) – which is also right in line with Furth's emphasis on the biological and developmental anchoring of both the cognitive and the affective – and the learning processes that get their energy from the resistance potential will typically be of a predominantly accommodative nature as well as being strongly emotionally obsessed. This has to do with the overcoming of considerable obstacles for life fulfilment, and it will typically involve a reorganisation of both cognitive structures and affective patterns.

But these accommodations will often differ in nature from the apparently sensible and balanced accommodations that are typically referred to in Piaget's work. Just as Furth, with reference to Freud's theory of drives, had to distinguish between constructive and restrictive assimilation, it might therefore be appropriate to correspondingly distinguish between, on the one hand, *constructive or offensive accommodation,* in which the resistance of the environment is accepted and leads to a reconstruction that contributes to new and more comprehensive and differentiated opportunities for knowledge and action – and on the other hand, *restrictive or defensive accommodation,* in which the resistance is perceived as more or less insurmountable, and the reconstruction comes to be about building up or reinforcing defences, about repression, alienation or the development of prejudice. I will return to these conditions in a more detailed analysis in chapter 6.

On the psychological-structural level it is a case of external resistance being countered by an inner psychological response that can set off an accommodative process possibly leading to qualitatively new knowledge or a personal development of an offensive or defensive nature. If you cannot get the one you love, you have to either accept it and in so doing perhaps accept that you do not have the requisite qualities – or else you develop some defensive justifications to explain it away.

Piaget does not appear to have been interested in the far-reaching significance of such a form of psychological resistance as a precondition for, or a part of, cognitive development. His predominant interest in the formal logical structures meant that such matters were not considered, and this probably forms part of the reason for his (and Furth's) preference for assimilative processes.

In my opinion, the notion that the one type of process should take precedence over the other is mistaken, and Piaget's insistence on assimilation as the life-constructing aspect of the process of equilibration can only be reasonably explained as a reaction to the overvaluing by others of accommodation, which is of course also life-constructing, but less directly so. Assimilation and accommodation are two superordinate types of learning processes that are always mutually dependent, and so neither can be dispensed with. In our complex and changeable modern society life, requirements alter from day to day, so to speak. Therefore both offensive and defensive accommodations increasingly take the nature of essential survival requirements, not just in special crisis situations, but also in the confusion and changeability of everyday life.

In the more traditional motivational psychology, the whole of this resistance problem has actually long been connected with more traditional learning, e.g. in Daniel Berlyne's theory of curiosity as learning motivation. The core here is that if a conflict involving a disproportion between the perception of an actual situation and an existing knowledge or expectation is perceived as challenging without being overwhelming, it will lead to the form of motivation that Berlyne calls "arousal". The concept can be interpreted as a psychological response – arising from an "arousal potential" that can be understood as that aspect of ordinary human capacity I have called the resistance potential. On the action level, the consequence according to Berlyne will be a curiosity that can be either perceptual and lead to exploratory behaviour, or it can be conceptual and lead to response-seeking or epistemic behaviour (Berlyne 1960).

In practice it is, of course, impossible to clearly distinguish between the potential for life fulfilment, or "desire" as Furth calls it, and the potential for resistance to conditions that stand in the way of this life fulfilment. It is more like two aspects of a survival potential corresponding to the polarisation that is again found in Freud as the conflict between the pleasure principle and the reality principle, or between libido and aggression.

The psychodynamic or motivational basis for learning thus lies in this double potential, and not only in the desire for life fulfilment as described by Furth. All learning requires psychological energy, and this energy comes from either the desire for life fulfilment, the desire for resistance, or a combination of both, and both potentials can ultimately be traced back to the specifically human basis for the biological struggle for survival.

However, although in practice it is not always possible to make a distinction, there is an important theoretical distinction between the life fulfilment potential and the resistance potential, for the life fulfilment potential can in principle be realised through assimilative processes alone, while the resistance potential is inextricably linked with accommodation.

Summary

On the basis of the previous section, the conditions concerning the inter-action between the cognitive and psychodynamic dimensions of learning can be summarised as follows:

1. A capacity to learn is part of the human potential for life fulfilment and individual development and survival as well as that of the species, and as such is basically of a libidinal nature. This potential for life fulfil-ment constitutes the psychodynamic basis for learning – this is where the energy for learning comes from. Both the cognitive and the emo-tional functions serve the potential for life fulfilment, including both development and consolidation.

2. In the first years of life, the cognitive and the emotional functions are integrated, but in the pre-school years they gradually become more distinct to form two ever-connected aspects of any learning process.

3. The cognitive learning processes lead to the formation of psychological *structures,* but these structures will also always be emotionally "ob-sessed", and the nature of this "obsession" is significant for how well the item learnt is remembered and in which situations it can be mobi-lised.

4. In the affective sphere, relatively stable emotional *patterns* are devel-oped, but these will also always be influenced by epistemic develop-ments. In assimilation there is an emotional influence typically of a less conscious nature, while it often appears more conscious in connection with accommodative processes.

5. Development occurs in both the cognitive and the affective spheres in an interaction between assimilative and accommodative processes. A distinction can be made between constructive assimilations that pre-dominantly promote development, and restrictive assimilations that pre-

dominantly assist consolidation. A corresponding distinction can be made between offensive accommodations that predominantly concern forward-looking reconstruction, and defensive accommodations that are predominantly used for the defence and the protection of existing structures.

6. In parallel with the separation of the cognitive and the affective, the pre-school years see a separation from the potential for life fulfilment of the resistance potential, which is mobilised when the potential for life fulfilment comes across any substantial obstacles. Where the potential for life fulfilment is a dynamic basis for both assimilative and accommodative processes, the resistance potential will typically be mobilised in connection with the overcoming of obstacles and will therefore predominantly be the basis for accommodations.

7. Life fulfilment and resistance, knowledge and emotions, assimilation and accommodation; all of these thus constitute an interwoven pattern of functions that together characterise the internal psychological aspect of learning.

5. Personal Development and Reflexivity

Learning and personal development

In the previous chapter I dealt with the relationship between the cognitive and the emotional dimensions in learning and found that these two dimensions are each involved in their separate ways in the complex and interwoven pattern of learning. However, there is also a learning sphere in which the cognitive and the psychodynamic form an integrated whole in such a way that the two dimensions cannot be distinguished from each other analytically. This concerns what in psychological terms is broadly referred to as "personality" and its various functions or qualities.

Personality is usually understood as *the individual as a whole with all its qualities, motives, skills and knowledge* – but as skills and knowledge are dealt with specifically within cognitive psychology, these spheres normally occur in personality psychology only as aspects of more general qualities, which integrate the cognitive and the emotional as a whole.

The personality spheres are typically those we normally understand as qualities and characteristics of such a breadth or generality that they cannot be classified under more specific knowledge, skills, comprehension or emotional categories – and they usually have a significantly reciprocal relationship. If, for example, one says that a person is "tolerant", it will normally imply that this tolerance applies across many or all spheres, although perhaps with varying strength. It is thus something that is difficult to specify and measure, but which on the other hand plays a major role in life.

In terms of learning there is the particular aspect of personality and personal qualities that they are to some extent anchored in certain individual genetic predispositions – such as what was at one time understood by temperament. But these predispositions develop and form through life's influences, so some learning is also occurring. Since it concerns complex conditions that reach right into the identity of the individual, this learning will typically take the form of displacements, in the same way as in the emotional sphere. It will also be demanding and as a rule involve lengthy processes, and will require a considerable personal effort, taking energy from both the life fulfilment potential and the resistance potential – which all together implies that there must be a substantial interest or motivation there for such a development to take place. Put in everyday terms, you only change your personality or substantial parts of it if you perceive that there are good grounds for doing so.

Personal development as a general qualification

In learning – and particularly institutionalised learning within the educational system (cf. chapter 10) – personal development in general and the development of specific types of personal qualities have since the 1960s increasingly become an area of substantial interest and study.

This interest has a double basis in both development in society's qualification demands and the more general cultural and societal development, and here I would like to consider these matters with a view to pinning down more closely their perspectives with regard to learning.

The most directly significant in educational terms has without doubt been the development in the qualification demands of our society. Previously the perception of these requirements concentrated on professional qualifications of a general or more or less directly vocational nature, but development throughout the last 20-30 years has been characterised by increasing focus on qualification requirements based more on personality or what today is often referred to as competencies.

In connection with a research project on general qualifications I was involved in analysing these matters in greater detail (Andersen et al. 1994, 1996), and in the course of this work the current personal qualification requirements were summarised in the following categories:

"*Intellectual qualifications,* that typically cover definitions such as rational, systematic and analytical thinking, sociological imagination, problem solving, change of perspective and skills in diagnostics, evaluation, planning etc. – centring on the individual's capacity for rational behaviour.

Perception qualifications, concerning precise sense perception, typically including precision in observation and interpretation – centring on what is defined as sensibility in academic terms.

Self-control qualifications, covering definitions such as responsibility, re-liability, perseverance, accuracy, ability to concentrate, quality and ser-vice orientation – centring on the individual's inclinations and capacity to act in accordance with general instructions.

Individuality qualifications, typically covering definitions such as inde-pendence, self-confidence and creativity – centring on the individual's ability to act alone, especially in unforeseen situations.

Social qualifications, covering definitions such as co-operation and com-munication abilities, congeniality and sociability – centring on the in-dividual's ability to interact with others.

Motivational qualifications, covering a range of definitions such as ini-tiative, dynamism, drive, openness, keenness to learn, adaptability etc. – centring on the individual's potential to keep up with and contribute to the 'development' (the much-used category 'flexibility' is often used as a group description for this sphere, but it also partially includes so-cial qualifications)."

(Andersen et al. 1993, p. 204-205 – Illeris 1995, p. 60-61).

All these categories contain both cognitive and emotional elements, but in varying proportions. Motivational qualifications, as their name suggests, appear to be of an emotional or psychodynamic nature to a large extent, while intellectual qualifications and perception qualifications are more on the cognitive side, with the other categories occupying various positions in between.

With reference to the teaching and learning that can promote this kind of personal development, the project concluded that the vocational and the general aspects – and thus also the cognitive and the personal – in the practical organisation of education may be understood and treated as two aspects of the same thing:

> "Briefly, education that is to strengthen general qualifications in a goal-directed way must be neither pure instruction, learning of skills or rote learning, nor pure personal development or therapy. It must on the contrary be organised in such a way that it combines a concrete, typical vocational or academic qualification with opportunities for expanding the participants' motivation to develop understanding, personality and identity." (Illeris et al. 1995, p. 188).

Altogether, development in society's qualification demands thus can be seen to prompt an educational effort for attempting the development of a very broad range of personal qualities by the organisation of teaching to combine a professional and a personality-oriented approach. In practice this typically occurs through problem-oriented and to some extent participant-directed projects with a concrete professional content that also involves, recalls and deals with relevant personal function spheres (Illeris et al. 1995, Andersen et al. 1996).

Late modernity and reflexivity

If we look at the educational system's growing interest in personal development in a broader societal perspective, the statement of aims in the Danish Act of General Education of 1975, with the latest adjustments in 1997, can serve as a characteristic example. This states that the school must:

- "further the pupils' acquisition and knowledge, skills, working methods and ways of expressing themselves and thus contribute to the all-round personal development of the individual pupil"
- "endeavour to create such opportunities for experience, industry and absorption that the pupils develop awareness, imagination and an urge to learn, so that they acquire confidence in their own possi-

bilities and a background for forming independent judgements and for taking personal action"

– "prepare the pupils for active participation, joint responsibility, rights and duties in a society based on freedom and democracy." (Danish Ministry of Education 1995, chapter 1).

In the first section there is a direct reference to "an all-round personal development", and it is generally clear that the learning that is aimed at in schools these days comprises both cognitive and emotional elements. The basis for these statements lies only partly in the development of vocational qualification requirements. When it comes to schools, it must be seen in a broader societal perspective concerning the transition from an industrial society to a service and information society – or seen in a cultural and consciousness perspective, to "late modernity" or "post modernity".

In relation to personal development, what the German youth and culture theorist Thomas Ziehe has called *cultural liberation* (Ziehe & Stubenrauch 1982, p. 17ff) is central to this development. We – and particularly the young – have been liberated *from* all the old norms and traditions that previously controlled our lives, for good or bad, *to* choosing and forming our own lives to a far greater degree. This means that *individuality* has come into focus in a new way, and in terms of learning, interest concentrates on the concept of *reflexivity*, which – as stated in chapter 3 – involves one constantly putting what one learns in relation to oneself, i.e. to one's understanding of oneself, and what meaning the influences one faces have for oneself. Ziehe very briefly defines reflexivity as "the opportunity to relate to oneself" (Ziehe 1985, p. 200), and describes it in another context as:

"... if we were constantly filming ourselves with a video camera, observing ourselves and commenting on it. All members of modern society are basically part of that structure, but it is most obvious among the young. – To be 'modern' today means to be able to name and formalise definite goals for oneself, which one relates to strategically and uses in one's self-reflection." (Ziehe 1991, p. 29).

In actual fact Ziehe suggested the term "the second modernisation" for these developments and their societal background, and he points out that pedagogical changes that have taken place from the 1970s onwards are no longer on a level with the situation and forms of consciousness of the young (Ziehe 1998).

The English sociologist Anthony Giddens is also very interested in these matters and sees them from a slightly different perspective:

> "It is often said that modernity is marked by an appetite for the new, but this is not perhaps completely accurate. What is characteristic of modernity is not an embracing of the new for its own sake, but the presumption of wholesale reflexivity – which of course includes reflection upon the nature of reflection itself. – Modernity is constituted in and through reflexively applied knowledge, but the equation of knowledge with certitude has turned out to be misconceived. We are abroad in a world which is thoroughly constituted through reflexively applied knowledge, but where at the same time we can never be sure that any given element of that knowledge will be revised." (Giddens 1990, p. 39).

Both Ziehe and Giddens stress that reflexivity is not only an intellectual phenomenon, but to a great extent also concerns experiential and emotional matters and self-comprehension and formation of the identity, generally. Giddens goes further: he also uses the expression *reflexivity of the body* for the modern upgrading of body awareness, identifies a hidden *institutional reflexivity,* i.e. that society's organs and institutions today must also function reflexively, constantly referring to and legitimising their existence and function – and talks generally about *reflexivity of modernity* as a characteristic of the time (Giddens 1990, 1991).

On the same level the German sociologist Ulrich Beck characterises the new epoch as *the reflexive modernization* because reflexivity has become an individual and societal necessity, and in the light of the breakdown of the grand narratives, the dominance of market mechanisms, globalisation etc., he talks of the *risk society* because the individual must choose his own life course without any certainties to guide him or her (Beck 1992).

Finally, I would like to name in this connection the German sociologist Niklas Luhmann, whose approach can be termed system theoretical – the concept of system being used about individuals, groups, organisations, and function systems such as markets, and systems are characterised by being self-referential, self-reproductive and closed to the surrounding world that does not form part of the system, but is a condition for its existence. Luhmann sees the world today as being characterised by an *emergent order,* i.e. that it cannot be understood from any overall principle, but each sphere and each system has its own basis. As self-referential systems, late-modern people must thus control their own existence and function in an ever-changing world, and this demands reflexivity – which in this context seems to appear as a central condition for existence for people today (see e.g. Luhmann 1995).

At first glance there appears to be a relationship between the focus of these modern observers on the individual's relationship to him- or herself, and a number of classical orientations within humanistic psychology, e.g. Gordon Allport's ideal of "the mature personality" (Allport 1967), Carl Rogers' "fully functioning person" (Rogers 1961), or Abrahams Maslow's notion of "self-actualization" as the ultimate goal for existence (Maslow 1954). But while such orientations have been open to criticism for being individualistic and without roots in society (Illeris 1978, p.18ff, 1981, p.70), the concepts referred to here take societal conditions as a starting point for the comprehension of typical developments in the individual. Central to these developments are *reflexivity* or *self-reflection,* which are both psychological categories that describe characteristic human modes of function in late modernity, and sociological categories concerning society's modes of function and the relationship between the individual and society.

Self-experience, reflexivity and biographicity

The late modern concept of reflexivity is therefore not primarily concerned with learning and thinking, but nevertheless involves considerable consequences for the nature of learning. It can be broadly linked to the development of personality and various more specific personal qualities, but in relation to learning, reflexivity concentrates first and foremost on the development of the *self* and the functions of the self.

The self is a philosophical and psychological concept with a somewhat turbulent history, which can be interpreted as a mirroring of the development in the relationship between the individual and society at different times. The central point is that the self takes the nature of a relation, i.e. the relation or the perception the individual has to, or of, him- or herself – in contrast to the concept of personality, which as previously stated, centres on qualities the individual has or is attributed with. Thus in a broad sense the self can be characterised as *a comprehensive concept that covers a person's experience of him- or herself,* but within the psychoanalytical tradition, there is also a lengthy and more detailed discussion of the definition of the self, the psychology of the self, and the relationship between the self and the ego (see e.g. Kohut 1977, Goldberg 1978).

In the present context, however, I would like to refer to the concept of the self that was developed by the American psychologist mentioned earlier, Carl Rogers, because he directly links changes in the organisation of the self with the concept of "significant learning" which I compared to Piaget's and Nissen's concept of accommodative learning in chapter 2 and to Mezirow's concept of transformative learning in chapter 3. Rogers basically perceives the self as an innate tendency for activity that through interaction with the environment develops into

"the organized, consistent conceptual gestalt composed of perceptions of the characteristics of the 'I' or 'me' to others and to various aspects of life, together with the values attached to these perceptions." (Rogers 1959, p. 200).

If we maintain the parallel between "significant learning" and accommodation and transformation, this leads to the assertion that changes in the self occur through accommodative and transformative processes concerning the organised, consistent conceptual whole, which structures the individual's perception of him- or herself and others, and of various aspects of life. This is therefore a specific type of accommodation characterised by the involvement of self-experience and self-relating, i.e. the individual relates himself to himself, or what I described as reflection in the form of mirroring in chapter 3.

Personal development and development of personal qualities generally occur through accommodations that in an integrated fashion comprise both cognitive and emotional factors; but within the particular field that is concerned with self-experience and self-relationing, development occurs through reflexivity, i.e. through accommodations in which influences from the interaction between the individual and the environment are processed by means of the particular form of reflection that can be characterised as mirroring.

In terms of learning, reflexivity is, like reflection, in most cases a particular form of accommodation. Both forms are characterised by having the nature of displaced elaboration, i.e. to some extent there is a time lag in relation to the influences causing them. But what is special about reflexivity is that it involves the organisation of the self.

Several of the analysts in this sphere that were mentioned in the previous section also emphasise that such reflexivity is not necessarily limited to internal processes, but can also occur through interpersonal communicative processes, in which one uses other people as a kind of sparring partner, and performs the mirroring actively and externally as an aid to gaining insights into one's own self-comprehension by observing the reactions of others, and listening to their evaluations.

Reflexivity must today first and foremost be understood in relation to the general societal conditions that mean that the individual constantly has to choose his or her way, not only externally, between all sorts of offers, but also internally, in terms of life course, lifestyle and identity. But with this, reflexivity also comes to have significance for some of the personality qualifications that were dealt with earlier in this chapter, e.g. typically qualities such as independence, self-confidence, sociability, sensibility and flexibility.

Therefore no clear boundary can be drawn between personal development and reflexivity, but one could perhaps say that personal development increasingly takes place through reflexivity. In a learning situation, both typically take place through processes in which the relevant qualities and conditions are challenged, and where there is also an opportunity for, and perhaps support for, a qualified process. And both demand a huge personal effort, which presupposes a significant motivation.

Finally it must be mentioned that these processes cannot always be immediately comprehended as being forward-looking or positive. Personal development and reflexivity may also involve the development of resistance, defensiveness, distortions and blocks that in various ways can be rigid and restrictive for the person in question. There will be a closer analysis of this in chapter 6.

Biographicity is a modern concept that sums up reflexivity and personal development. The German biographicity researcher Peter Alheit (cf. chapters 9 and 11) defines with this concept how modern people experience the fact that to a great extent they can form their own lives:

> "Biographicity means that we can redesign again and again, from scratch, the contours of our life within the specific contexts in which we (have to) spend it, and that we experience these contexts as 'shapeable' and designable. In our biographies, we do not possess all conceivable opportunities, but within the framework of the limits we are structurally set we still have considerable scope open to us. The main issue is to decipher the 'surplus meanings' of our biographical knowledge, and that in turn means to perceive the potentiality of our unlived lives." (Alheit 1995, p. 65).

Biographicity has developed rapidly in recent years, in step with "normal biography" construction principles breaking down, i.e. there may not be a natural continuity between family background, education, work and identity, but a perception that those are issues one can and must take a stand on. Alheit also talks of a feminisation of the life process, because to be an adult does not always mean having full-time work – as it previously did for men (cf. Schulze 1992, Alheit 1995).

In the present context it is important to be aware that biographicity is something that concerns how we *perceive* and *interpret* our lives in relation to the opportunities we have and the choices we make. For in this lies also the fact that biographicity can be understood as an overall framework for learning through reflexivity, which after the breakdown of the external traditional norm-oriented framework, holds the individual's self-comprehension and identity together.

Summary

The factors concerning learning in connection with personal development and reflexivity can be summarised in the following points:

1. Personality and personal qualities encompass cognitive and emotional elements as an integrated whole.

2. Personal development, like other forms of learning, occurs through an interaction between assimilative and accommodative processes. It will typically be a lengthy and gradual process, with characteristics of displacement, and will require considerable motivation, often getting its energy from both the life fulfilment and resistance potential.

3. A number of personal qualities are included these days as important societal qualifications. These can be summarised in the categories of intellectual qualifications, perception qualifications, self-control qualifications, individuality qualifications, social qualifications and motivational qualifications.

4. A particular part of the personality is the self, which comprises the individual's self-experience and self-relationing. Developments in the self are of increasing significance in our late-modern society, where the individual has to make a lot of personal choices, both with regard to the surrounding world and him- or herself, without the guidance of generally applicable norms and traditions.

5. Developments in the self typically occur through self-reflection or reflexivity, i.e. reflection that involves the individual's relationship to him- or herself by means of mirroring. Like other forms of personal development, such processes require a considerable motivational base.

6. In educational terms, personal development and reflexivity seem to be best promoted through processes that involve and challenge relevant characteristics in the participants and support a qualified elaboration and adjustment.

7. In the concept of biographicity, personal development and reflexivity are summarised as the perception and interpretation of the way we choose to live our lives.

6. When the Intended Learning Does not Occur

Mislearning and differences

In the previous chapters I have chiefly dealt with the part of learning that concerns the internal psychological acquisition process, linked only peripherally to the social interaction process. However, it is far from always the case that the influencing situations experienced by the individual are transformed into an internal psychological acquisition process – and especially in education and other contexts that form the setting for a specific kind of learning, it is clearly a problem when this learning does not occur or perhaps occurs only partially or in a distorted form. Therefore, before I proceed to look more closely at the interaction processes in learning, it would be appropriate to look at what can hinder the acquisition process generally, and the intended acquisition in particular. It is practically a matter of course that learning psychology has chiefly been concerned with what happens when someone learns something. But in terms of education and pedagogy, it is at least as important to be interested in what happens when pupils or participants do not learn anything, or learn something other than what was intended.

One of the few learning theorists to have considered this subject in detail is the English sociologist Peter Jarvis (1992), whose work I will look at again in the next chapter. Jarvis divides "non-learning" into three categories: *presumption* implies that one already thinks one has an understanding of something and therefore does not register new learning opportunities. *Non-consideration* implies that one might register new opportunities, but does not relate to them, perhaps through being too busy or too nervous of what they might lead to. *Rejection* means that on a more conscious level, one does not want to learn something new in a particular context.

Jarvis' categories thus cover three degrees, or levels, of consciousness in non-learning and thus introduce an important line of approach. However, the levels are defined only through short general descriptions without distinct criteria. I will therefore content myself here with taking them as a source of inspiration, and instead use a distinction between *mislearning* of a more chance nature and *resistance* and *defence* respectively, which can be linked in different ways to psychological conditions in the person concerned.

In many non-learning situations there will thus be simple mislearning, i.e. somehow or other there will be what we in ordinary terms call a misunderstanding, or perhaps unclear communication or a failure of concentration, leading the individual to not quite understand or grasp what is going on, and in an educational situation, what was meant to be learnt.

Mislearning is easiest to relate to in connection with academic teaching in spheres where it can clearly be established what is right and what is wrong. I have found a very ordinary example of this in the work of American psychologist Robert Mager, who has worked on programmed learning. Having the task of developing a programmed course in elementary electronics, he found through a preliminary testing of the students that although they all claimed to know nothing about electronics, they all had a fair amount of knowledge and understanding of the subject, of which a certain amount was misknowledge and misunderstanding (Mager 1961). They had all learnt something about electronics, without having learnt it formally – and some of what they had learnt was wrong.

However, this example only concerns the most tangible and easily confirmed mislearnings, which are relatively easy to correct – that is, if they are detected. They can certainly be serious, for if one assimilates further information on a mistaken basis, the misunderstanding will naturally become more pervasive. In a subject such as mathematics, for example, it is easy to see how a single mislearning can lead on to another, so that extensive and intricate contradictory structures of correct and mistaken learnings build up, which can contribute strongly to the student in question ultimately giving up, having learnt nothing except that "I just can't understand maths."

If one looks at other subjects or spheres, however, it quickly becomes more complicated; what is, for example, mislearning in the context of the interpretation of a text where many different interpretations are possible? And in the personal sphere, there is an infinite number of development possibilities, all with far-reaching consequences for the individual. None of the possibilities can be asserted to be the correct one, but some possibilities can be understood as wrong or problematic if they later lead to serious difficulties for the person in question.

In education, mislearning must naturally be avoided as much as possible, but it is only in limited situations that it is possible to make unambiguous distinctions between error and non-error. And if, for example, the pupils are always told what is right and what is wrong, what they may and may not do and so on, they are unable to develop a sense of judgment, or independence or responsibility – this cannot really be called mislearning, but the learning is distinctly misplaced in relation to the environment the pupils have to relate to.

Where errors are unambiguous, one can of course attempt to avoid them, and correct them when they do occur. But otherwise, it is just as important to remember that there will always be *different* learnings because learning, as previously emphasised, always concerns something new being linked to what was already in place – and that which is already in place differs from person to person. Empathy, dialogue and tolerance are needed. Progress, both for the individual and more generally, can be something that happens when something is understood in a different way from normal.

Resistance: conflict and potential

Another reason for the non-occurrence of the intended learning can lie in resistance on the part of the person who is supposed to be doing the learning. Already in chapter 4 I have dealt more fundamentally with the resistance potential, its development and its significance for learning. The resistance potential is typically activated when the individual is hindered or limited in his or her life fulfilment, and this can occur both in specific situations or more generally if the individual finds himself in contexts he perceives himself to be in conflict with, e.g. a more or less unwanted school or training course, a specific subject, a specific teacher or the social situation in the class or team. The background can vary enormously, from something quite personal that emerges in certain specific types of situations, to a more general resistance, rooted in a more general perception of limitation or repression.

Activation of the resistance potential does not have a general blocking effect on learning, but it is rarely the originally intended learning that occurs. On the contrary, there will typically be restrictive or defensive accommodative processes occurring – e.g. the pupil who ends up learning that he or she just can't understand maths, viewing the teacher or other pupils in a negative light and attributing all kinds of negative qualities to them, or more broadly, that school and education "stink", or are at any rate nothing the person concerned can get anything out of. In adult education we often come across participants with this negative kind of attitude towards education, which developed during their years in school, and which has to be overcome if there is to be a meaningful educational process (Illeris 2001). In particular cases and in single situations that are especially provocative, resistance can also take the form of more or less uncontrolled aggression.

However, resistance can also lead to accommodations of a more constructive nature with far reaching results to follow, partly because the resistance potential can be a very strong incentive, which in a constructive process can unite with the life fulfilment potential in an effort to find and develop alternatives to those conditions perceived as unacceptable.

In institutional education, participants' resistance is almost always viewed on the face of it as something negative by the teachers and other representatives of institutions. It is at best troublesome, but can also easily undermine planned activities and cause them to go off course, and in a broader perspective, it can also cause similar problems for the framework, milieu and self-comprehension of the institution.

Nevertheless it is often in connection with resistance, or at least elements of resistance, that the most important transcendent learning occurs. Personal development in particular, which is currently accorded such significance in education, often occurs through a process characterised by resistance. And it must not be forgotten that resistance is a central element in a democratic society, for part of the way democracy functions is that public resistance should be able to restrain or correct those in authority. In society as a whole, in education, at work and in other spheres of everyday life, resistance can be what leads to conditions changing and developing in step with new circumstances and new needs.

Seen from a learning perspective, resistance contains a great potential which can however be difficult to deal with in institutional education (this subject has been discussed in Danish as "passive aggression", Berliner & Berthelsen 1989). Viewed pedagogically, it concerns on the one hand creating a space for learning and situations that can allow room for participants' resistance, and on the other acknowledging resistance as a legitimate form of expression as well as giving it both the challenge that is its natural precondition and the support that can promote important learning.

This might sound wonderful, but in ordinary education it can be tremendously demanding to relate to the participants' resistance, and institutional frameworks can impose limits that make it extremely difficult to carry out a constructive resistance process – the resistance might well, for example, be directed at those very institutional frameworks, or it could be supported by social indignation and frustrations with restricting conditions, which in the educational environment can be hard to relate to, even if the resistance is perceived as altogether justified.

All the same it should not be forgotten that in many cases education forms the only context where participants have a realistic opportunity to allow their resistance to unfold and to adapt it in a constructive and progressive manner, and that this can be the source of the most far-reaching potential for learning. Frustrated resistance will typically be converted into defence and blockings that can hinder further learning.

The entire discussion on the social sorting process that is constantly demonstrated in the school and educational system, has a lot to do with certain types of resistance that are perceived as acceptable and legitimate in the institutions, while others are not, and this difference typically follows certain social distinctions – school is organised and functions on the premises of the already privileged members of society. There is nothing new in this, and the problem cannot be solved simply on a pedagogical level, but there will always be situations where the pupils' resistance can be dealt with in a more or less constructive way.

Defence, rejection, blocking and distortion

While resistance thus contains great learning potential, both positive and negative, defence as a basic outlook is always negative or restrictive in relation to learning, even though it can be absolutely necessary for the individual.

Where situations and influences that are perceived as threatening, restrictive or altogether unacceptable do not provoke a directly resistant reaction – perhaps because they are not immediately provocative, or because the person concerned does not have the reserves to rise to the challenge – instead there will typically occur the development of a psychological defence.

The concept of psychological defence mechanisms is closely linked to Freud and appeared very early on as a key concept in the development of psychoanalytical theory. The classic example is *repression* as a defence against unacceptable drive impulses, psychological conflicts and recognition of traumatic experiences, but eventually Freud also referred to many other mechanisms of defence such as *regression, projection* and *isolation,* and in the classic book on the subject, his daughter Anna Freud enumerates a long list of different types of mechanisms of defence (Freud 1942, p. 45ff).

Later, the German social-psychologist Thomas Leithäuser, in connection with the development of the theory of everyday consciousness – which I will return to in the next section – identified other types of mechanisms of defence that regularly occur in current learning contexts, examples being *reduction* ("Of course I know this" – of something new and actually unknown), *harmonisation* (emphasising unimportant common traits in conflicting conditions), *displacement* ("not my department"), *levelling* ("this is really no problem") or *personification* and *scapegoat mechanisms* (Leithäuser & Volmerg 1977, here reproduced from A.Andersen et al. 1993, p. 24).

In terms of learning, the mechanisms of defence can first and foremost entail a *rejection,* i.e. one simply will not let the impulses in question into the consciousness; for one reason or another, one will not accept them or become involved with them, and one ignores them, so naturally no learning takes place. And where the rejection is subjectively important and perhaps has to be repeated several times, it can take on the nature of a *block-*

ing, i.e. it appears automatically and heavily, and perhaps assumes neurotic features such as a *phobia,* often involving strong anxiety reactions.

However, more common than blocking or phobia is the reaction, in some ways more refined, that can be termed a *distortion,* i.e. the unacceptable impulse is not perceived as it is, but is distorted into something acceptable. In this connection a particular phenomenon which Piaget calls *distorting assimilation* should be mentioned; this is the notion that children assimilate to their wishes and fantasies instead of to reality (cf. Furth 1987, p.38).

Distorted assimilations of this kind will for the most part be corrected later without any major problems, but another form of distorted assimilation occurs very widely in both children and adults, when one comes across situations or impulses that are incompatible with the cognitive structures already developed. In such cases one ought, according to Piaget's theory, to undertake an accommodation that can bring the cognitive structures into agreement with reality. But very often there is instead a rejection, or one distorts the impulses to make them fit the existing structures in order to "manage" them by means of assimilative processes that – as pointed out earlier – demand less energy and are less troublesome than accommodations.

This kind of distorted assimilation typically occurs in connection with what we call prejudice. Prejudice entails a mistaken understanding, concerning a particular subject, having been built up for various reasons, which it would cost a great deal for the individual to give up; therefore the individual systematically distorts any impulses that contradict it. Today this type of reaction goes far beyond mere prejudice. Rejections and distortions occur systematically and massively in modern society in the form of what is called *everyday consciousness* – which I will deal with in greater detail in the next section.

Everyday consciousness

The theory of everyday consciousness, as already mentioned, was developed by the German socio-psychologist, Thomas Leithäuser – to a large extent together with psychoanalyst Birgit Volmerg – in extension of the Frankfurt School tradition of combining Freud-oriented psychology and the Marx-oriented conception of society (Leithäuser 1976, Leithäuser & Volmerg 1977 – see also chapter 7).

Leithäuser bases his argument on the notion that everyday life has become independent, fragmented and impoverished, because the productive sphere is dominant, and all other aspects of life are eventually ordered in accordance with its economic rationality.

Everyday life today is characterised as consisting of a long succession of separate situations, that apparently all have their own meaning, but are perceived as unconnected because the underlying common denominator, i.e. that everything will submit to capitalistic economic rationality, is not immediately apparent. For each of the various types of situations we must adopt various roles, as wage earner, as parent, as consumer, as road-user, as resident, as TV viewer, as voter etc. And just as the situations are unconnected, neither does there need to be any reciprocal connection between the various roles. It is, for example, an established fact that interviews on work conditions can take a very different course and have a very different content depending on whether the workers are interviewed at work or at home.

What is common to all these various fragments is time structure. Our lives are increasingly ruled by the clock. What is important here is, of course, the division wage labour makes between work time and "leisure" time. Within wage labour, time is structured in varying degrees by breaks and meetings and so on – and within the education system by the timetable; this also accustoms children to accept an externally imposed time structure without any connection to the content of the activities that are being structured. Our leisure time is correspondingly more and more subject to time structures – just think of what significance TV programmes now have for the internal structure of our home lives. In order to deal with this unconnected diversity, modern man makes use of a number of routines that mean need is repressed, postponed and made to conform to the time structure. Need repression and postponement naturally occur in every society; this is a basic precondition for the formation of a society. But with the time structures that have developed in modern society, this situation has reached a point where a highly developed internal constraint is demanded of every single member of society in order that it be able to function. The routines also free us from the necessity of keeping ourselves open and candid in every one of the innumerable situations we come across in our everyday life. That would quite simply be practically and psychologically overwhelming – and we are able to distance ourselves from all the atrocities that appear every day on our TV screens, or the irresistible offers from the supermarkets angling for our limited funds.

On the other hand modern mass-communication provides a torrent of potential interpretations and possible meanings, which are just as unconnected as the time structure, but are well able to form strong emotional links between the confused everyday events and the repressed dreams and ideas, and all the angst and disarray that is a consequence of repression.

Corresponding to the practical routines we must also therefore rationalise our consciousness, and this typically occurs through the development of what Leithäuser calls everyday consciousness. Everyday consciousness has taken over the place where previously coherent religions or other ideologies structured our conception of the diversity of our everyday lives. But just as everyday life has been fragmented into a continuous succession of situations, everyday consciousness is not a coherent conception like the ideologies, but is rather characterised by fragmentation, stereotypes and unmediated contradictions.

In the present context it is of particular interest how everyday consciousness evolves in the individual as a psychological structure. Leithäuser and Volmerg describe this by means of the concept of *theme-horizon-schemes* – i.e. psychological schemes or structures that maintain a specific theme within a specific horizon, limited by an everyday situation. By means of these schemes we are able to routinely interpret the themes we come across in the many detached situations of our everyday lives, without actually reflecting on them or forming an independent opinion of them.

In this current context it is worth noting that the two modes of function for the theme-horizon-schemes named by Leithäuser and Volmerg correspond to a great extent to my earlier deliberations on the Piagetian theory: an event that could give rise to disturbances is either rejected, i.e. the impulse is defined away and not adopted into the psychological structures; or the impulse is disqualified within the field of consciousness to a non-observation or non-perception by being distorted so that it fits into the previously established structures, in the relevant theme-horizon-scheme.

In this way we avoid relating to the huge stream of new impulses to which we are all subject in today's society. We need to do this in order not to be overwhelmed, but at the same time transcendent learning is thus obstructed. This can only take place through a so-called *thematisation,* i.e. an accommodation that transcends everyday consciousness.

Such thematisation requires psychological energy – in the Piaget-oriented conception it will concern constructive accommodations that lead to existing theme-horizon-schemes being reconstructed as schemes of a less limiting nature. In a Freud-oriented conception it concerns overcoming mechanisms of defence. Psychological energy presupposes motivation, and motivation is rooted in life fulfilment potential and resistance potential.

Thematisations are fundamentally essential because modern society is so complex, and the important financial and power structures so impenetrable, that the individual has no immediate possibility of forming a coherent understanding of how things work.

Everyday consciousness has the nature of a generalised mechanism of defence, and just like other mechanisms of defence, it has both positive and negative aspects, and defensive and offensive features. The positive aspect consists primarily of the fact that we would be completely unable to cope with our lives without such a defence; we would be overwhelmed and soon end up in a mental hospital (which a lot of us actually do, anyway). The negative aspect concerns the fact that part of our life fulfilment is confined in routines, impoverishment, falsity and prejudice. The defensive aspect deals with the notion that we use distortions when the surrounding world becomes too much for us. The offensive aspect is the ability to convert defence into a counter-attack; in situations where the challenge becomes *too* insistent and we are able to mobilise a certain reserve of energy, we can take up the challenge and do something about the situation, internally on our own behalf, or externally through individual or collective actions.

In an educational context such a defence will typically be developed to different degrees in the different participants, and for some it can contribute strongly to rejecting the teaching. In general, defence is probably the psychological mechanism that most contributes to the occurrence of a different learning than that intended, and as a rule a high degree of security, permissiveness and motivation is required for the learner to get over this defence, for to a certain extent it is needed for the maintenance of self-worth and identity. But at the same time, overcoming defence is often the most decisive factor for achieving progressive learning, both academic and personal.

Habits of expectations and sets of assumptions

In the previous section I have given a fairly detailed explanation of Leithäuser's theory of everyday consciousness. But several other theorists have formed similar conceptions, particularly the British-American Stephen Brookfield and the American Jack Mezirow in the field of adult education, both of whom have been mentioned earlier. Their accounts are perhaps less clearly rooted in psychological theory than is Leithäuser's, but appear primarily as an essential background for understanding the practical problems that manifest themselves in adult education and for working out how to deal with them from an emancipatory perspective, cf. for example, the discussion of Mezirow's concept of "transformative learning" in chapter 3.

Brookfield chiefly uses the word "assumptions", and in larger contexts corresponding to the concept of everyday consciousness, he talks of "sets of assumptions" or the participants' "worlds of assumptions" (Brookfield 1987, p. 44ff, 1990, p. 177ff), while Mezirow prefers the expression "habits of expectations" (Mezirow 1990, p. 4, 1991, p. 4ff), which he links together with the more precisely defined concepts of "meaning schemes" and "meaning perspectives" (cf. again chapter 3).

Both Brookfield and Mezirow emphasise that assumptions and expectations are often acquired as integrated elements, rarely made explicitly clear, of socialisation in childhood – Brookfield writes, for example:

"How do we acquire in childhood the assumptions that we begin to examine critically in adulthood? Assumptions are the seemingly self-evident rules about reality that we use to help us seek explanations, make judgments, or decide on various actions. They are the unquestioned givens that, to us, have the status of self-evident truths. People cannot reach adulthood without bringing with them frameworks of understanding and sets of assumptions that undergird their decisions, judgments, and actions." (Brookfield 1990, p. 178).

However, it can also – more in line with Leithäuser – concern conditions that are relevant in everyday adult life. In a relatively early work, Mezirow distinguishes between unconscious *psychological assumptions* of an inhibitory nature, and *cultural assumptions*, that are embedded as basic values or attitudes in the cultural or sub-cultural environment important to the individual (Mezirow 1985, p. 145).

Absolutely in line with Leithäuser's concept of thematisation, Brookfield and Mezirow find that most learning of importance in adulthood consists largely in breaking through elements of such underlying and controlling assumptions and habits of expectations:

"Learning may be defined as the process of making a new or revised interpretation of the meaning of an experience, which guides subsequent understanding, appreciation, and action. What we perceive and fail to perceive and what we think and fail to think are powerfully influenced by habits of expectation that constitute our frame of reference, that is, a set of assumptions that structure the way we interpret our experiences. It is not possible to understand the nature of adult learning or education without taking into account the cardinal role played by these habits in making meaning. – Becoming critically aware of our own presuppositions involves challenging our established and habitual patterns of expectation, the meaning perspectives with which we have made sense out of our encounters with the world, others, and ourselves. – Reflection on one's own premises can lead to transformative learning." (Mezirow 1990, p. 1, 12 and 18).

Both Mezirow and Brookfield give many directions on how such transcendent learning can be promoted in adult education – including, for example, Brookfield's work with *"critical incidents"* in which adults are to write reports on important events and experiences they have had in various spheres, and which he subsequently analyses with them what were the basic conditions that made the experience in question significant for them (Brookfield 1990).

Leithäuser's theory of everyday consciousness thus provides a description of important general conditions hindering transcendent learning that is deeply rooted in psychology and social theory; Mezirow and Brookfield deal with the same conditions from a more practically oriented perspective. However, there is a great deal of common ground between the two approaches in their actual perceptions of what is at stake.

Late-modern forms of consciousness

From a current perspective, Leithäuser's theory of everyday consciousness in particular can also be seen as a kind of forerunner for the late- or post-modern consciousness and culture theories described in chapter 5. In recent years there has been a further division of life into various unconnected spheres, and more than anything, a rapid acceleration in the commercialisation, globalisation and pace of change of society. There are continual changes in the very basis of our lives, and this appears to have such far-reaching consequences for opportunities for learning and personal development that the defence provided by everyday consciousness can no longer cope with it.

I do not wish to elucidate further on late- or post-modern culture and consciousness forms at this point, but would just like to sketch out a few main points of significance for learning conditions, starting with the British-Australian postmodernist adult education researcher Robin Usher, who has taken particular inspiration from the French sociologist Jean-Francois Lyotard and a number of other French postmodernists (see e.g. Usher 1993, 1998, 2000, Usher & Kosmidou 1992, Usher et al 1997, Lyotard 1984).

Usher's central point is that people today do not have a coherent, authentic and rational self that can learn from experiences in a sensible way, autonomously and independently of emotional and social ties. Rather, the self is irrational, emotional, embedded in the body with all its needs, and stamped socially and societally.

The notion of the autonomous and rational self is a construction of an ideal that evolved together with modern individualistic society and serves the interests of the authorities, particularly as a kind of target concept for discipline within the school/educational system using the systematic repression of emotional, bodily and social perspectives.

As I understand Usher, he regards the self that is operated with in psychology as an idealised false picture of personality formation, which many have perhaps tried to live up to, though very few have been able to in reality, for under the smooth surface there are always very different impulses moving. And in the post-modern period which Usher perceives that we are in, this hopeless notion neither can, nor should, be maintained, for it is connected to the notion of a coherent world order, which cannot, nor ever could be proven.

On the contrary, the world is divided, unconnected and constantly changing, and the self is correspondingly fragmented, unstable and enquiring, always on the move, never at peace, marked by the overflow of influences and apparent opportunities for choice which pervades post-modern life.

Viewed from the learning theory perspective I have attempted to build up in the previous sections, this kind of personality conception means that there is typically no attempt to unite the various schemes continually constructed by the individual through assimilative processes by means of accommodative reconstructions of a unified whole, such as those in Piaget's conception. The important accommodations are attached to changeability, to constant re-evaluation and updating, connecting and disconnecting of schemes, that each cover the individual's comprehension of life's different parts.

Leithäuser's concept of limited theme-horizon-schemes can thus be continued into an image of post-modern forms of consciousness, but the notion of thematisations that can break through the divisions of everyday consciousness and create coherence and wholeness in comprehension must be replaced by an image of constant renewal, connecting and disconnecting of schemes, that are constantly seeking to be adjusted and updated in accordance with continual changes in the environment – an image that may be more suited to the possibilities in Mezirow's transformative learning, even though it was not really post-modern instability that formed the basis of Mezirow's conception.

In a constantly changing and developing process of the kind Usher describes, it is clear that the mechanisms of defence must remain in the background. There is no coherent self or fixed identity that must be defended; all is permitted, and the main concern is keeping up, "the art of navigating in chaos", as the Danish author Finn Thorbjørn Hansen (1997) puts it. The individual is open to the new and the unknown, for what is always important is to change and keep abreast of things – constant development is both a requirement and a condition.

However, as I see it, at any rate, this also means that where before there was defence, now there is vulnerability. Openness to changes and developments also becomes openness to uncertainty and violation. One would like to keep up all the time, but no one can manage it all, and our risk society does not have a safety net.

It is in this context that psychologists, sociologists and cultural analysts have moved towards reflexivity as an opportunity for the individual and society to keep track of the permanently unconnected and the changeable (cf. chapter 5). But where modernity's rational self was forced to surround itself with strong mechanisms of defence to hold on to identity and self-respect, post-modernity's reflexive self has been forced in its very flexibility and change orientation to tolerate the vulnerability that openness brings.

And where modernity's pedagogical goal could be to break through the defence so that the individual could progress, post-modernity's pedagogical goal can be to dam up the flexibility so that it does not lead to emptiness and loss of orientation (cf. Ziehe 1998). Whether reflexivity alone can manage this may remain a central question for learning theory. Reflexivity is of necessity accommodative in nature, and in order to have meaning and strength, there must be assimilatively formed structures that the accommodations can draw upon. But in post-modern society there is not much scope for the stable construction of assimilative schemes in the cognitive sphere or stable patterns in the affective sphere – and learning cannot consist of accommodations and reflexivity alone.

Summary

When the intended learning does not take place, from the perspective of learning theory, there may be various factors present, which can be summarised as follows:

1. Due to perhaps misunderstanding or failure of concentration, there may be a *mislearning,* which can lead to further mislearnings later on. Mislearnings of this type can usually be corrected when they are discovered. In many cases it cannot be immediately discerned what is right and what is wrong, and this is *different learning.* In personal spheres mistaken learning or development can lead to serious psychological problems.

2. There may be *resistance* from the learner's side, because the learner feels limited or repressed in the actual situation or in a broader context. Resistance can lead to either restrictive or defensive accommodations and to more or less uncontrolled aggression. But resistance can also set off constructive and transcendent processes and, particularly in the personal sphere, important developments can result from resistance and perhaps get energy from both the resistance potential and the life fulfilment potential.

3. Very often absent or mistaken learning is connected with the development of a psychological *defence* that can manifest itself in various ways, typically through *rejection* and in more pronounced cases *blocking or phobia,* or through *distortion* – e.g. through *distorted assimilations,* meaning that when impulses are not in accordance with the existing psychological structures, instead of setting off accommodative reconstructions, they are distorted to fit the existing structures (or prejudices) and can therefore be adopted assimilatively.

4. *Everyday consciousness* is a systematised defence that is necessary for all as protection against the constant bombardment of various and often very damaging impulses which everyone in present society comes up

against. A system is formed of so-called theme-horizon-schemes, that pick up new impulses within a specific thematic sphere and either reject them or systematically distort them. *Habits of expectations* or *sets of assumptions* are other terms for such structures.

5. Everyday consciousness, habits of expectations and sets of assumptions can be penetrated by accommodative *thematisations* or *transformations* that open the way for a transcendent comprehension.

6. In connection with *late-modern* or *post-modern forms of consciousness,* important accommodations are to a lesser extent oriented towards the connecting of different schemes to linked comprehension, and to a greater extent towards constant changes that can pick up developments in a constantly changing divided environment. This openness to change leads to a weaker development of psychological defences and thus an increased vulnerability to uncertainty and hurt. In terms of learning, it can bring an increased need for both reflexivity and the development of firmer structures through predominantly assimilative processes.

7. Interaction, Social Learning and Socialisation

The social dimension of learning

In the introductory chapter it was pointed out that learning comprises in an integrated manner both internal psychological acquisition processes and social interaction processes. I also stated that my attempt to examine this complex field would start with the internal processes and gradually broaden the perspective to include social interaction processes. In chapter 2 there was a discussion of the cognitive dimension of learning, starting with Piaget's theory, and as this discussion gradually became more and more comprehensive in the course of the following chapters, with the inclusion of the emotional dimension and factors such as resistance and defence, social and societal factors have also come into the picture to a certain extent, particularly in connection with areas such as reflexivity, everyday consciousness and post-modern forms of consciousness.

This chapter will focus on the interaction processes of learning as well as the social and societal dimension, using the internal psychological processes for reference. For although the two types of processes belong inextricably together in a totality-oriented conception of learning, to a certain extent they have to be separated for a closer analysis. These are two very different types of processes, with different internal structures and functions.

It must first be emphasised that while the cognitive and emotional dimensions of learning are primarily rooted in the individual's biological-genetic constitution, and influenced both by individual and societal developments, the social-societal dimension is rooted in the social and societal contexts of which the individual forms a part. These contexts are not biological-genetic but historic-societal in their constitution. For the internal psychological dimensions, the individual is the setting, while the action takes place through the individual's meetings with the surrounding world. For the interaction dimension, it is the surrounding world that is the setting, and the action is the individual's deeds in relation to this surrounding world.

This also means that the interaction between the three dimensions is not simply an exchange of the same nature between three equal poles.

When the dimensions were introduced, in chapter 1, it was noted that there is a direct integration or exchange between the two internal psychological dimensions, and in chapter 4 this connection was defined thus: cognitive structures are always emotionally obsessed, and the emotional patterns are always affected by cognitive influences; in addition, emotions and motivations are what mobilise and regulate psychological energy in both the cognitive and the emotional aspects of learning.

Thus, it is the totality of the two internal psychological dimensions that is in the interaction with the surrounding world and the social-societal dimension. As an image it can be illustrated as follows, in relation to the tension field of learning:

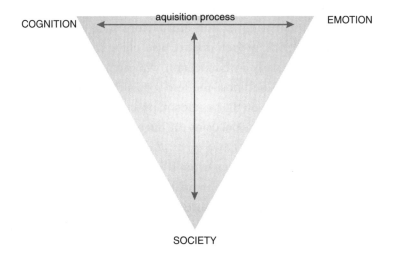

Figure 4: The interaction between dimensions in the tension field of learning

Along the tension field's top horizontal side there is a constant exchange or connection between the cognitive and the emotional pole, and it is this totality that interacts with the social-societal pole.

On the basis of this interpretation, this interaction and the social-societal dimension will be dealt with in more detail in the following.

Forms of interaction

It is perhaps surprising that although I talked at a superordinate level in chapter 1 about "interaction processes between the individual and his or her material and social environment", this interaction has subsequently been linked to the social and societal dimension – what happened to the interaction with the material surroundings?

Naturally the individual is involved in interaction with the material surroundings all the time, but the nature of this interaction is always transmitted socially and societally. In today's society this transmission is predominant and very visible – the imprint of mankind on the material world is so widespread today that it is extremely difficult to find an element of "untouched nature". Viewed in relation to learning, the material is under submission to the more dominant social. This fundamentally means that mankind's mental condition is that of a social being, his psychological functions can only develop in a social space – because we are talking of humans, the societal dimension is given.

And although it may be possible to find a piece of untouched nature, our perception of this nature is necessarily socially influenced – we know that it is called the "sea" or they are called "stars", and that people relate to these phenomena in specific ways: that the sea is something you can swim in, sail on and even drown in, and that the stars form various constellations and that they are inconceivably distant from us etc. Thus, it is not possible to separate interaction with the material surroundings from interaction with the social surroundings – in psychological and also in learning conditions they make up a totality that is always transmitted socially.

As I also talked about in the introductory chapter, there is, in addition, the important factor in today's society that this transmission can occur both in a direct social interaction and indirectly through a large number of different media that stretch from written and artistic expressions to the vast range of electronic equipment. Naturally this is of great practical significance for learning opportunities, but when it concerns learning, the forms of transmission must not be treated on the basis of a media perspective, but rather psychologically, from the perspective of how the individual as learner confronts his or her surroundings, whether they are transmitted directly or through media.

From the point of view of psychology, it can be said that interaction begins with what can be called *perception* in its simplest form, where the surrounding world comes to the individual as a totally unmediated sense impression. The individual is passive, but an impression encroaches and is registered – this may be most simply illustrated with a scent impression, which people rarely seek actively, but typically perceive when it imposes itself on them.

Something different happens when we talk about *transmission*. This aspect of interaction typically involves someone from outside having an interest to some degree or other in passing on something to others, or in influencing someone, in transmitting specific sense impressions or messages either generally or to specific others. The receiver can be more or less interested in the transmission in question, and accordingly will be more or less active in relation to it.

Most generally in relation to interaction we talk of *experience*. In general language use, both perception and transmission can be included in the term "experience", but one can also choose to limit the use of the word so that experience presupposes a particular activity, i.e. that the learner is not simply receiving, but also acts in order to benefit from the interaction. (In chapter 8 I will return to the concept of "experience" and try to establish a more qualified definition).

A particular form of considerable interest in learning where the learner actively complies with the learning opportunities is *imitation,* in which the learner attempts to do something in the same way as another person acting as a model or, in a more goal-directed form, as an instructor. Imitation is a very widespread form of interaction in the pre-school years, both in direct copying and in role-play and so on, where the children more generally copy others as they perceive them. But imitation also plays a large role in teaching and similar situations – the Dreyfus brothers point out, for example, that one reason computers will never be able to replace teaching and social learning is because they do not have the capacity for imitation (Dreyfus & Dreyfus 1986).

The next extensive form of interaction I would like to address is *activity,* which as previously explained (cf. chapter 3) is the expression within the cultural historical tradition for a goal-directed endeavour, i.e. the learner actively seeks influences that can be used in a particular context which the person concerned is interested in.

And finally I would like to mention *participation* as the most extensive and also the most general form of interaction. This is characterised by the fact that the learner is in a common goal-directed activity, a community of practice, as Etienne Wenger (1998) calls it, in which the person concerned has a recognised position and thus also an influence.

As has emerged, this sketch of various categories of forms of interaction is structured on the basis of the learner's involvement in the interaction. It would be easy to think of other categorisations based on other parameters, but in terms of learning, the choice of the involvement dimension as the structuring element includes the concept that the likelihood of learning occurring and the degree of "direction" (as opposed to chance) in this learning generally follows this parameter – or to quote a basic opinion in the cultural historical tradition's concept of learning:

"The one who does the work gets the qualifications."
(Hermansen 1996, p.63).

Hermansen himself has certain reservations regarding this saying, partly because not every work provides qualifications – work may be monotonous or repetitive – and partly because further qualification presupposes that practical work will be supplemented with systematising or theoretical considerations.

The forms of interaction set out above thus serve here only to provide some structural ideas of how interaction can work, and hint at the significance of active involvement in this connection; I do not intend to use these forms of interaction as starting points in the following sections, since they are not clearly defined and substantiated, and in practice they often overlap. But they can provide a sort of reference framework when I refer to various approaches and theories I believe to be significant in the understanding of the interaction processes that are found in learning.

In the next section I will briefly summarise some main trends in the comprehension of the interactive aspect of learning, after which, in the following sections, I will look at various contributions to the subject that express more specific orientations.

The social embedding of learning

The close interpersonal interaction processes that are of direct significance for learning have traditionally been dealt with primarily in social and group psychological contexts, and only with diffused or limited references to learning contexts, as one can see typically in edited American and Scandinavian works from the 1960s and the early 1970s (e.g. Krech et al. 1962, Israel 1969, Eskola 1971).

The concept of *social learning* was first established in earnest at this time with Albert Bandura's work on the significance of close social ties for learning. It primarily concerned model learning and learning through imitation – phenomena that had often been dealt with before, not least by Piaget (1951) – and which Bandura and his work associates studied in a traditional behaviouristic fashion. One result they came to was that the learning is influenced not only by the behaviour of the model, but also by the positive or negative response the model receives to his own behaviour, as witnessed by the learner.

From this they developed the theory of *vicarious learning*, which asserts that the reinforcing influences of learning are not aimed directly at the learner – which again presupposes that certain mental adjustment processes occur that cannot be measured or registered and which therefore reach beyond the comprehension horizon of the behaviouristic paradigm (Bandura & Walters 1963, Bandura 1977). Bandura's work was thus primarily linked to the type of interaction processes that are here called imitation, and was also transcending in that it revealed the limited opportunities for explanation of the behaviouristic approach to learning.

At the same time as Bandura opened the way for an elaboration of the prevailing conceptions of social learning, the learning concepts of Vygotsky and particularly Piaget began to make a serious impression on American psychology. This can be seen in the work of some of the most central figures in pedagogical psychology at that time, e.g. Jerome Bruner (1960) and David Ausubel (1968). And around the same time the Brazilian Paulo Freire published "Pedagogy of the Oppressed" and turned a considerable part of the comprehension of learning upside down with his convincing references to South American agricultural workers' societal conditions (Freire 1970). And in Europe the new Marxist and socio-linguistically oriented socialisation theories began to place both developmental psychology and social psychology in a new perspective (e.g. Gottschalch et al. 1971, Gutt & Salffner 1971, Bernstein 1971, Brückner 1972, Lorenzer 1972 – I will return to this theme later). Thus, the traditional American disciplines of learning, group and social psychology and the new concept of "social learning" came under pressure, and attention was increasingly directed to the significance of societal conditions.

Currently an ambiguous picture is emerging in extension of this. The traditional group and social fields of psychology have returned to a certain extent, but in new and more complex forms, in which they mingle with many of the impulses from the 1970s that now most often appear in more moderated forms. The term "social learning" crops up in many contexts, but even so has never quite achieved the status of an independent sphere of research – the term is not, for example, used by one of the currently most prominent figures in the sphere, the English educational sociologist referred to earlier, Peter Jarvis, who prefers to talk about "learning in a social context" and similar expressions. I will in any case briefly summarise Jarvis' conception here, as I view him as a typical representative of the concept of social learning today, within the English-speaking currents at any rate.

Jarvis emphasises that learning occurs in a tension field between the individual and the social:

"The process of learning is located in the interface of people's biography and the sociocultural milieu in which they live, for it is at this intersection that experiences occur. – When children are born, they are born into a society whose culture preceded them and will almost certainly continue after their lives are over. Culture, therefore, appears to be objective and external. But the children have inherited no, or minimal, instincts to help them live within society and conform to its culture; thus they have to acquire that culture. In the first instance, then, learning is a matter of internalising and transforming something that is apparently objective to the individual. – However, there comes a time when they begin to think for themselves, ask questions, and generally experiment. – Children gradually become more independent; they usually develop a mind of their own and then process the external cultural stimuli and respond to them in a variety of ways. – Individuals begin to act back on the social world that has formed them." (Jarvis 1992, p. 17, 22 and 23).

There is no doubt that Jarvis recognises both the internal acquisition processes and the interaction processes, as they are called in this book. In a book on adult learning he devotes an entire chapter to Kolb's cognitive learning theory (cf. chapter 2). But in the same place he also defines his position in the following way:

"Most learning theory in adult education has taken a predominantly psychological perspective, which is not surprising since adult education has been concerned with both adult development and traditional approaches to learning. – This study, however, is more concerned to examine the learning processes from a social perspective." (Jarvis 1987, p. 2).

Without making a clear distinction between inner acquisition processes and social interaction processes, Jarvis strives to put it all into a social perspective with emphasis on the active role played by the learner. In this way he represents a trend to incorporate the internal processes into the perspective of the social processes, with the social processes here including the more general socialisation, more goal-directed teaching and influence processes and the learner's own self-directed activities (what I have termed transmission, experience and activity), while imitation has more or less slipped out of sight.

However, others go further than Jarvis in their insistence on the significance of the interactive. The most consistent attitude in this direction is found in *social constructionism*, typically represented by the American psychologist Kenneth Gergen (1994). The basis for the social constructionist conception – somewhat in line with Robin Usher's conception as summarised in chapter 6 – is that

> "the site of explanation for human action moves to the relational sphere. – Social constructionism traces the sources of human action to relationships and the very understanding of 'individual functioning' to communal interchange." (Gergen 1994, p. 69 and 68).

Social constructionism goes a decisive step further than the underlying view of the concept of social learning:

> "For example, social learning theorists talk about the 'situation specificity' of behaviour. They suggest that our behaviour is dependent not upon personality characteristics but upon the nature of the situations in which we find ourselves. Behaviour is therefore 'specific' to a particular situation. – According to this view we should expect a person to be different in different situations, whereas for the traditional 'personality' view these differences are problematic. – But there is ... good reason to believe that a person is never a coherent system of consistent elements. – What might it mean then, to say that personality is socially constructed? One way of looking at this is to think of personality ... as existing not within people but between them. – Take some of the personality-type words we use to describe people: for example, friendly, caring, shy, self-conscious, charming, bad-tempered, thoughtless ... words which would completely lose their meaning if the person described were living alone on a desert island. – The point is that we use these words as if they referred to entities existing within the person they describe, but once the person is removed from their relations with others the words become meaningless." (Burr 1995, p. 25, 26 and 27).

Social constructionists do not as such deny that learning processes occur internally in an individual. But they find it uninteresting, because the nature of these processes and the content of them are always determined by relations in the social field. They agree with Piaget and other constructivists that the world and society are not objective elements that can be acquired through learning processes. The surrounding world is perceived in both cases as something that is actively constructed. In a constructivist approach this construction occurs in the individual by means of meetings with the surrounding world and interactions with it. In a social constructionist approach the construction occurs socially as developments in the community.

In my understanding, however, the two approaches do not need to oppose each other. In accordance with the introduction to this book, the way I view it is that social constructions occur in the communities which constantly interact with individual constructions in the internal learning processes. The social constructionists rightly point out the significance of the social field, but this can easily lead to the significance of the internal psychological processes in the individual being overlooked or underestimated. Friendliness is developed socially and only has meaning in a social context, yet it is individuals who acquire and practise friendliness.

At any rate, today one must distinguish between the socio-psychological approaches to learning, which have been dealt with in this section, and those that lean more towards more socialisation theory, which I have already mentioned, and which I will analyse more closely below.

The Frankfurt School and the Hanover School

Socialisation denotes the process through which the individual acquires current societal norms and structures, thus becoming part of the society in question. The process includes both an individual and a social-societal aspect in line with this book's conception of learning. Rather than signify a particular part of the learning process or a particular form of learning, socialisation may therefore be perceived as a specific viewpoint on learning and development, namely, the societal viewpoint. In this lies the notion that the significance of learning is perceived based on the relationship that develops between individual and society, and that can occur directly through teaching and other forms of goal-directed transmission, and to a great extent also indirectly, by the individual gaining experience of how things work and how different people behave.

There have thus always been considerable elements of socialisation theory in learning, developmental, personality and social psychology, but a more direct and targeted socialisation theory approach first seriously developed in extension of the work of the so-called Frankfurt School concerning the scientific school of thought called *critical theory*.

It concerns the approach that developed in the years between the two world wars at the "Institut für Sozialforschung" in Frankfurt, other places in Europe and especially the USA after Hitler came to power in 1933, and from the early 1950s again in Frankfurt. Central people in the first generation of the Frankfurt School were particularly Max Horkheimer, Theodor Adorno, and later, Herbert Marcuse. The main academic point lay in the intersecting field between philosophy, sociology and psychoanalysis, and in many ways, the problems that were focused on concerned the relationship between individual and society, often seen in a contemporary historical perspective. The approach was primarily a coupling between the Marxist conception of society and the psychoanalytical conception of the individual – but both in a critical interpretation in which there was also room for other approaches, while certain Marxist and psychoanalytical interpretations were rejected – not least the dialectical materialistic conception of Marxism that was predominant in the Soviet Union – and the theories were applied to current societal and political problems.

A major work from the early period was Horkheimer's and Adorno's "Dialectic of Enlightenment" that took the form of outlines and dialogues, but still describes the Frankfurt School's objective of critical enlightenment (Horkheimer & Adorno 1944). For Adorno too, aesthetic and artistic dimensions took a central position. Of more direct interest in the present context is the extensive investigation of the authoritarian personality structure that was perceived as a basis for the success of Nazism (Adorno et al. 1950 – cf. chapter 10). And finally it must be mentioned that Marcuse gained some degree of status as the student rebellion's philosopher, particularly with his books "Eros and civilization" (Marcuse 1955) and "One dimensional man" (Marcuse 1964), that in different ways deal with new forms of alienation in the post-war period.

The second generation of the Frankfurt School is most strongly signified by the philosopher Jürgen Habermas, who took over management of the institute in Frankfurt in 1965. Habermas has dealt with a broad range of subjects, including the relationship between theory and practice (Habermas 1963/88), the elucidation of various interests in knowledge (Habermas 1968/89a), a number of books on language, communication and public life (especially Habermas 1962/89b and 1981/84) and the relationship between system and lifeworld (Habermas 1981/87). To summarise very briefly, Habermas attempts to oppose modernity's technical or instrumental rationality that increasingly characterises society, with a communicative rationality, discourse, the ideal speech situation and lifeworld, as approaches that can maintain a humanistic emancipatory practice and "knowledge-constitutive interest".

Habermas has also addressed the theory of socialisation in a short work (Habermas 1971), but it is first with the "branch" of the Frankfurt School that has sometimes been called the Hanover School that this interest became concentrated on the socialisation theory approach.

The Hanover School comprises a number of researchers who can scarcely be described as a group, but all have this in common: they are all inspired by and/or have had connections to the Frankfurt School, and they work or have worked in Hanover. I have already made reference to two of the members of the Hanover School in an earlier chapter, namely Thomas Ziehe with his conception of cultural liberation and interest in current youth and education problems (chapter 5) and Thomas Leithäuser with the theory of everyday consciousness (chapter 6). Two early contributors were Peter Brückner with his highly critical book on "The social psychology of capitalism", which drew attention to many repressive aspects of socialisation (Brückner 1972), and Alfred Krovoza, who was particularly interested in the repression of sensuality and paid particular attention to the human resistance potential (Krovoza 1976), which made him a source of inspiration to the conception of resistance that is described here in chapter 6. Another significant member of the Hanover School is Oskar Negt, whose conception of experience will be dealt with more fully in the next chapter.

However, the most important work among the Hanover School's treatment of the concept of socialisation is Alfred Lorenzer's materialistic theory of socialisation, which I will deal with below, after which I will also consider Regina Becker-Schmidt's gender-oriented contribution in this chapter.

Lorenzer's materialistic theory of socialisation

Alfred Lorenzer's theory of socialisation was mainly developed in his book "Materialistic theory of socialisation" (1972). His work is a clear extension of the Frankfurt School's attempt to bring together Marxist and psycho-analytical conceptions, and he sets this out with a sort of manifesto:

> "This investigation pursues the question: how can the child's develop-ment be seen as a natural process and as a social process of develop-ment at one and the same time? – What is alluded to here is not the harmless old cliché about a weaving together of natural aptitudes and cultural influences. Rather, the investigation is fully concerned with the confrontation between two theories that seem mutually exclusive: psychoanalysis and historic materialism. – If psychoanalysis understands human structures of experience – action, thought, feelings, perception – as determined by drives, historic materialism must maintain that these very structures must be seen as dependent on history, on the encounter of humans with external nature, as it is here and now..." (Lorenzer 1972, p. 7).

In the present context it is important to point out that to a great extent Lorenzer relates to Piaget's work, which he acknowledges, while to a certain extent distancing himself from it (Lorenzer 1972, p. 8 and 83ff). Lorenzer agrees with Piaget because they both basically view

> "the child's development as a differentiated weaving together of devel-opment and maturation steps." (Lorenzer 1972, p. 8).

But at the same time Lorenzer distances himself from Piaget:

> "Piaget bases his ideas on the assumption of logic, that unfolds from itself, and sees the individual's societal determination as something that

simply sits above the subjective-personal individual development."
(Lorenzer 1972, p. 8).

Piaget's insufficient treatment of societal conditions is an oft-repeated point
of criticism with which I entirely agree (and which I attempt to take into
account in this book). But beyond this I simply see the basic difference
between Lorenzer and Piaget being that while Piaget explicitly focuses on
cognitive development (cf. chapter 4), Lorenzer just as clearly maintains
that his

"problem formulation aims first at emotional processes and not at cognitive." (Lorenzer 1972, p. 85).

As I see it, Lorenzer is a little wide of the mark in his comprehension of
Piaget's concept of logic. This logic – or intelligence or structure – that Piaget
asserts unfolds from itself (i.e. through certain specific stages), consists of
certain genetically determined modes of function, namely that mankind is
disposed to elaborate impulses from the environment through assimilative
and accommodative processes, and organise them in structures. This is a
sort of interpretation of the way the central nervous system works, i.e. it
corresponds exactly to the reference to development as a natural process
which Lorenzer emphasises in the first lines of his book as one aspect of the
basis he is working from. About the other aspect, the content of the structures or the social process of development, there is hardly a disagreement.
But there are big differences in practice, for the very reason that Piaget is
mostly interested in the development of knowledge and logical thought, while
Lorenzer is more interested in the personality and emotional development
and the social-societal basis. (See also my consideration of the relationship
between the cognitive and the emotional in chapter 4).

In extension of these features it is thus my opinion that Lorenzer's conception of subjectivity as *internalised structures of interaction forms* correspond on a fundamental level to the conception of learning's duality of
internal psychological processes (internalising) and interaction processes
(forms of interaction) on which this book is based. And I also see Lorenzer's
conception as parallel to the conception of the psychological cognitive

structures and affective patterns that I have developed earlier in this book, with Piaget as my starting point.

However, Lorenzer's approach is naturally different from that which I have already set out, since it is the interaction processes or forms he is primarily interested in. In addition, within this sphere it is particularly the generally socialising content in the processes Lorenzer attaches most importance to, not least that part of socialisation or personality formation that is embedded in the unconscious.

Lorenzer is thus exclusively concerned with the earliest interaction that occurs between the child and its primary relation object in what Lorenzer calls in a generalised form, the *mother-child-dyad*. Here the child forms its most fundamental subjective structures in its intimate interactions or exchange relations through *accordances*. But Lorenzer also very clearly points out that even here there will be frustrations. The mother will not be able to completely meet the child's needs, and frustrations are also necessary for the child to develop into a societal individual.

Later the field of interaction broadens, the child's structures develop and become differentiated, and the unconscious, sensuously spontaneous interaction forms are gradually supplemented by two further types of interaction forms: the linguistic symbolic interaction forms that are internalised into the conscious layer, and the sensuously symbolic interaction forms that lead to the creation of the so-called *protosymbols,* which can be characterised as broader and more open symbol formations that transmit the tensions between the conscious and the unconscious layers in relation to socially prescribed practice, and form the basis for the identity and the imagination.

However, in any stage of the development process there can also occur what Lorenzer calls *systematically broken practice,* i.e. repeated discordances, incomprehensible to the child, which can lead to the interaction forms in question being driven out of the linguistic level and becoming unconscious *clichés*. Lorenzer emphasises that

"insocialisation of cliché-determined behaviour serves societal purposes, ...makes the subjects available at the service of an existing order(and) blocks potential discussions of the action norms that belong to the be-haviour complex in question." (Lorenzer 1972, pp. 142 and 143).

Socialisation is thus a process that will always embrace both development and limitation or damage, and will never be able to be the frictionless transfer of societal conditions to the individual that is the underlying basis in much of developmental psychology.

I view Lorenzer's theory (here very briefly sketched out) on a fundamen-tal level as a conception of the structure and functions of the interaction processes that are in agreement with the basis of this book: it concerns various types of social processes that include, through the participating people, authorities and media, the existing societal structures, norms and contradictions, forming the basis for the internal psychological acquisition processes that occur in the individual. However, I will not pursue Lorenzer's theory any further, for it is only concerned with learning in a very general sense, and it is only on this particular level that it is of interest here.

In the following section I will look more closely at two special current views of the significance of the social field for learning today, namely the German feminist researcher Regina Becker-Schmidt's gender-oriented conception, which can be understood in direct extension of Lorenzer's theory, and the Flemish adult education researcher Danny Wildemeersch's grass-root-oriented draft. After this I will return to the Russian cultural historical school and various contemporary elaborations from this, and finally in this chapter I will consider the Swiss-American Etienne Wenger's "social theory of learning", which draws inspiration from both Russian and American learning research.

Social learning, contradictions and ambivalence

Like Alfred Lorenzer, Regina Becker-Schmidt's work elaborates that of the Frankfurt School. Her field is feminist studies, and she first focused in particular on unskilled women in industry. She has since worked more broadly on gender research and gender theory. Thus, she has not aimed at developing the concept of social learning ("soziales Lernen") generally, but uses it in her research into the learning processes that are effective for women in our society (esp. Becker-Schmidt 1987).

In this connection, Becker-Schmidt starts with the extreme contradictions that characterise the lives of women:

> "The learning content, which is what our considerations of social learning are all about, is linked to women's reality, to the conflicts in female lives, which the societal organisation of gender relations necessarily result in." (Becker-Schmidt 1987, p. 9).

Basically it concerns the contradiction between wage work and reproduction in the private sphere, including motherhood. But even within each of these fields, the situation for women is full of contradictions, for the role of women in relation to society is full of ambiguities: femininity is both idealised and undervalued at one and the same time; it is women who deal with all of the practical and social problems of everyday life, they humanise the world, so to speak, but societally they are not valued, neither in terms of wage nor status, and socially they have to put up with scorn and humiliation.

Psychologically these basic contradictory conditions are converted into *ambivalence*. The needs of women are alternately exceeded and denied. Women are brought up to systematically renounce things, they learn to put up with enmity, oppression and conflict, to resign themselves to things, to come to terms with things. Becker-Schmidt describes, for example, how the function of housewife has become isolated and essentially shallow, due to the fragmentation of the family and the increasing use of technology in housework (Becker-Schmidt 1987, p.77ff).

Becker-Schmidt's problem concerns how women learn to live with these contradictory realities, and how they can be liberated from them. It is in this context that her use of the concept of social learning must be understood. Generally, social learning concerns how people learn to live with the contradictions and conflicts of reality, and the development of the capacity to deal with both external and internal conflicts and keep an open mind towards ambiguity.

Two key concepts in this context are *ambivalence tolerance* and *ambivalence defence*. Women have to learn to live with ambivalence, to recognise it and develop a psychological resistance to it:

> "Ambivalence therefore has its response on both internal and external fragmentation. Our psychological reality is just as controlled by conflicting desires as the social reality is pervaded by contradictions. In both cases 'mixed feelings' express subjective and objective conflicts. – When we question ourselves, face conflicts and endure, that is 'ambivalence tolerance'; when we shrink from them, that is 'ambivalence defence'. – Our analyses attempt to put both levels of conflict together: the level of conflicting psychological drives and impulses and the level of contradictory social reality." Becker-Schmidt 1987, p. 8).

Social learning thus implies acknowledging ambivalence and its causes. This can happen through *reality testing*, i.e. putting experiences into context in time and space, to emotionally "feel" and to logically "think about" (cf. chapter 5 on reflexivity). One can try to transcend the customary patterns, accept dislike by moving into the unknown, give names to the contradictions and the ambivalence – that develops ambivalence tolerance. It requires willpower and energy (cf. chapter 2 on accommodative processes and chapter 6 on everyday consciousness and thematisation) – and the motive to make these efforts may lie in a notion that it could be better, not to understand as such that the contradictions could be solved, but that they could be handled better if you acknowledge them, also thereby gaining the opportunity to understand and accept ambivalence (Becker-Schmidt 1987, p. 62ff).

As the Danish gender and education researcher Kirsten Weber points out, Becker-Schmidt's approach is hopeful because it suggests a way out through the concept of ambivalence tolerance (Weber 1995, p. 91). It must also be said that Becker-Schmidt's analyses were of middle-aged women, and there are signs that the situation is about to change. In one respect cultural liberation and the late-modern opening of opportunity horizons (as discussed in chapter 5) bring a turning point in the rigid matter of gender contradiction. On the other hand, the same developments seem to imply that ambivalence is spreading to become a basic condition of an existential nature for everyone (cf. Ahrenkiel & Illeris 2000).

Although Becker-Schmidt's analyses and considerations of the concept of ambivalence are so clearly rooted in the life situations and consciousness patterns of women, it may soon be obvious that they are relevant on a general level regardless of gender. They basically concern socialisation, and therefore they chiefly concern the general influence of the interaction processes, but they also include considerations of the development of activities for the conscious handling of contradictions and ambivalence.

Social learning and social responsibility

An entirely different approach to the concept of social learning can be found in the work of the Flemish researcher Danny Wildemeersch, who works on adult education from a social perspective and is particularly interested in educational perspectives in connection with grass-roots activities and the like. Wildemeersch defines social learning as

> "combined learning and problem-solving activities which take place within participatory systems such as groups, social networks, movements and collectivities, operating within 'real life' contexts and thereby raising issues of social responsibility." (Wildemeersch 1999, p. 39).

Social learning thus occurs in *participatory systems*, which operate in a tension field between creativity, power and responsibility, and the learning takes place around four axes characterised as action, reflection, communication and negotiation. This is illustrated by a complicated model (which I do not reproduce here, since the author expressly continues to view it as "the provisionally last stage of our work in progress" – Wildemeersch 1999, p. 41).

In the present context it is significant that the thinking and the model attempt to span both the external societal conditions and the internal psychological conditions. There may be some inspiration from Kolb's model (chapter 2) in the presentation of the internal psychological level, but at the same time this model's limits are transcended, for the individual processes in Wildemeersch's model are directly integrated in the social or collective processes in which the participatory systems are engaged.

Wildemeersch thus connects social learning with the processes that occur in dedicated forward-looking problem solving. This also includes a concept of *social responsibility,* which in several contexts Wildemeersch has been aiming at (Wildemeersch 1991, 1992, Jansen et al. 1998). This concept has not been precisely defined, but it is clearly more wide-reaching than the concept of "responsibility for one's own learning" that has become current in the debate over Danish education (cf. Illeris 1998) – as it spans right from the external societal responsibility regarded by many today as absolutely essential in a large number of contexts, both local and global, to the responsibility a participant may have in a goal-directed group project, and the personal responsibility for our own actions and our own lives.

In terms of learning, social responsibility forms a particularly significant relationship with reflexivity (Wildemeersch 1991, p.156ff). If reflexivity is not to end up in individualistic selfishness, lacking any social perspective, it must be connected with a sense of social obligation. Wildemeersch also uses expressions such as "critical reflectivity" and "aesthetic reflectivity", which respectively imply a critical distance and a social connection (Wildemeersch 1998, p.98-99).

Social learning and social responsibility are thus for Wildemeersch a way to behave, which develops – or perhaps does not develop – societally as a part of socialisation, and comes to be seen in a new light in extension of late-modern developments that in one respect have put reflexivity on the agenda and in another are handing more and more societal functions over to the market mechanism and to individuality.

When someone constantly has to make a choice between apparently boundless possibilities, and even has to choose his or her own life course and identity, there is no avoiding reflexivity, which settles everything in relation to oneself. In this way, learning through reflexivity becomes a necessity, however demanding it may be, and it becomes vitally important to qualify this form of learning (Wildemeersch 2000).

It is a discussion with far-reaching consequences, for without the general development of a reflexivity that is always a match for the development of a market society, the in-built mechanisms within this development will lead to an ever-stronger impoverishment of the world's resources, both material and human. The basic qualification for balanced learning with both reflexivity and responsibility is that the learning content should be perceived to be meaningful with regard to oneself. This basic qualification is far from always fulfilled in institutional education, but is basically present in grass-roots activities and the like.

Thus, Wildemeersch is active around the boundary between the critical and the pedagogical normative. Social learning is societally determined and for that very reason must be qualified. In terms of learning, this concerns experience, transmission and activity.

The heritage of the cultural historical tradition

I will now return to the Russian cultural historical school, which has always emphasised the viewing of learning from a societal perspective and thus in principle relating coherently to the internal learning processes and interaction processes. Vygotsky in particular harboured ambitions to link the two aspects together:

"What Vygotsky sought was a comprehensive approach that would make possible description and explanation of higher psychological functions in terms acceptable to natural science. To Vygotsky, explanation meant a great deal. It included identification of the brain mechanisms underlying a particular function; it included a detailed explanation of their developmental history to establish the relation between simple and complex forms of what appeared to be the same behavior; and, importantly, it included specification of the societal context in which the behavior developed. Vygotsky's goals were extremely ambitious, perhaps unreasonably so. He did not achieve these goals (as he was well aware). But he did succeed in providing us with an astute and prescient analysis of modern psychology." (Cole & Scribner in Vygotsky 1978, p. 5-6).

Vygotsky's in-depth studies of language, thought, learning and development were thus embedded in a materialistic societal frame of comprehension that, as far as the social dimensions of learning are concerned, qualified his theories more decisively than other learning theory developments between the two world wars, such as that of Piaget and the then predominant behaviouristic psychology in the USA. In a contemporary context, however, it emerges as a drawback of the Russian theories, particularly when they occur in an educational perspective, that their societal connection is so clearly linked to the Soviet-Marxist conception of society of that time. For although they contain many important and positive comprehensions, particularly of the significance of work and social community, there is for good or ill a huge distance from there to today's late-modern capitalistic market society – and it also seems problematic that communist society is in principle viewed as free from conflict.

The approach of the cultural historical school has nevertheless been continued, even outside Russia, in comprehensive studies using Leontjev's concept of human *activity* in particular as a pivotal point (Leontjev 1981 – cf. chapter 3). I especially regard Yrjö Engeström's work as a significant contemporary elaboration of the cultural historical tradition, while at the same time viewing it as a liberation from some of its ties to Soviet-Marxism. Although in my inclusion of Engeström's work in chapter 3 (on reflection) I related particularly to his transcendent conception of the internal learning processes, it should be borne in mind that this conception was developed within a fully prepared framework, in which the individual is in a community or society that has developed regulating norms, usable tools, both material and symbolic, and a societal division of labour (cf. Engeström 1987, p. 73ff, 1996b, p. 131ff). An important characteristic in Engeström is that he links the cultural historical tradition together with Bateson's concept of *double-bind* (cf. chapter 3), for this brings a strong conception of conflict into the picture, contradicting the idealised communist view of harmony.

Another comprehensive elaboration of the cultural historical tradition may be found in the so-called "critical psychology" or "Berlin school" of West Berlin, which gradually evolved into an independent psychological direction or position under the leadership of psychologist Klaus Holzkamp (esp. Holzkamp 1972, 1983). I have previously quoted (in chapter 4) from Ute Holzkamp-Osterkamp's comprehensive work on motivational psychology, which has an important and established view on the relationship between knowledge and emotions. Klaus Holzkamp's own last important contribution was a comprehensive book on learning, which he basically views as a particular form of subjective action, and therefore deals with from the subjective perspective of the learner – in strong contradiction to the externally-determined dominating perspective of learning in school and education (Holzkamp 1995).

In contradiction to the cultural historical tradition and to Holzkamp's own earlier work, in this book the concept of subjectivity has a central position. But this is a completely different conception of subjectivity than that developed under the auspices of the Frankfurt School by researchers such as Lorenzer, Leithäuser and Becker-Schmidt, to whom Holzkamp makes no reference. While the Frankfurt School's concept of subjectivity in continuation of psychoanalysis is characterised by internal tensions and conflicts, Holzkamp's concept of subjectivity is rational and goal-directed. Holzkamp himself deals fairly briefly with this contradiction, and characterises psychoanalysis as an

"earlier subject-scientific thought tendency in the history of psychology. – Freud's theory is (and therein lies its potentially clarifying nature) – simply in making the contradictions and breaches comprehensible and (within the framework of what is possible) surmountable in striving for their realisation – irretrievably committed to human sense as the most important life value." (Holzkamp 1995, p. 29 and 30).

And Holzkamp then quotes Freud:

"The voice of the intellect is a soft one, but it does not rest till it has gained a hearing. – In the long run nothing can withstand reason and experience." (Freud 1962, p. 49 and 50).

The quotation is correct, but it is taken from a text in which Freud is dealing with religion, and it may well be something of a misrepresentation to use it in an attempt to place Freud somewhere in Holzkamp's conception of rationality – just as a view of Freud as standard-bearer for irrationality would be equally mistaken. Freud, and the Frankfurt School and the Hanover School after him, was primarily oriented towards conflicts and contradictions, and the contradiction between Holzkamp's and the Frankfurt School's conceptions of subjectivity cannot be explained away. For outsiders, the contradictory relationship between the two German "schools" seems highly unfruitful – but apart from this Holzkamp's last book denotes for me an important step in the direction of understanding the significance of the subjective.

Thus it is my view that the successors to the cultural historical tradition, particularly with the contributions of Engeström and Holzkamp, are well on the way to working their way free from their ties to the Soviet positions, and I have taken considerable inspiration from Engeström's work in the sphere of general learning theory (cf. my application of Engeström in chapter 3).

Communities of practice as a framework for social learning

A new and in many ways quite comprehensive theory of social learning – or in the author's own words "*social theory of learning*" (Wenger 1998, p.4) – also has links with the Russian cultural historical tradition, but springs primarily from anthropological studies in industrialised and non-industrialised societies, although its connection with these has gradually faded, and it now has clearer parallels in both social constructionism and Wildemeersch's studies of learning in social movements.

The first steps to this theory are to be found in Jean Lave and Etienne Wenger's book on *situated learning* (Lave & Wenger 1991), which does not actually contain any proper learning theory, but focuses primarily on the social conditions for learning, a subject I shall return to in chapter 10. But in a further elaboration of the ideas of this work in a book on *communities of practice* (Wenger 1998), Wenger has developed a comprehensive theory on the social dimension of learning, which may be seen as a very ambitious and detailed attempt to overcome the distance between the social and the individual dimensions of learning.

Wenger is absolutely clear that learning has dimensions other than the social:

"There are many different kinds of learning theory. Each emphasizes different aspects of learning, and each is therefore useful for different purposes. To some extent these differences in emphasis reflect a deliberate focus on a slice of the multidimensional problem of learning, and to some extent they reflect more fundamental differences in assumptions about the nature of knowledge, knowing, and knowers, and consequently about what matters in learning." (Wenger 1998, p. 3-4).

Wenger's conception that learning embraces various dimensions seems right in line with the basic view of this book, but while I attempt to specify and discuss the dimensions in relation to each other, Wenger gives priority to the social context even though in his introductory model, which brings together his overall conception and approach, the concept of "learning" (not "social learning") is centrally positioned. Four main conditions of learning are placed around this, of which practice and community clearly relate to the social context of learning, while meaning and identity reach out towards its individual dimensions, even though Wenger mainly sees them from a social perspective.

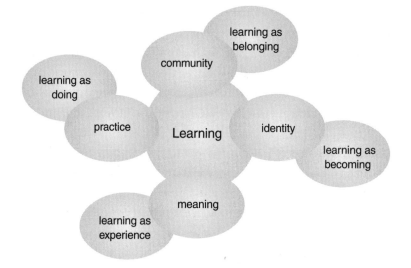

Figure 5: A social theory of learning (from Wenger 1998, p.5)

Wenger himself gives the following explanation for the model:

"A social theory of learning must ... integrate the components necessary to characterize social participation as a process of learning and knowing. These components ... include the following:

1) *Meaning:* a way of talking about our (changing) ability – individually and collectively – to experience our life and the world as meaningful.

2) *Practice:* a way of talking about the shared historical and social resources, frameworks, and perspectives that can sustain mutual engagement in action.

3) *Community:* a way of talking about the social configurations in which our enterprises are defined as worth pursuing and our participation is recognizable as competence.

4) *Identity:* a way of talking about how learning changes who we are and creates personal histories of becoming in the context of our communities.

Clearly, these elements are deeply interconnected and mutually defining. In fact, looking at (the figure), you could switch any of the four peripheral components with learning, place it in the center as the primary focus, and the figure would still make sense.

Therefore, when I use the concept of 'community of practice' in the title of this book, I really use it as a point of entry into a broader conceptual framework of which it is a constitutive element. The analytical power of the concept lies precisely in that it integrates the components of (the figure) while referring to a familiar experience." (Wenger 1998, p. 4-6).

The social dimension of learning is tied to community and practice, and creates meaning and identity, and therefore learning presupposes action and participation and converts them into experience and development. These key words and their positions in the model provide a valuable illustration of the significance of the community of practice for learning, which is elaborated through Wenger's further descriptions and finally converted into important consequences for the development of organisation and education.

The most important quality of the theory lies in its comprehensive and coherent understanding of the social level – while the psychological and societal levels are only brought in as extensions or examples. This is probably also partly why neither internal psychological nor societal conflicts have any important role to play in the theory. As a learning theory it expands the concept of social learning, but in relation to individual development, it lacks the perspective of conflict, and although there is a concept of experience, it is not in the same dialectic mode, (and therefore developmental and conflict-oriented mode), as in the concept of experience developed in extension of the socialisation approach of the Frankfurt and Hanover Schools. I will discuss this further in the next chapter.

Summary

In this chapter I have looked at the interactive aspect of learning. This is a very broad field, spanning from close personal interactions to socialisation in all its breadth and complexity, and on to media-transmitted interaction. I have therefore only been able to present a small part of what I consider to be most relevant in this sphere and most suited to contribute to a structural comprehension. It can be somewhat difficult to sum this up in clear points, but I shall try anyway:

1. Learning occurs in an interaction between internal psychological acquisition processes and social interaction processes. The interaction processes comprise both direct interaction between people, and the individual's interaction with the material, the societal and the media-transmitted world, including societal socialisation.

2. In terms of learning, the interaction processes can be roughly grouped in six partially overlapping main categories according to the degree of the learner's involvement and activity. These can be titled perception, transmission, experience, imitation, activity and participation.

3. It is characteristic that the interest in learning in recent years by the development of concepts such as social learning and, very radically,

social constructionism, has moved in the direction of interaction processes. In this situation it is important to maintain a conception of the internal psychological processes as an integrated part of learning.

4. Social learning is primarily linked to participation and action in communities of practice, and the development of meaning and identity occur as mutual social processes.

5. Socialisation denotes the processes by which the individual acquires current societal norms and structures, thus becoming a part of the society. Thus, all learning plays a part in socialisation, and all socialisation is a form of learning. When we talk about socialisation, however, a specific societally-oriented approach is brought to bear on learning.

6. Socialisation always comprises both development and limitation – corresponding to the individual's life fulfilment and resistance potentials. Socialisation is thus in itself a contradictory process that cannot run without friction, and always develops ambivalence to some extent.

7. In our present-day late-modern society there is a trend towards increased openness in the forms of interaction, while the market mechanism increasingly permeates all our influences. This development places further demands on the individual's self-regulation, reflexivity and responsibility.

8. Experiential Learning

Learning and experience

"From experience you shall learn" goes an old Danish folk expression, and there is no doubt that in everyday language, in both Danish and English, experience is reckoned to be better and more profound than "ordinary learning", having another dimension of personal significance and involving personal commitment. But experience is also a central concept in learning theory, and in the following sections I will set out how and with which criteria this concept can be used as a common framework for understanding learning, that in an important way both covers and brings together the three dimensions I have discussed in detail earlier in this book.

I must immediately emphasise – as in chapter 2 – that I use the word "experience" in a more demanding and qualified sense than it is given in everyday English, more so even than as used by Kolb in his book on "Experiential Learning" (Kolb 1984) and many other researchers and debaters in this field. My use of the concepts "experience" and "experiential learning" goes beyond distinguishing between the immediate perception and the elaborated comprehension; it implies also that the process does not relate only to cognitive learning (as is, for example, the case in Kolb's work), but covers all three dimensions of learning.

However, it is this book's contention that *all* learning includes these dimensions to some degree, although the weighting can be rather unbalanced in some contexts. When I claim that experience is immediately understood as something other and something more than ordinary learning, I am referring to a qualitative difference. On the other hand it is not possible and not in accordance with the nature of learning, to make a sharp distinction between what is experience and what is "ordinary" learning. One of the consequences of the complex nature of learning is that there will be many places where they overlap – just as when Piaget asserts on the one hand that all learning comprises both assimilation and accommodation, while at the same time he operates separately to a great extent with both assimilative and accommodative processes (cf. chapter 2).

The concept of experience I am setting out here does not therefore solely concern the notion that all three dimensions are involved, for they are all in principle always involved, but *all three dimensions must also be of subjective significance for the learner in the context.* Experience has important elements of content and knowledge, i.e. we acquire or understand something which we perceive to be important for ourselves. Experience also has a considerable emotional element, i.e. we are committed affectively and motivationally to the learning taking place. And finally, experience has an important social and societal element, i.e. we learn something that is not only of significance to us personally, something that also concerns the relationship between ourselves and the world we live in.

Thus, experience is set out as the central concept in the learning conception of this presentation: experience is characterised by incorporating the three dimensions spanned by the learning conception presented here in an important way – and is therefore better suited in my opinion than, for example, the cultural historical tradition's concept of activity to encompass the entire scope of learning.

As I have already stated (chapters 3 and 7), the concept of activity does not include, or not adequately at any rate, the emotional dimension. In part this means that individual psychological tensions, contradictions and instances of ambivalence significant for learning will tend not to be considered. It also means that in teaching, the significance of the learner's participation in activity management is often undervalued.

It could be argued here that with the application of the concept of experience there has been a corresponding tendency to overlook or downplay the cognitive dimension of learning. I am not, as such, in disagreement with this, but in those cases I see it as excessive focusing on psychodynamic and social-societal factors. For this removal or downplaying of the cognitive is not found in the ordinary full comprehension of the concept of experience, and should therefore not appear in a more qualified professional application – in contrast to the concept of activity, which is seen as a scientific concept in the cultural historical tradition's own selective perception of science, which has a tendency to work round the psychodynamic field and its significance. Freud performed a great service by confronting such forms of science, and therefore it is also my view that the relation of the concept of experience to psychoanalytical approaches, together with its roots in an ordinary language tradition, is what gives it its place as a key concept for a total learning approach.

I will attempt to illustrate this here by referring to the two most important approaches that form the basis for the perception of the concept of experience as it is used in Danish pedagogy: firstly, the progressive approach developed in the USA in the early 1900s, particularly by the philosopher and pedagogue John Dewey. And secondly the approach of German sociologist Oskar Negt, who like Ziehe, Leithäuser, Lorenzer and Becker-Schmidt, works in extension of the Frankfurt School and has played a large role as a theoretical reference for the development of experiential pedagogy in Denmark for over 20 years (cf. Webb & Nielsen 1996).

Dewey's concept of experience

While the majority of Dewey's development of pedagogical practice and theory took place around the turn of the twentieth century, he dealt in detail with the concept of experience later in a short work entitled "Experience and Education" (1938/63) based on a series of summarised lectures.

Dewey has a broad definition of the concept of experience in accordance with its everyday meaning. We experience things all the time, but what is important in pedagogical terms is – as I have also stated before – the quality of the experiences,

> "to discriminate between experiences that are worth while educationally and those that are not. It may seem superfluous to argue that this discrimination is necessary not only in criticizing the traditional type of education but also in initiating and conducting a different type. – Does not the principle of regard for individual freedom and for decency and kindliness of human relations come back in the end to the conviction that these things are tributary to a higher quality of experience on the part of a greater number than are methods of repression and coercion or force? Is it not the reason for our preference that we

believe that mutual consultation and convictions reached through persuasion, make possible a better quality of experience than can otherwise be provided on any wide scale?" (Dewey 1963, p. 33 and 34).

Thus Dewey's criteria for this distinction lies in general humanism and he further attempts to root it in a rather unclear concept of growth, which concerns to what extent

> "an experience arouses curiosity, strengthens initiative, and sets up desires and purposes that are sufficiently intense to carry a person over dead places in the future …(and not) operate so as to leave a person arrested on a low plane of development, in a way which limits capacity for growth." (Dewey 1963, p. 38 and 37-38).

In connection with this Dewey presents two integrated principles or dimensions as being central to upbringing, namely the principles of *continuity* and *interaction*.

> "The principle of continuity of experience means that every experience both takes up something from those which have gone before and modifies in some way the quality of those which come after." (Dewey 1963, p. 35).

Hence Dewey believes that

> "It is then the business of the educator to see in what direction an experience is heading … (and) to take the moving force of an experience into account so as to judge and direct it on the ground of what it is moving into." (Dewey 1963, p. 38).

The second central principle, that of interaction, means that

> "…a transaction (is) taking place between an individual and what, at the same time, constitutes his environment" (Dewey 1963, p. 43).

Dewey understands the environment in this context as

> "a world of persons and things which in large measure is what it is because of what has been done and transmitted from previous human activities." (Dewey 1963, p. 39).

Thus, the experiences are created by the interaction between the individual's active influence on the physical environment and the social and bodily influence of the environment on the individual.

Through the principles of continuity and interaction the experience process is created, and they provide

> "in their active union with each other ... the measure of the educative significance and value of an experience." (Dewey 1963, p. 44-45).

Despite the reference to interaction, however, Dewey's concept of experience has often been criticised as individualistic and lacking a societal dimension. The American-Danish educational sociologist Thomas Webb gives a more balanced criticism, with a full description of how he gradually came to doubt the value of the Dewey inheritance he had brought with him from the USA, because in practice, despite Dewey's own intentions, it often seems to lead to a form of indirected child-centred or laissez-faire pedagogy, perhaps

> "owing to a lack of understanding for the realities inherent in cultural obstacles for social change." (Webb 1997, p.24).

Although Dewey was clearly aware that individual experience is always embedded in a social context that is code-termining for the experience and can be traced back to societal factors, the nature of these societal factors only appeared in his analysis in the form of criticism of traditional pedagogy. Dewey referred to a democracy-ideal to which upbringing and teaching are under an obligation (esp. Dewey 1916), but the ideal was general and abstract and was not placed in relation to the fundamental economic and power structures in the capitalistic society it was to be realised in.

Negt's concept of experience

It is in the societal sphere that Negt's concept of experience decisively transcends Dewey's – and for Webb and others has contributed to substantiating the conception of an experiential pedagogy that is not just feasible in practice, but also has better potential for actually realising Dewey's ideals.

Negt's concept of experience is mainly dealt with in the book "Public Sphere and Experience" (Negt & Kluge 1993), where it appears in a broad civilisation-critical context, which revolves round the question of the opportunities for the working class to experience their own situation and opportunities in our present (late) capitalist society. The concept of experience is thus only directly defined through an oft-quoted and fairly intricate statement from the philosopher Hegel:

> "The dialectic process which consciousness executes on itself – on its knowledge as well as on its object – in the sense that out of it the new and true object arises, is precisely what is termed experience." (Hegel 1967, p. 142).

With this reference, Negt draws on a long philosophical tradition leading from Kant, through Hegel, to the Frankfurt School. But although the approaches are very different, the distance from Dewey is not in my view all that great as far as the concept of experience itself is concerned. What Hegel calls the dialectic process which consciousness executes on itself is the same as what Dewey is attempting to capture through his claim of continuity. And what Hegel calls the dialectical process on its knowledge as well as on its object is present in Dewey's claim of interaction.

This can also be seen as that which is dealt with in this book as, respectively, the internal psychological, and the external social and societal partial processes in learning – by which means the central point in Hegel's statement is that both these processes are dialectic in nature, i.e. they take the form of interplay or tension that may lead to a synthesis, an overlapping agreement. In the internal psychological processes, the dialectic lies between the psychological structures developed previously and influences from the environment (cf. the approaches of Piaget and Ausubel, chapter

2). In the external interaction processes, the dialectic lies in the interaction between the individual and the environment.

However, a general definition of the Negt approach to experience that is both more accessible and more complete can be found in the work of the Danish educational researcher Henning Salling Olesen:

> "Experience is the process whereby we as human beings, individually and collectively, consciously master reality, and the ever-living understanding of this reality and our relation to it. Experiences in the plural exist, as in everyday language, but they are to be understood as partial products of this process. Experience is thus a subjective process as it is seen from the point of view of the person experiencing. It is also a collective process because when we experience as individuals, we also do so through a socially structured consciousness. It is, finally, an active, critical and creative process where we both see and adapt. – This concept of experiences is inherited from the German sociologist Oskar Negt..." (Olesen 1989, p. 8).

In this definition it is interesting to note the reference to the duality of experience, as both a subjective and a collective process – a duality that again corresponds to this book's approach to learning as an internal psychological and an external interactive process. It also seems remarkable that despite the explicit reference to Negt, it could have been written, word for word, by Dewey, for this indirectly shows that the difference between Dewey's and Negt's conceptions of experience do not lie in the actual nature of the experience itself, but in the question of how the current societal structures actually affect the formation of the experience.

To quote Salling Olesen again, in the Negt conception it is all about the fact that *"reality is not immediately apparent"* (Olesen 1981, p. 21), i.e. that there are central societal factors that cannot be immediately experienced, such as, for example, the relationship between utility value and exchange value, or the reduction of the workforce from a general human potential to being an item that can be bought and sold on the market. Although the central capitalistic structures are man-made and therefore may also be changed, they are experienced as natural, like a kind of "second nature", and thus the entire experiential base is displaced.

So, basically, in a capitalistic society the experience opportunities for workers are already fundamentally distorted; it is not immediately possible to experience the conditions that are decisive for the workers' social situation. Therefore the ultimate goal of experiential pedagogy is not, as in Dewey, certain general concepts of personal growth and an upbringing to fit into a democratic society, but rather that *"people regain their status as societal subjects"* (Olesen 1981, p. 23) – or how the working class can break through the distortion of immediate experiences, experience the structural conditions for their experiential development, and then fight to change these conditions.

It is an important aspect of Oskar Negt's work that there is direct reference to workers' education as a counterpart to the fundamental distortions in the bourgeois public – and there has been much discussion over how and to what extent Negt's conception can be more generally adapted to ordinary education. This has not, however, prevented the Danish experiential pedagogy movement from adopting Negt's conception, far more so than Dewey, who is more of a figure for the more theoretically-trained and humanistically-oriented pedagogues to refer to and thus link to the progressivist tradition.

A contributing factor to Negt's impact has naturally been that he, contrary to Dewey, is contemporary with the experiential pedagogy movement and debate. Another, more concrete, factor has been his involvement in the Glocksee School, an experimental school in Hanover, without any particular link to the working class, but more like a Danish left-wing free school. At the end of the 1970s there was great interest in the Glocksee School among the left wing of Danish pedagogy – probably especially because it united a progressive, free school practice with theoretical analyses on a Marxist and psychoanalytical basis.

In an article on the Glocksee project, Negt moves away from the worker-specific basis and provides a more general societal and psychological argument for the school's experiential pedagogical approach (Negt 1976). But Negt's treatment is of an overall and theoretical nature, and one should look to his colleague Thomas Ziehe (1978, 1980) for more direct peda-gogical discussions of the Glocksee School's activities.

While Negt thus represents the theoretical position of the concept of experience, which has been most important for the development and com-prehension of experiential pedagogy in Denmark, more practical inspira-tion has probably been gained from Ziehe's work, which unites practical pedagogy with analyses of modern-day cultural liberation and new forms of youth consciousness (Ziehe & Stubenrauch 1982, Ziehe 1985, 1998, cf. chapter 5).

Learning by experience

In this section I will attempt to set out some conclusions concerning the concept of experience based on the approaches outlined above and in relation to previous chapters in this book.

Firstly, it is important to draw attention to the totality of the concept of experience in relation to learning. The concept comprises all aspects of learning in principle, including internal psychological learning processes and social interactive processes, knowledge-related aspects and emotional aspects, and all forms of learning and forms of interaction. But for learn-ing to be described as experiential in the way this concept has been set up here, various specific qualitative criteria must be fulfilled:

Firstly, the learning must be of considerable subjective significance with regard to the cognitive as well as the emotional and the social-societal learning dimensions.

Secondly, the learning must be part of a coherent process – there must be continuity, as Dewey puts it. Even if we focus exclusively on single experiences, it only makes sense to use the expression experiential learn-ing when the single event can be understood in the context of earlier expe-riences and future opportunities for experience, for only through this can the single experience gain its significance. Any form of "building block thinking" that fails to take this into consideration can be said to have mis-understood what the concept of experience is basically about. (Thus we also encounter a difference in relation to the concept of learning as such, for in some cases it can be possible and meaningful to talk of learning as a more isolated phenomenon).

Thirdly, the interaction process between the individual and the social and/or material surroundings must be of such a nature that the individual can be said to be a subject in the situation, i.e. that he or she is present and is self-aware. Whether that person behaves as such in that particular situation can obviously be hard to determine in practice. But in principle it is important to draw the line at situations in which the learner only plays a passive role and is uncommitted. It is not impossible to learn something in such a situation – there are plenty of examples in ordinary school teaching; but this kind of learning cannot be called experiential, for if you are not involved as a subject there will not actually be any interaction process, but instead what is typically called a filling process – or "banking" as Paulo Freire (1970) calls it.

Fourthly, it is important that the formation of experience is always socially mediated. It does not occur in individual isolation, but of necessity requires a social context. Naturally this should not be understood as meaning that there cannot be occasions in which people gain their experiences alone, but for the very reason that it is a continuing process, the isolation is only momentary, and the context in which it takes place will always be socially marked. The social nature of experience is thus a necessary consequence of the fact that mankind is a social being, unable to develop without sociality.

Fifthly and finally, in Negt's conception at any rate, the influences from the environment that the interaction is concerned with must be such that they reflect or exemplify relevant societal material and/or social structures. This is what lies in Negt's conception of "the principle of exemplarity" or "exemplary learning" (Negt 1971, Christiansen 1999, p. 60ff). Here too there can naturally occur a limitation problem in practice – a subject which I will not go into in more detail here, but will instead refer to fuller treatments of the form of project work (Illeris 1999).

Thus, in many ways there can be a merging of the concept of experiential learning and some of the interpretations of the concept of social learning, which were dealt with in chapter 7. This is primarily the case with Regina Becker-Schmidt's conception of social learning – which is not so surprising in consideration of the fact that Negt and Becker-Schmidt work in the same place and work on the basis of the same scientific tradition, and Becker-Schmidt also fully discusses her stand on Negt's concepts on experience and the exemplary principle in the direct context of the concept of social learning (Becker-Schmidt 1987, p. 68ff).

Neither do I see any important contradictions between Negt's conception of experience and Danny Wildemeersch's concept of social learning – although the parallel is less clear and explicit than that in the case of Negt and Becker-Schmidt. It is in fact probably more difficult to unravel the relationship between Negt's concept of experience and Wenger's concept of learning, and there are obvious differences when it is compared with the other representatives of social learning and similar subjects, as discussed in Chapter 7. In my opinion, it is in these very differences that the concept of experience displays its particular value as a superordinate for the forms of learning that really are significant for the learner.

Experiential pedagogy in Denmark

In Denmark the concept of experience has come to play a central part in educational thinking since "experiential pedagogy" crystallised after about 1980 as a kind of common term for a number of pedagogical endeavours and patterns of work that emphasise the formation of experience of the participants, understood as a total learning based on the requirements, problems and interests of the participants (cf. Webb & Nielsen 1996).

Throughout the 1970s there was a sparkling optimism and faith that new pedagogical creations would not only give pleasure to the participants and help them develop, giving them better qualifications more in tune with the times, but would also help to change society in a more liberating and democratic direction, perhaps even contribute to the bringing forth of a positive socialist revolution.

A common slogan for a large part of these activities was that we should "use the experiences of the participants as a starting point", and this particular statement was often understood as the maxim of experiential pedagogy. Another and slightly more open statement talked of "connecting to the experiences of the participants", and in some cases it could be "con-

tributing to/preparing the formation of experience for the participants".
In the most directly practice-oriented book on the subject there was even
a technical description of the concepts of experience coupling, experience
connecting and experience formation, that in a rather heavy-handed way
cut the concepts down from the theoretical and idealistic spheres to the
everyday level of teaching (Jacobsen et al. 1980).

In practice, however, the subject proved to be more complex – and on
the basis of an analysis of three ambitious experiential pedagogical projects
that were carried out around 1980 in schools, upper secondary schools
and basic vocational education respectively, it could be quite clearly concluded that

> "ideal experiential pedagogical processes must be about the pupils' im-
> portant, subjectively perceived problem areas, that are to be elaborated
> in a continuing experiential process based on their existing patterns of
> experience and governed by a forward-pointing action perspective."
> (Illeris 1984, p. 32).

Here it is probably the words "problem areas" and "action perspective"
that are significant. The point was that looking back towards previous experiences is less interesting for pupils than looking forward towards new
challenges and experiences. The implementation of experiential pedagogy
in practice had therefore to build on fundamental principles of problem
orientation, participant direction, exemplarity and solidarity – and when it
was to take place within the framework of institutional education it could
typically be done through the application of the pedagogical work pattern
developed under the name *project work* (Illeris 1999).

Currently there appears to be a tendency for project work to be perceived in a broader sense, so that it now comprises several different forms of
creative processes – thus coming in line with the form of "culture of education", culture-producing school activity, which Jerome Bruner orients himself towards in his later book, in which he summarises his experiences from
a long career as a learning and educational researcher (Bruner 1996).

Summary

The various considerations of the concept of experience can be summarised as follows, based on the examination of them in this chapter:

1. Experience is defined here as an overriding concept that in a total and subjectively important way, embraces the cognitive, emotional and social-societal dimensions of learning, the internal psychological acquisition processes and the social interaction processes. However, learning is only formation of experience when a number of other qualitative criteria are fulfilled:

2. In order for learning to be characterised as formation of experience, the subjective must be part of a coherent process involving earlier experiences and future experiential opportunities.

3. In order for learning to be characterised as formation of experience, the learner must be actively present and be self-aware in his or her interactions with the social and/or material environment.

4. In order for learning to be characterised as formation of experience, it must be rooted in a subjectively relevant social context.

5. In order for learning to be characterised as formation of experience, it must further reflect or exemplify important societal material and/or social structures.

6. Experiential learning typically concerns the important subjectively perceived problems of the participants, which are worked through in a continuing experiential process on the basis of previously established patterns of experience and governed by a forward-pointing action perspective.

7. Project work is a typical pedagogical work pattern that prepares the way for this kind of formation of experience, as the work form can be broadly interpreted to embrace all forms of structured creative culture production.

9. Learning Sequences, Learning Jumps, Stages and Models

Circular, spiral and sequential models

The previous chapters have been largely devoted to the individual learning event and its nature and dynamic, although in the case of the concept of experience it was linked to a large extent with more coherent processes. But whether or not it concerns experiential learning, it is characteristic that almost all learning occurs in more or less comprehensive processes or sequences of actions that build on one another in a coherent way – and particularly in education it is this kind of learning sequence that is targeted. This chapter concerns different approaches and models of compound learning sequences of varying lengths. (It must be noted at this point that there are also what might be called relational models that are not concerned with sequences, but show how various elements stand in relation to each other, such as Wenger's learning model in chapter 7. However, I am dealing with process models only here).

Earlier in the text I introduced one kind of process model, with my discussion of Kolb's learning cycle in chapter 2, and there are in fact many examples of the learning sequence being understood as circles in the same way that Kolb transposed Piaget's, Dewey's and Lewin's learning conceptions into his cycle model. However, in chapter 2 I also mentioned that Donald Schön's studies of experts' problem-solving appear to contradict the cycle model because it is characteristic that no specific sequence can be identified, but in the situation the individual draws analogously on the relevant cues of varying nature that are available as a result of the presuppositions of the person concerned.

A natural elaboration of circle models is obtained by linking several circles together, such as Kolb shows in his consideration of Dewey's learning conception (Kolb 1984, p.23). This then becomes a spiral model, as it is presented as circles building on top of, or as extensions of, each other so that a new circle begins where the previous one ended.

A typical example of a spiral model can be found in American Jerome Bruner's proposal for "the spiral curriculum" (Bruner 1960, p. 13, 33 and 52ff). This was based on his challenging thesis that

"any subject can be taught effectively in some intellectually honest form to any child at any stage of development." (Bruner 1960, p. 33).

The challenge is "just" to find forms of presentation and examples that correspond to the child's stage of development – and so it becomes a spiral learning process in which the same points are returned to in new ways in step with the child's development.

A more advanced spiral model is the English researcher Tom Schuller's triple helix for development throughout the course of life (Schuller 1997, 1998). The model is inspired by the biochemical structure in a DNA molecule, and shows as a simplified model how Schuller views biological, psychological and social development as three independent and yet intertwined sequences that together reflect the life course of the individual (figure 6a).

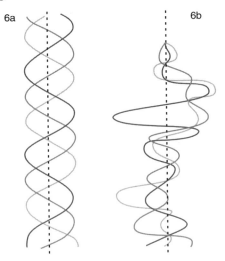

Figures 6a and 6b: Tom Schuller's triple helix. The idealised model (6a) and the "reality" model (6b). The biological, psychological and social development of a life course (Schuller 1998, p. 32-33).

In reality, however, development does not take place in so simple and harmonious a manner as this idealised model might suggest, and there are fluctuations and tempo variations for each of the development strands, so an illustration of a life as it is lived might look like that shown in figure 6b.

On the basis of the approach in this book it would be more appropriate to convert this model into a quadruple helix by dividing psychological development into a cognitive strand and an emotional strand, from the age of about six, at any rate, as discussed in greater detail in chapter 4.

Another type of process model, closer to the basis of this book, i.e. Piaget's theory of learning, was produced in Denmark by Jens Bjerg et al. (including Thomas Nissen) as a kind of sequential wave or exchange model, that shows in an idealised form the interaction between assimilative and accommodative learning processes:

assimilative processes

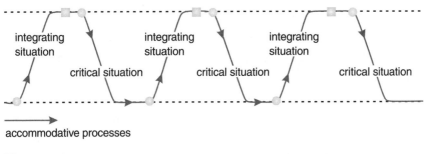

accommodative processes

▦ appropriate time for identification of specific competencies (observation of level of attainment)

◯ appropriate time for observations as basis for change of phase, including pedagogical estimation of emotional and psychosocial conditions

Figure 7: The interaction between assimilative and accommodative learning (Bjerg et al. 1976, p. 45).

The model shows how a learning sequence shifts from (predominantly) assimilative processes through a critical situation to (predominantly) accommodative processes, back through an integrating situation to (predominantly) assimilative processes, and so on – and it also indicates points of time in a sequence of this kind that can be ideal for pedagogical observations of attainment levels and observations of phase changes, respectively. Bjerg's model is of course very much simplified – as a model always has to be – but is also a good illustration of the fundamental approach this book is based on.

A better-known model, that in principle illustrates the same idea, is that of the American social and organisational psychologist Chris Argyris, for "single loop" and "double loop" learning in organisational and management development (Argyris 1992):

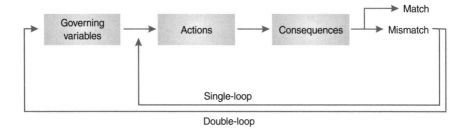

Figure 8: Single loop and double loop learning (Argyris 1992, p. 8).

Argyris is concerned with learning in organisations (cf. chapter 10). Organisations exist to fulfil certain specific goals, and they do this through actions. These actions can lead to the expected consequences, so a "match" is obtained, or the consequences can be inconsistent with what was expected, resulting in a "mismatch". In cases of mismatch it may be possible to then attempt another solution within the same frame of reference, making this a single loop in terms of learning, or alternatively, it may be possible to attempt to pass beyond this framework, these "governing variables", making this a double loop.

On the one hand, Argyris' model is special because it is so closely linked to organisations; the actions can, for example, be ascribed to individuals or the organisation itself, and the only learning that is of interest is that which leads to altered practice in the organisation. On the other hand there are clear parallels between this model and the fundamental conceptions of Piaget, Bateson and Mezirow, that there is a considerable distinction between learning that builds on existing presuppositions, and learning that involves changes to or transcendence of these presuppositions – and Argyris' model has the obvious advantage of being easy to understand and being linked to a specific practice context. However, it must be said that Argyris' model lacks a more explicit theoretical root, although it is clear that he (just like David Kolb and Donald Schön) draws on a conception basis that predominantly relates to Kurt Lewin and gestalt psychology.

Learning jumps

What definitely separates Bjerg's and Argyris' models from the circle and spiral models is the graphic emphasis of the uneven nature of learning sequences – that a learning sequence can involve qualitative breaks. Thomas Nissen has discussed from a theoretical point of view how it may be possible to imagine both the individual's knowledge development and the collective knowledge development of mankind generally established by unbroken assimilative processes alone, and how such a situation will fail in the long run, because the environment will always be changing:

> "One can imagine the whole of human development as combined assimilative processes. – Assimilative learning can lead to a good deal of refinement and technical competence, wisdom and culture, but always with the goal for the individual of creating conditions and preserving presuppositions for a defined life pattern. – If the life conditions change, for the individual and society, the assimilative learning can no longer ensure the individual's adjustment. The time will come when the reductive activities either bring about a removal of the individual's personal responsibility or take the form of a 'holy' war, that quickly consumes its initiator." (Nissen 1970, p. 51-52).

When there are important changes in life conditions, both the individual and society must be able to adjust themselves radically in order to keep up, and must be able to transcend the adaptation that was appropriate to the earlier conditions; this applies not only to the major changes in life conditions that have taken place throughout the history of mankind, but also to the sweeping changes that constantly occur in modern society in the conditions of life of both the individual and society as a whole. (The problem today is not that mankind has trouble making these transcendent steps, but that there are so many changes, and they are so far-reaching, that no-one is truly in a position to keep up with them; cf. the discussion on every-day consciousness in chapter 6).

A comprehensive understanding of learning sequences must therefore include the idea that there can and must be breaks or *learning jumps*. In Piaget and Nissen jumps of this kind are understood as accommodations, Rogers talks of significant learning, as already mentioned, and Argyris deals with the double loop – while in the circle and spiral models attention is not directed towards jumps in learning. Also Vygotsky's concept of the zone of proximal development, dealt with earlier, involves the notion of a learning jump from the current zone over the "distance" that marks the transition to the development zone (cf. chapter 3). And in a number of other theories that are only more or less indirectly concerned with learn-ing in a narrower sense, it can be seen that the idea of a learning jump appears on several levels.

In a slightly broader framework than the direct learning theoretical, within the Frankfurt School and the Hanover School (cf. chapter 7) there is some understanding of human consciousness development in a capital-ist society as limited by a number of radical societal conditions of a mate-rial and ideological nature, with, however, the opportunity for breaking through these limits, perhaps in the form of *sociological imagination and formation of experience* (Negt 1971, Negt & Kluge 1993 – cf. chapter 8), *thematisations* (Leithäuser 1976 – cf. chapter 6) or *reality testing* (Becker-Schmidt 1987 – cf. chapter 7). In the prevalent corresponding Danish conception in the 1970s, the concept of *consciousness-raising* was to a great extent an expression for a similar conception of a qualitative break.

More recently, there is a quite parallel conception in Mezirow's con-cept of *transformative learning* (Mezirow 1991 – cf. chapter 3) and again in the work of German culture and biography researcher Peter Alheit, who has developed a concept of *transitional learning* (Alheit 1994, 1995 – cf. chapters 5 and 11); these both set out explicitly the idea that awareness of the structures that have hitherto directed one's life course also provides one with the possibility of altering them.

In a more classic framework, there is also a corresponding conception that is clearly understood as a breakthrough or a jump in the concept of *catharsis,* which was central to Freud's early theories (Freud & Breuer 1956).

Catharsis means cleansing or expulsion, and in Freud and Breuer it denotes the curing of hysteria that can occur through an emotional abreaction; it was also later used more generally to refer to the overcoming of the reasons for psychological misdevelopments, which can occur through a psychoanalytical process.

Finally I must mention the notion of learning jumps in development that is central to the conception of human phylogenetic development as advanced by the Russian cultural historical school discussed earlier (Luria 1976, Leontjev 1981) – in which it relates to "the law of transition from quantity to quality" in the conception of Marxism valid in the Soviet Union, so-called dialectical materialism:

> "Development does not simply mean that something changes (quantitative development) or that something unfolds, but in development, completely new forms can in fact arise (something changes). – The qualitative jump denotes the break that occurs when a gradual or quantitative development turns into something qualitatively new." (Hansen 1990, p. 56).

Stage models

From the understanding that a learning sequence can include important qualitative jumps, it is not far to the development of various forms of phase, stage or step models for different types of learning and development sequences.

A typical example of a model of this kind is the American Dreyfus brothers' five-step model for the development of "human intuition and expertise" (Dreyfus & Dreyfus 1986 – cf. chapter 10). In an attempt to describe how human intelligence is superior to any computer in certain vital points, there is a description of how we pass through stages such as *novice* and *advanced beginner,* then *competence* and *proficiency* to reach *the stage of expertise.* This does not consist, as it would in a computer, of us quickly and logically surveying and analysing vast amounts of information, but instead means that we find ourselves in a comprehensive experience within a field, enabling us to intuitively find relevant possible solutions in a problem situation – a conception that also fits with the description of experts' means of functioning that the aforementioned Donald Schön achieved through empirical studies (Schön 1983).

However, the Dreyfus brothers' model does not clearly specify what the criteria are for the various phase transitions, and therefore this model does not fulfil the requirements for a psychological stage model which, with reference to Piaget, Danish life-span researcher Johan Fjord Jensen has advanced in five overall principles: that the stages shall be *sequential,* i.e. they must come in a specific order and build on one another so that no stage can be skipped; they must be *universal,* i.e. they must apply to everyone, regardless of time and place; they must be *complex* in the sense that the later stages include the earlier in an increasingly complex order; they must each comprise a period with *structural equilibrium* so that they include all relevant elements in a common structure that lasts until the next phase transition; and finally they must be qualitatively *different* (Jensen 1993, p. 91).

These extensive requirements are largely met by the two great stage theories of psychology, that is, Piaget's theory of the cognitive development of the child and Freud's theory of the psychosexual development of the child (see e.g. Furth's comparison of the two theories as described in chapter 4). But these two theories only concern childhood to puberty, and against these Fjord Jensen presents various stage theories for the total life course from the more modern life-span psychology, first and foremost Erik H. Erikson's step model (Jensen 1993, p. 112ff).

Erikson's model was first presented in 1950 in the book "Childhood and Society" (Erikson 1950), later elaborated on in "Identity, Youth and Crisis" (Erikson 1968) and other works, and can be found in its final form in "Life Cycle Completed" (Erikson 1982).

The concept of the model is that the course of a human life runs through a number of psychosocial stages, and that the transition from each stage to the next is promoted through an existential crisis, in which a basic complex of problems must be clarified. If this clarification is successful, the individual goes on to the next stage strengthened; if it is not successful, there is a fundamental misdevelopment.

Psychosocial Crises

	1	2	3	4	5	6	7	8
Old Age VIII								Integrity vs. Despair, Disgust. WISDOM
Adulthood VII							Generativity vs. Stagnation. CARE	
Young Adulthood VI						Intimacy vs. Isolation. LOVE		
Adolescence V					Identity vs. Identity Confusion. FIDELITY			
School Age IV				Industry vs. Inferiority. COMPETENCE				
Play Age III			Initiative vs. Guilt. PURPOSE					
Early Childhood II		Autonomy vs. Shame, Doubt. WILL						
Infancy I	Basic Trust vs. Basic Mistrust. HOPE							

Figure 9: Erikson's life stage model (Erikson 1982, p. 56-57).

The most thoroughly considered aspect of Erikson's work is the crisis of youth concerning basic identity formation, which can lead to the development of a viable personal identity or to an identity confusion of varying degrees (Erikson 1968) – a conception which has also been strongly criticised for being oriented towards societal adjustment and conformity (see e.g. Illeris et al. 1982), and which is in clear contradiction to current postmodernist theories that claim harmonic identity formation is impossible in our existing society (see e.g. Usher et al. 1997, Usher 2000).

I do not, however, wish to look further here at the individual stages in Erikson's model, but will make use of the very clear construction. Erikson himself describes his model as epigenetic, using a concept borrowed from studies of embryology, where it originally means that the various organs develop step by step as part of a previously existing whole entity based on innate inherited predispositions, and furthermore, that the individual stages' most important contradictory conditions can be found in earlier forms in the previous stages, and are elaborated on in a general way in the later stages. Erikson thus views the stages as biologically founded, but psycho-social in their concrete formation.

In terms of learning, every phase transition is characterised by multi-faceted crisis solving, or what one might call a complex of an accommodative or transformative nature, broadly spanning existential problems that involve the cognitive, the emotional and the social-societal sphere. This brings Erikson's model largely in line structurally with the model Bjerg et al. created of Piaget's learning conception, which was considered at the start of this chapter – though naturally on a superior level. (Erikson notes in his last book with a certain degree of satisfaction that Piaget spoke positively of his model and stages approach – Erikson 1982, p. 76).

In life-span psychology there are many other stage approaches, all deviating from Erikson's model in different ways. The most significant are dealt with in detail in Fjord Jensen's book, and at the end he is able to put them together to create a model in the form of a double life arch:

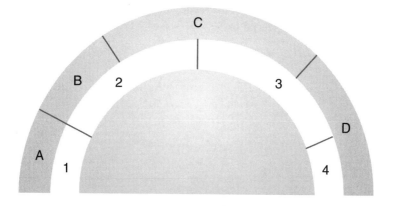

Figure 10: The double life arch. Social life ages: A. Childhood. B. Youth. C. Adulthood. D. Old age. Interpretive life ages: 1. Childhood. 2. First adulthood. 3. Second adulthood. 4. Old age. (Jensen 1993, p. 182).

The point of the model is that in adult life there are two types of stages that typically appear displaced: the social life ages and the interpretive life ages:

"With one part of life and consciousness, the person belongs to society, but with the other he belongs to himself. From one viewpoint he is on a life course that is regulated by the structures of that age culture, with its own social-biological milestones and age-related rituals. In belonging to this, the person becomes part of a social age culture with its own life ages. From another viewpoint he is on a life course which he regulates himself with his own interpretations. As such he is driven by personal needs of development and expression." (Jensen 1993, p. 182).

Looking at this approach in relation to Tom Schuller's triple helix discussed earlier, there emerges an image of biological and social development intertwined in a single cadence of stages, while psychological development – which can perhaps be separated into a cognitive and an emotional strand – follows a second cadence of stages.

Another and quite different way of viewing the course of life is that of David Kolb, who perceives it as having three main stages generally characterised by an ever-closer connection of the four learning modes (see chapter 2) into an integrated total:

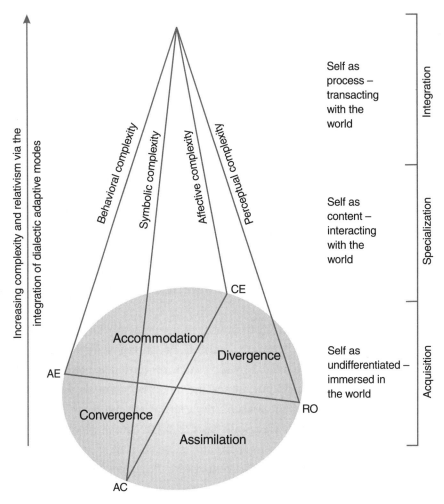

Figure 11: Kolb's model of lifelong growth and development (Kolb 1984, p. 141)

The first stage, which covers childhood to puberty, is characterised by *acquisition,* and the self is still undifferentiated and embedded in the environment – this stage can also be divided into sub-stages in accordance with Piaget's theory. The second stage, up to what Fjord Jensen calls the life turn, which can occur at a variety of ages (cf. chapter 11), is characterised by *specialisation* (on the basis of Kolb's description I would prefer to call it qualification – in relation to career, family and society) – the self is content or case-oriented, and absorbed in interaction with the surrounding world. Finally there is the third stage, which according to Kolb not everyone reaches, characterised by *integration* – the self takes on the nature of a process; one relates to one's own life course and the role one plays in relation to the surrounding world.

Learning and life course

As the previous section shows, there are many different attempts to explain and present compound learning sequences. But there are also certain important parameters that appear again and again in the various approaches and models.

Firstly, there is the question of the *duration* of the sequences. Some of the models primarily refer to lesser learning sequences in a specific sphere – this is how Kolb's learning cycle should immediately be understood, as well as the sequential model of Bjerg et al. and Argyris' double loop model, although all three of these can be related to more comprehensive partial sequences such as a professional learning sequence over a set period. Other models are to be found on various intermediate levels, such as the Dreyfus brothers' expertise theory and Piaget's and Freud's theories of developmental stages in childhood. And many models refer to the life course as a whole – this applies to Schuller's helix model and the various life stages models. Finally, the cultural-historical school's conception concerns the phylogenetic development of the entire human race.

Secondly, there is the question of different *learning or development spheres*. This is only explicitly set out in Schuller's helix model and Fjord Jensen's double life arch, but on the basis of these two examples it is possible to look at other models and attempt to work out which spheres they refer to. It is fairly clear, for example, that Kolb's growth and development model primarily relates to what Schuller calls psychological development and Fjord Jensen calls interpretive development.

Finally there is the question of the *nature* of learning or development – in which there is a clear distinction between approaches and models that depict even progress, and models that involve various steps or stages, separated by more or less crisis-inspired jumps or transitions.

A complete approach to learning and development sequences must include all three of these dimensions. It must allow for sequences of widely varying duration, ranging from the linking together of two or more specific learning events in a particular sphere, to the life course viewed as a total entity (I here omit phylogenetic development as an example of perspective). It must also allow for individual sequences being mainly cognitive, emotional or social in nature, or being involved in two or three of these spheres, and it must allow for the fact that the sequence may be conditioned by, or be involved in, interaction with a biological maturation or ageing process. Finally, a complete approach must understand that only limited learning sequences can be considered without learning jumps, and that there will be the potential for learning jumps in all sequences.

A graphic presentation of this kind of total approach to learning and development sequences does not appear to be possible, at least not in a two-dimensional form. However, it is possible to imagine a combination of Schuller's triple helix (which, as I explained before, should in my opinion be quadruple), Erikson's step model and Kolb's growth and development model. There would be three or four strands that each take the form of steps or broken sequences, which could be more or less independent or intertwined depending on the pattern, and which become ever more integrated throughout the course of life.

However, a combination model of this type would only provide an overall framework. Within this framework there would be a myriad of various small and medium-sized sequences in all spheres, which would also have their jumps and steps, and which could be united with or split from other sequences in a colossal intertwining that would be completely confused yet at the same time structured – in Piaget's conception of the structure concept as a system of transformations which, inside its limits, is maintained and enriched by the transformations themselves (Piaget 1968).

A combination model of this kind could perhaps be called a "*staircase-house model*", understood as a colossal number of large and small stairs on different levels and intertwined with one another within the overall construction, which is composed of the various large stairs of the life course.

It is important to be aware that there can also be "delearning" in the sense of someone deliberately abandoning something learnt previously and replacing it with a totally new understanding (whereas deliberate delearning without some sort of replacement does not seem to be a possibility), and there can be what Engeström terms "horizontal learning", understood as corrections or alterations that do not take the learner further in terms of levels (Engeström 1996b) – or translated into the model: there can also be stairs leading down or crossing over on the same level.

It is clear that a combination model of this type would in some way or other reflect the nature of the neural networks in the brain and central nervous system, which are the bearers of learning, and it is also clear that the model – as pointed out by the Dreyfus brothers (1986) among others – had to distinguish itself from, and transcend, even the most advanced computer models by virtue of the capacity of human learning to develop functions that carry meaning and create a wholeness.

Summary

It is difficult to summarise the most important points of this chapter, but I shall attempt it as follows:

1. A number of learning events can take place in a compound learning or development sequence, which may be an even and progressive, predominantly assimilative sequence, but in most cases there will be broken sequences including both assimilative periods of construction and accommodative learning jumps.

2. Learning and development sequences can be of varied duration, from limited sequences in a specific learning sphere (e.g. in a school subject), to comprehensive overall sequences that relate to the individual's personal development as a whole.

3. A distinction can be made between predominantly cognitively-related, emotionally-related and socially-related sequences, but these spheres

can also appear in an integrated form in other sequences, and they can be conditional on or coherent with a biologically-conditioned maturation or ageing process.

4. The individual's learning and development sequence as a whole can be visualised within the framework of a gigantic "staircase-house model", where large numbers of learning sequences of a more or less specific or integrated nature intertwine themselves like large and small stairs with jumps and platforms within the framework of the overall life course which is composed of larger step or stage sequences.

10. Spaces Of Learning

The learning situation influences the learning result

The last chapter represents the end of my discussion of how learning generally occurs. The next two chapters will concern certain important characteristics of the conditions of learning, with the external conditions being dealt with in this chapter, and the internal conditions in the next – since both the external and the internal conditions are important elements in learning as it actually occurs.

With regard to the external conditions, I will focus on the types of "space" in which learning occurs. I will not base my discussion on what significance the overall societal conditions have for learning – even though they undoubtedly play an important role, which becomes clear, for example, on reading texts from the Russian cultural-historical tradition that presuppose a communist society to be the pinnacle of a long historical development. Rather, I will look at the various types of space or frameworks for learning situations offered by present-day society, and look also at how the overall societal conditions influence these spaces. The spaces or spheres I wish to take up are everyday learning, learning in practice or apprenticeship, learning in schools and other educational institutions, and learning at work; finally I will take a short look at the concept of collective learning – and I will immediately point out that for the learner these spaces naturally cannot be seen independently of one another: learning that occurs in a specific place both influences, and is influenced by, learning in the other spaces in which the person concerned is involved.

My reason for taking up these conditions is that the situation or the framework within which the learning occurs always plays a part in influencing the learning result. In chapter 4 I dealt with the subject of how emotions both "obsess" the cognitive structures being developed, and at the same time form their own patterns on a more general level. In this context emotions must be understood in a broad sense: this does not simply concern momentary sentiments, social sympathy or antipathy, or what mood the learner is in when the learning occurs. It also refers to the attitude the learner has to the learning context, and on several levels: at school, for example, it would be typically to the teacher, to the subject, to that particular school and to school in general. It is this last level I particularly want to look at. What significance does it have for learning for it to occur in a school, in a practice context, in a business or in a collective context or movement?

When discussing the significance that the framework conditions and the situation have for learning, making it natural to refer to the concept of *situated learning*, which was developed by American anthropologist Jean Lave, based partly on experiences with apprentice-type training traditions in non-industrialised countries, and later elaborated in depth in collaboration with Etienne Wenger (Lave & Wenger 1991, see also chapter 7).

The concept has had considerable exposure in recent years, including in Europe. In my view, however, it is rather problematic. At first glance it appears as a general concept, which, in line with my earlier considerations, asserts that all learning takes place in a specific situation, and that this situation is significant for the nature of the learning and for its result. Thus Lave and Wenger write that the concept

"took on the proportions of a general theoretical perspective, the basis of claims about the relational character of knowledge and learning, about the negotiated character of meaning, and about the concerned (engaged, dilemma-driven) nature of learning activity for the people involved. That perspective meant that there is no activity which is not situated." (Lave & Wenger 1991, p. 33).

In this context Lave and Wenger make another very interesting point which further deepens the situation's general significance for learning, viz.

"that even so-called general knowledge only has power in specific circumstances. Generality is often associated with abstract representations, with decontextualization. But abstract representations are meaningless unless they can be made specific to the situation at hand. Moreover, the formation or acquisition of an abstract principle is itself a specific event in specific circumstances. Knowing a general rule by itself in no way assures that any generality it may carry is enabled in the specific circumstances in which it is relevant." (Lave & Wenger 1991, p. 33-34).

Thus according to Lave and Wenger it is not simply that the concrete situation influences the learning that occurs, but it also has significance for which existing learning results are activated. When the learning occurs in an interaction between existing structures and new impulses (cf. chapter 2), the environment and the learning situation influence not only the learner's perception of the new impulses, but also which existing structures are involved in the internal elaboration processes.

In my opinion, had Lave and Wenger kept to these positions, their concept of situated learning could have proved a clear and productive contribution to learning theory. However, it seems as if they do not quite want to acknowledge these general points of view and elaborate on them, for they are following a different agenda. Their ultimate message is not that all learning is influenced by the situation in which it occurs, but that a specific type of situation has certain particular learning qualities, i.e. situations that can generally be termed *legitimate peripheral participation* and typically appear in connection with *apprenticeship* – I shall return to this subject later in chapter 10. I would just like to note here that Lave and her collaborators now appear to be pushing the concept of situated learning into the background. In a current Danish publication in this sphere, the concept is avoided for the most part, except in a few direct references to Lave and Wenger's 1991 book (Nielsen & Kvale 1999), and in his book on "Communities of Practice", Wenger totally ignores the concept of situated learning and only in a few places refers to "situated experience" (Wenger 1998).

This only leaves the very basic statement that all learning is decisively influenced by the situation in which it occurs – and so also by the external framework of the situation, and ultimately, by the overall societal conditions that determine this framework. Therefore, in the following sections I will look at a few typical framework situations for learning in our society, and the opportunities and limitations they involve.

Everyday learning, tacit knowledge and informal learning

When various types of learning spaces are to be considered in the context of situations in which learning takes place, there is a link with the fact that life in modern society is divided up into a number of different spaces or spheres that are directed by different rationales and do not have any immediately obvious connection – as has already been discussed in chapter 6 on everyday consciousness.

As a parallel to everyday consciousness, a concept of *everyday learning* may be proposed, as that learning which occurs informally and apparently by chance in everyday life as one moves around the spaces of one's life, without consciously intending to learn anything, but often busily absorbed in getting everything to function and more or less understanding it.

In everyday learning one comes across a flood of impulses and impressions, and acquires ways of selecting, relating to and navigating among them in the confusion of life in order to get through the day, yet all without any conscious adjustment. One may also talk – to use an expression borrowed from Hungarian-English philosopher Michael Polanyi – of the *tacit dimension* of learning (Polanyi 1966), which involves the acquisition of *tacit knowledge*. A person can be in possession of knowledge, even though this knowledge may not have, nor may be given, a verbal form – and such knowledge is very often what is in reality directing our behaviour.

It is not that the tacit dimension is clearly attached to everyday learning, but rather the contrary, that a very large part of everyday experience is converted into tacit learning. However, even in more goal-directed learning contexts within various learning spaces, the acquisition of tacit knowledge will occur in parallel with explicit knowledge – and "knowledge" is actually an imprecise word in this whole context, for understanding, insight, emotions, values, opinions etc. are all involved.

Another concept in this sphere is *informal learning*, which may be characterised as the more goal-directed form of everyday learning that occurs in non-industrialised societies, where learning has not yet gained its own institutionalised space. Before the concept of situated learning was developed, Jean Lave referred to informal learning of this type in her anthropological studies, characterised in these eight points by herself and Patricia Greenfield:

" 1. Embedded in daily life activities.

2. Learner is responsible for obtaining knowledge and skill.

3. Personal; relatives are appropriate teachers.

4. Little or no explicit pedagogy or curriculum.

5. Maintenance of continuity and tradition are valued.

6. Learning by observation and imitation.

7. Teaching by demonstration.

8. Motivated by social contribution of novices and their participation in adult sphere."

(Greenfield & Lave 1982, p. 183).

Naturally there are substantial differences between informal learning of this kind in a pre-industrial society that is more or less static in nature, and the learning opportunities in a modern society. All the same, Lave and many others believe that modern society could benefit from allowing itself to be inspired by these features of informal learning, and it was on this basis that she later worked with Etienne Wenger to develop the concept mentioned earlier of "legitimate peripheral participation" – and Wenger has moved on further with his concept of "communities of practice." (Wenger 1998, cf. chapter 7).

Practice learning and apprenticeship

Thus, there is clearly an understanding that even in modern society it can be appropriate to attach more goal-directed learning to a specific social or work practice, and formalised types of *practice learning* are typically found both in the vocational training that in a number of countries is a more or less direct descendent of the old master-apprentice relationship, and in the short-term trainee arrangements which in Denmark take place in the last year of school and in a large number of professional training courses, e.g. teacher training and training for social or health work. In addition, various induction arrangements are put on in many cases when someone begins a professional career after completing theoretical training.

The concept of "legitimate peripheral participation" is linked to the kind of practice learning that is like an apprentice relationship. It means that the learner learns through his or her participation in a community of practice, in which everyone accepts and is prepared for the fact that the learner is starting off in a peripheral position and will gradually, through participation in more and more of the community's activities, learn cognitively, emotionally and socially the work areas of the community, and through this, slowly reach a more central position and finally achieve full membership of the community (Lave & Wenger 1991). "Legitimate peripheral participation" can also be found in a number of other contexts (cf. Nielsen & Kvale 1997, 1999).

In Denmark there has been much criticism of Lave and Wenger's approach. Such criticisms are typically directed at the apprenticeship system as being an authoritarian and conservative form of training that does not guarantee the theoretical insight needed, with the theorists' new interest in apprenticeship being a new romantic dream with no basis in reality. A partial response to this criticism has been to broaden the concept beyond formal apprenticeship as stated above, also to moderate the extremely categorical position taken up at the beginning:

"We must (and need to!) re-think the role and status of apprenticeship. If the purpose of education is competence, and if competence includes, among other things, non-propositional knowledge, non-personal knowledge, body knowledge, non-rule based skills, etc., and these types of knowledge and skills are not established (at least not intentionally and in full) by means of scholastic teaching, then the different forms of non-scholastic (situated) learning become essential and not just peripheral. – Apprenticeship offers a relevant form of non-scholastic learning. But 'apprenticeship' is a slippery term applied to many different forms of learning and it does not constitute a learning method (singular). And apprenticeship is not just learning in an instrumental sense: it also involves socialisation and has, at least in some of its different current and historical implementations, an authoritarian and oppressive character. The knowledge learned through apprenticeship in different settings is not only knowledge (in a strict sense): For better or for worse, it includes moral values, ideologies, prejudices, and so on. So if we want to rehabilitate apprenticeship, it has to be a critical rehabilitation. – The task is, among other things, to find the most fruitful combination, or rather integration, of theoretical reflection and apprenticeship (and related forms of situated learning). An integration on the individual level as well as on the institutional level." (Wackerhausen 1997, p. 201).

Statements of this kind open up the way for dialogue with other approaches that are critical of traditional teaching methods in schools, and for collaboration with the current line of thought that aims at closer links between educational functions and vocational practice.

This line of thought is partially based in work on the development of computer-based artificial intelligence and some of the difficulties encountered in this. The development of artificial intelligence involves an attempt to cultivate the structures of knowledge processes and is thus a sort of parallel to the theoretical base of formal education. But it has become clear that the structures of human knowledge processes are extraordinarily complex, or to put it more directly: humans can do things that even the most advanced computers in the world cannot. This has led to a new way of analysing the development of human competence, emphasising the upholding of complexity and uniqueness in how competence development occurs in professional practice.

The most decisive breakthrough for this approach came with the Dreyfus brothers' highly challenging book "Mind over Machine" (Dreyfus & Dreyfus 1986). The book points out the great theoretical constraints on artificial intelligence, and so indirectly also on traditional school learning, which is based on the same limited and formalised conception of human competence. In contrast to this, Dreyfus and Dreyfus present a model for the development of human expertise, as explained in chapter 9. This model leads from novice level to expert level in five steps. What is important here is the gradual acquisition of practical knowledge or *know-how* through experience and imitation, for, according to Dreyfus and Dreyfus, expertise does not consist of the logical management and analysis of large quantities of information, but rather of comprehensive experience within a certain field, allowing the person concerned to intuitively pinpoint relevant potential solutions in a problem situation.

Dreyfus and Dreyfus have been quite strongly criticised in Denmark, though less for their basic assumptions on the relationship between artificial and human intelligence than for the five-step model they have developed. It has been alleged that the model is unclear and builds on a very narrow base, that it is limited, undynamic, self-fulfilling, elitist and conservative, that it lacks an understanding of the significance of social conditions; and questions have been posed as to how one can transcend experience-based competence and move on.

However, this kind of criticism cannot be levelled at another researcher in this field, American psychologist Donald Schön (cf. chapter 3), who does not refer to computers and artificial intelligence, but forms his basis on the problems faced by theoretically-trained graduates when they emerge into professional practice. With his concept of *the reflective practitioner*, Schön has focused on the exchange between practical experience and knowledge bases (Schön 1983, 1987).

In practice, according to Schön, relevant competence is characterised by the mastering of relevant routines, in which knowledge and action are two aspects of the same item, *knowing-in-action*. The reflective practitioner is, however, able to transcend this level when situations occur that go beyond the established routines, and this takes place through *reflection-in-action*, a process in which knowledge, experience and proposals for a solution form a whole that characterises the reflective practitioner – and which is very suggestive of the Dreyfus brothers' concept of expertise (as noted in chapter 3, in this context, Schön uses the concept of "reflection" in a rather different way from how it is perceived in this book).

Schön's work has perhaps not attracted quite the same media attention as the Dreyfus brothers' challenging of ideas of artificial intelligence. But his proposed solution is far more firmly rooted in practical experience: the development of a productive exchange between formal education and practical experience by means of such things as trainee arrangements and the inclusion of practice in training where the most important thing is to maintain interaction between theoretical professionalism and practical experience. He also suggests giving higher priority to project types of work in formal education – so there may be the possibility of an agreement between more realistic solution proposals from those who represent practice learning and suggestions from people who base their educational ideas on the concept of experience and other similar concepts (cf. chapter 8).

One thing seems sure in this context, at any rate: the educational problems of modern society will not be answered through calls for substantial increases in apprenticeships and trainee courses. It is already a big problem in Denmark in many spheres to find enough suitable trainee positions to meet demand under the current arrangements, and any large increase in this sphere would simply be unrealistic.

It is basically the case that while learning in practice was previously quite normal – as it still appears to be in non-industrialised countries today – it is a fundamental structural circumstance of modern industrialised capitalistic societies that businesses attempt to leave all non-profit-making activities to the state, including the securing of a qualified workforce. This trend can only be countered by either compelling businesses to take responsibility for it, which would in many ways be inappropriate, and could also easily lead to insufficient qualifications, or by making such training schemes more financially attractive to businesses by means of grants and so on.

In a context of this nature, any business in a private capitalist society will necessarily operate more or less fully with what has been called an "apprenticeship calculation", in which the costs of the apprenticeship, both direct and indirect, must either be offset by subsidies or by the apprentice working so long on a low wage that the strain on the business at the start of the apprenticeship will be recouped in increased earnings at the end. But even when these conditions are met, it would seem that in general only specific types of businesses are keen – in major hi-tech and automated work there is only rarely a place for unqualified staff, who, quite apart from the problems and delays they may cause, may also introduce an unnecessary risk of considerable additional costs resulting from quite minor errors and production disturbances in complex, largely automated functions.

Viewed from a learning perspective it must first be maintained that learning through practice participation, apprenticeship, on-the-job training and so on is naturally, like all other learning, characterised by the nature of its surrounding framework. If it is quite informal learning, as occurs in open situations or in daily life situations in non-industrialised societies, it will be the individual situation and its context that influences the learning. But if it is a formal learning situation or practical course, various institutionalised structures will apply.

It has already been stated that Lave and Wenger's critics pointed out power and authority conditions as having an impact on learning in apprenticeships – and it seems obvious that the very conditions which Lave and Wenger idealise with their concept of legitimate peripheral participation also have their downside in the form of the submission which necessarily occurs. Any learning will in principle be acquired with a consciousness that this is how *one* does it. If the apprentice has a positive relationship with that "one", i.e. to the tradition and those who represent it, there will be a tendency towards an uncritical and limiting assimilative adaptation. And if the apprentice has a negative relationship to the situation, it can easily lead to defence and blocking (cf. chapter 6) – though maybe also to a more constructive resistance (cf. chapter 6).

Under any circumstances, apprenticeship does not, as it is, fulfil the precondition for the formation of experience that the learner be actively present and self-aware (cf. chapter 8), or the precondition in the concept of activity that it be a motivated and goal-directed activity (cf. chapter 3). Apprenticeship reflects more directly than school learning the societal power structures and market structures – for better or for worse, as Wackerhausen's statement above has it – and it accordingly provides both opportunities and problems for learning.

School learning is institutionalised learning

Regardless of any emphasis on the advantages of practice learning, it is an unavoidable fact that the majority of the learning in our society that should be organised by the state must necessarily take place in schools and other educational institutions. As already explained, it is a fundamental motif in a modern capitalist society that the provision of a qualified workforce is the responsibility of the state, and the work sector cannot to any great extent take upon itself the provision of training activities that are not directly related to the particular needs of an individual business. Apart from this, society requires new generations to socialise together to a substantial degree, and this must of necessity also take place under the auspices of the state.

There already exist some meticulous descriptions of how the school and education system in Denmark have developed in close connection with the development of our industrialised capitalistic society and its qualification requirements (e.g. Simonsen 1976), and Norwegian sociologist Nils Christie has described in a more illustrative fashion how the necessity for a school developed in conjunction with the modernisation of society in a French village throughout the 1800s (Christie 1971). It has also been clearly shown how the fundamental function of school was, and basically still is, to discipline the growing generation to function in the context of wage work and also to accept and extend the existing society (e.g. Knudsen 1980). The societal sorting function, and through this the reproduction of the social inequality of society, have also been carefully documented in Denmark and in other countries (e.g. Hansen 1995, Coleman et al. 1966, Jencks et al. 1972, Bowles & Gintis 1976).

The question now is what this unavoidable institutionalisation means for the learning that takes place in the school and education system.

On a more general level, the French sociologist Pierre Bourdieu has addressed himself keenly to this question. Back in 1970, he and Jean-Claude Passeron pointed out how schools' qualification and sorting functions are closely tied up with a legitimation function that justifies and continues both the prevailing ideology of that society and the sorting that takes place, so that social differences and societal grading are passed on from generation to generation, with certain few exceptions (Bourdieu and Passeron 1977). Since then Bourdieu has developed a comprehensive theory in which a highly significant function of school is that of being society's – i.e. the state's – most important institution for legitimising the current structures and ideological conditions, and socialising children to them:

"one of the major powers of the state is to produce and impose (especially through the school system) categories of thought that we spontaneously apply to all things of the world – including the state itself." (Bourdieu 1998, p. 35).

Bourdieu's description is clearly influenced by the French circumstances, where the school system does not embrace the same degree of freedom as in Denmark, and where nationalism takes on a somewhat different nature. However, the basic function of school and education is the same, and this is characterised by Bourdieu not simply as "disciplining for wage work" (Knudsen 1980), but as *symbolic violence*, which is to say that it makes sure that society's dominance and power structures are accepted and internalised by the individual.

Nevertheless, it must be noted that Bourdieu's very radical statements are to a certain extent contradicted, or at any rate tinted, by late-modern trends towards individualisation and globalisation. With individualisation there is a growing demand for the individual to individually influence common socialising by means of his or her choices; also, within the framework of society, to take on through this a higher degree of responsibility for his or her own trajectory – with the attendant success or failure. And with globalisation the ties to the state and nation are of necessity superimposed with a consciousness of the border-transcending nature of markets and of communication. English sociologist Anthony Giddens, for example, (cf. chapter 5) summarises this as follows:

> "One of the distinctive features of modernity, in fact, is an increasing interconnection between the two 'extremes' of extensionality and intentionality: globalising influences on the one hand, and personal dispositions on the other." (Giddens 1991, p. 1).

However, regardless of these important development trends, in order to understand the nature of the learning that takes place at school it is still crucial to realise that the act of going to school is basically a societal compulsion. This compulsion can be more or less direct; it can be a school obligation, as in most countries, or a teaching obligation, as it is in Denmark.

In terms of learning, it is crucial that from day one all the directly involved teachers, parents and pupils realise deep down that going to school, or in certain special circumstances, receiving another form of teaching, is something that you *have* to do. There is no getting out of it – the constitution dictates it – and this knowledge is fundamental legally as well as in terms of consciousness. This permeates all the learning that takes place, precisely because it is so fundamental that it does not need to be said. And it carries on working after the teaching obligation has ended, most strongly in youth training, which in our modern society is so essential for the individual's societal opportunities that it is almost an indirect compulsion; but it is also very often present in adult education, because the participants automatically bring to it the pupil and teacher roles to which they are accustomed.

Some of the ways this influencing of learning actually functions is maintained in the concept of *the hidden curriculum,* which encompasses a number of the daily school routines which are not determined in the curriculum or anywhere else, but which nevertheless play a strong part in socialisation through their constant daily repetition, year in, year out. The American Philip Jackson has pointed out that pupils thus become accustomed to waiting, to rejections, interruptions and social seclusion (Jackson 1990) – and the Englishman Peter Mortimore has been one of several to go further with this, stressing the vast amount of time wasted at school, although he has been more concerned with efficiency than with what this means for the participants in terms of socialisation (Rutter et al. 1979, Mortimore et al. 1988). In connection with a Danish survey, Bauer and Borg summarised the demands of the hidden curriculum on pupils as follows:

"The role of the pupil involves the pupil having to have motor and verbal control. This means that the pupil must be able to sit still for reasonably long periods, be quiet, and preferably speak only when encouraged to by the teacher – ...the pupil must have the self-discipline to be able to work on projects alone for lengthy periods in spite of the close presence of classmates and various interruptions – ...must be able to adapt to changing forms of authority and changing pedagogical strategies within short periods of time. At the same time the pupil must be able to endure a high degree of conformity. – ... must be able to give a good performance in competition with other pupils – ...be attentive, and this attention must be directed towards the teacher and the subject activities, which are to a great extent completely foreign to the pupil's own life context – ...be ready to ignore his or her own needs and experiences from family and leisure time. These demands often lead to a sham adjustment to the role, as the pupil hides his or her interests from the teacher and pretends to attend to the teacher and the subject activities. A sham attention of this kind brings with it an instrumental attitude to work – ... means that the pupil behaves passively and accepts the school's power – ... that the children must be able to postpone the fulfilling of their needs..." (Bauer & Borg 1986, p.29).

With regard to disciplining for wage work, it could be said that school socialises children to accept without resistance the performance of externally determined activities according to the bell – or to accept capitalist society structures as a kind of "second nature" (as it was termed in chapter 8).

Another factor that has a strong effect is schools' assessments of pupils, considering the significance this assessment has for each individual's later education and job opportunities. In Denmark, formal assessment is now postponed until the final year of ordinary school, but informal assessment starts on the first day of a child's school career. What has the greatest effect is the assessment that decides whether an individual can go on to further education or not. This subject has been thoroughly documented in Denmark by means of Steinar Kvale's survey of "grading behaviour", which shows how upper secondary school pupils' attitude towards the giving of grades permeates all their activities, and how the teachers tend to undertake a kind of collective repression of these factors that is in conflict with their self-perception and professional identity. Kvale concludes that

"There is a huge gap between the behaviour that is officially desired of pupils as a result of education, and the behaviour which is promoted in a school based on grading choices. Giving grades promotes discipline, not independence, it promotes competition at the cost of co-operation, it promotes a tendency to loneliness at the cost of a libidinal attitude to learning, and a superficial form of adaptive learning as opposed to a creative form of learning." (Kvale 1980, p. 189).

And Kvale finishes by hypothesising that

"Grade work in schools qualifies pupils for wage work in commercial life." (Kvale 1980, p.193).

More generally, Steen Wackerhausen has stated that school and the education system are bearers of *the scholastic paradigm,* i.e. that within the entire construction and practice of the system there hides a specific form of comprehension that is so obvious that it need not be stated, because everyone takes it for granted:

"The raison d'être of education is to cause or generate competence. – The scholastic tradition ... offers a scholastic education, i.e. an education whose core elements are knowledge and rules or principles. And since education is supposed to generate competence, the implicit or embodied conception of competence is that competence is constituted by exactly those elements: knowledge and rules (or principles). Or more unfolded and precisely: Competence is constituted by knowledge and rule-based skills." (Wackerhausen 1997, p. 196-197).

So, to make the scholastic paradigm quite clear in its self-bearing circular form: the aim at school and in education is to develop the specific knowledge and skills that are important precisely because they are developed here. And in working on this for so many years the pupil also develops in a way that is generally appropriate for the society that has developed and maintains the school and the education.

This in itself goes a long way towards explaining why there are not many concrete examples of how this influences everything that is learnt "academically" at school and in education for part of the point is that everyone is so in-socialised with these attitudes that they are not immediately noticed – this is what Bourdieu is referring to in his statement that the state sets the conception we use even when it applies to the state itself. I will, however, refer to a single contemporary example from a Danish study of mathematics teaching in a vocational training school:

"School is just as much a context as other practices, and the skills the participants develop are attached to the school and cannot just be transferred to other communities of practice. – In viewing school as one community of practice among others, where what one is qualifying oneself for is ever more central participation, I was able to understand why most of my pupils thought that maths was a wonderfully concrete subject, with no need to consider its relevance – despite the fact that very few of them would have to use maths at the current level in their later career. Maths did not gain its significance through future work or anything else external to school; maths gained its significance in school and through school, as a part of school's community of practice. – School as a community of practice is already assigned a discursive interpretation (author's note: a commonly-held unspoken understanding), and if these powerful discourses are not taken into account in an analysis, ideas of this kind will only be seen as produced by the community." (Hansen 1998, p.10-11 and 12).

"Not for school, but for life!" was the motto that used to be found, in either Danish or Latin, over the entrance to many school buildings. And this classical invocation expresses something central to schooling's false self-comprehension – for reality is precisely the opposite: all that is learnt for its content, or "academically", by pupils at school and in other institutional education is primarily perceived as learning for school, and if someone occasionally uses it for something outside school, it is perceived as a sort of surprising extra outcome.

What is learnt at school and in education is immediately perceived as *school learning*, learning for school's sake. So there is always a gap between education and "reality" in the society beyond – a gap which may, for example, manifest itself in the "practice shock" many experience when they finish their education and have to go out and actually "use their education in practice". School learning is obsessed and structured in such a way that in most cases there must be an accommodative restructuring both emotionally and in terms of content, before it can be applied outside the institutional context.

However, this entire situation is in many ways so inappropriate that it is no longer societally acceptable, even though it also fulfils an essential discipline function. Current society needs another form of socialisation and development of certain other competences than the knowledge and rule-bound ones traditionally represented by school and education. It is these changes that lie behind the current interest in practice learning – but as explained in the previous section, an emphasis on practice learning can only solve a small part of the problem.

Therefore school and education are necessarily plunged into a reorganisation process that is unending in its very nature. There will always be conflict between institutional qualifications and the development of societally-determined demands for competence, and the processes and times of reorganisation before their results can be seen will generally be of such long duration that apparently balanced states may only be achieved partially and by chance. Society can neither do without education nor manage it so that it keeps step with society's development. There will always be an uneasiness and a delay, which will also form a space for the unforeseen and the transcendent, which, paradoxically, society cannot do without either (cf. Illeris 1981, p. 53ff).

Learning at work, organisational learning and "the learning organisation"

One type of learning space that has attracted a great deal of attention in recent years is that of the workplace, i.e. businesses and organisations. This does not just apply to the question of practice in connection with training courses, which was dealt with earlier in this chapter, but in another way also to employees' opportunities for learning and gaining qualifications at work or in connection with it – and there are widely held opinions as to whether the business or organisation itself can learn something.

A comprehensive example of a theory complex on the psychology of work – including learning at work, not least among manual workers at shopfloor level – has been developed by a number of (East) German work psychologists, particularly Walter Volpert (1975, 1987) and Winfried Hacker (1986,

1998). Despite the theories' basis in the Russian cultural historical tradition (cf. chapter 3) and their connection with East European state communism, they also had a considerable influence on West German work psychology and industrial sociology even before the Berlin Wall came down, presumably by virtue of their great detail and thoroughness.

The theory turns on "the psychological regulation of labour activity" and learning is only a minor element of the theory. The basic conception asserts that when labour actions are performed, psychological structures develop in the person doing the work which mirror the structural nature of the work (cf. Leontjev's theory of object reflection, chapter 3). The human psyche is perceived as the element that illustrates and regulates the individual's actions, while it is also specified through work actions. In this way complex work leads to more complex and advanced psychological structures than, for example, assembly line work, and work organised on capitalist rules gets rid of structures that reflect the repressive nature of work, while work that is freed from repressive structures can lead in principle to ever expanding personality development.

Despite the thoroughness and complexity, this theory complex essentially builds on a rather mechanical conception of object reflection, and it has also been strongly criticised for a failure to include and understand subjective factors (e.g. Volmerg 1990). The psychological structures are perceived as a complicated mechanical or information technology system, reflecting the labour actions cognitively, affectively and attitudinally. Thus, the theory is also a very clear example of a conception that learning is determined, not only partially, but in fact totally, by the space in which it takes place.

There is another conception of learning at work that has roots in the cultural historical tradition in Engeström's elaboration of his comprehensive learning theory (cf. chapter 3) in practical organisation development, which he and his collaborators carried out predominantly within the public sector (see e.g. Engeström 1993, 1996a, Torvinen 1996).

This involves getting these organisations to function expediently, dynamically and efficiently with regard to their goals, but in practice a number of factors develop which seem to slow this down. Engeström here turns his particular attention to the basic contradictions in the organisation –

and which in public management are often allowed to develop and become further established as years go by because there are no external incentives to settle them.

Here Engeström's inspiration can be seen as coming from Bateson's concept of double bind. There may be almost insoluble contradictions, yet his attempt to find a solution anyway seems almost therapeutic in its essence. It involves presenting the contradictions in the structure and practice of the organisation to the staff in such a way that they cannot be explained away, overriding the organisation's self-comprehension and forcibly promoting a more realistic acknowledgement. Only when the contradictions have been acknowledged as blocks is there a basis for working positively to deal with them.

In Engeström, too, there is a clear connection between the organisation as a learning space and the nature of the learning that occurs – both when it concerns the development of contradictions and when the contradictions are to be dealt with so that the organisation can move on and keep up with the society of which it forms a part.

However, the most widely disseminated theory of learning at work today is without doubt that of American psychologist Chris Argyris, partly in collaboration with Donald Schön, who has been mentioned several times already in this book. Argyris and Schön use the term *organisational learning*, but I prefer to stick to "learning in organisations" – for it does not mean that the learning is particularly organisational in its nature, but rather that it takes place in, or is connected to, organisations – which in this case are typically large private businesses.

I have already discussed the concepts of *single loop and double loop learning*, developed by Argyris and Schön (1978) and transmitted in their widely disseminated model illustrated here in chapter 9. In their latest book, Argyris and Schön define the two concepts as follows:

"By *single-loop learning* we mean instrumental learning that changes strategies of action or assumptions underlying strategies in ways that leave the values of a theory of action unchanged. – By *double-loop learning*, we mean learning that results in a change in the values of theory-in-use, as well as in its strategies and assumptions." (Argyris & Schön 1996, p. 20 and 21).

There are clear parallels between these two concepts and Piaget's concepts of assimilation and accommodation (cf. chapters 2 and 9) – and similarly with Bateson's thinking, in which the transition to a higher learning level involves the learner keeping to the premises that are constituent to the lower level (cf. chapter 3). Argyris and Schön's model was, however, developed on the basis of comprehensive work with modern organisation development, and it is important to be aware that they do not present their contribution as a general learning theory – but simply as a theory of learning in organisations, where it is basically the organisation's goals and interests that form the perspective, while the learning and learning opportunities of the staff are perceived as important means of optimising this.

Argyris and Schön do not, therefore, go very deeply into considerations of learning theory, focusing instead on *defensive routines* and other factors in the organisation that can stand in the way of the staff's learning opportunities (Argyris & Schön 1996, p.99ff, cf. Argyris 1992, Part I). The foundation is that the organisation as such develops when the individual staff members develop themselves and, by virtue of their interactions, each other, through their learning processes that are individual in principle.

So it is quite clear for Argyris and Schön that learning in organisations can and must be influenced by the nature and goals of the organisation, which in the case of private companies includes making money and coping with the competition, but also developing and marketing products and providing a good workplace for the employees. These goals are fundamental, and therefore in principle it may be seen as positive that the goals and functions of the organisation influence the learning. The problem is that all possible routines and other constraints can get in the way of this kind of expedient learning, which must be dynamic and transcendent and can therefore also be demanding and threatening.

Argyris and Schön maintain that it is only the individuals in an organisation, and not the organisation as such, that can learn. The term *the learning organization* can still to a great extent be said to have developed in extension of Argyris and Schön's work in this field, and "organisational learning" and "the learning organisation" are often treated as almost identical concepts (e.g. Elkjaer 1999).

The learning organisation is defined by the concept's most prominent representative, the American Peter Senge, as an organisation in which

"... people continually expand their capacity to create the results they truly desire, where new and expansive patterns of thinking are nurtured, where collective aspiration is set free, and where people are continually learning how to learn together." (Senge 1990, p. 3).

There is no reason to look further at the principles of the learning organisation and the innumerable pieces of advice and directions that abound in this part of the field. It is more concerned with management and occasional clever statements than with learning theory.

On the other hand there is reason to pay attention to the unrestrained harmony contained in this definition. In the most widely read Danish book on the subject (van Hauen et al. 1995) it is presupposed without question that "collective labour" can be liberated among the employees who are striving to "create results". Not a word on fundamental contradictions in the wage work relationship, not a word on power relationships, not a word on conflicts – this kind of conception has no place in modern ambitious management thinking. On the other hand the approach appears to run into a lot of problems in practice, even in businesses right in the forefront of modern management and personnel development. At any rate, that is what the Danish organisational researcher Mette Morsing has found in a study of practice in a Danish company known for its modern personnel and management strategy – and, orienting herself much more towards problems and conflicts, Morsing concludes that

"it is the break between different forms of 'sense' that provides the opportunities for new thinking in practice." (Morsing 1995, p. 26).

On a more fundamental level, I see a central question in how far thinking on learning can go when it is based in the interests of an organisation or business. For it is not the organisation itself that can learn, but the people that make up the organisation – and the development of customs and routines and storage of information by the organisation is not the same as learning.

So, as a contrast to modern management thinking, I would like to briefly refer to a classic example of a Marxist consciousness-sociological analysis carried out by the German Ute Volmerg into the relationship between work conditions and the development of identity in connection with industrial labour. The analysis states that the key elements in the work conditions for the workers' identity development and learning opportunities concern *disposal opportunities* (i.e. possibilities for arranging their own work), *interaction opportunities* (i.e. possibilities for interaction and communication with others) and *opportunities for applying qualifications gained* (Volmerg 1976, p. 21ff). This does not as such contradict modern management thinking, which builds to a great extent on the opportunities for active development and participation of staff. However, in this instance, the concepts are developed from the rationale of the staff and not from that of the companies, giving them a quite different aspect.

A current Danish investigation by Christian Kjærsgaard into the educational motivation of workers, carried out in a medium-large and a large industrial workplace, and related to Volmerg's concepts, concludes:

" 1. That to a great extent the workers are aware and articulate concerning their own educational requirements.

2. That the qualification requirements of workers are co-determined by individual experiences and collective norms in relation to the work situation and expectations of development opportunities.

3. That subjective strategies form the basis for the individual worker's educational motivation.

4. That subjective needs for collectivity and for common debate among the workers play an important role.

5. That the contextual conditions through subjective adjustments are significant for the workers' attitude towards processes of change in the work and in education related to the business." (Kjærsgaard 1996, p.293).

It is a long way from this kind of down-to-earth investigation of educational motivation and learning orientation at floor-level in ordinary Danish companies – of which it must be said that the larger is to a great extent oriented towards modern management – to what Mette Morsing calls the *"good intentions and an almost idealising rhetoric"* (Morsing 1995, p.11) in modern literature on organisational learning. And when looking at learning in organisations, it is important to consider not only the high-flying theories, but also the existing realities.

In any case, there is no doubt that work as a space for learning has a strong influence on both the learning conditions and the learning that takes place. This is clearly seen in experiences from practice, and appears also as an unspoken presupposition in the perceptions of the companies, the staff and the theories. Learning *at* work is understood as learning *for* work. It may well include a more general aspect of personality development, but even this will be perceived from the perspective of work.

Collective learning and mass psychology

As a final "space" for learning, I will deal briefly with the concept of *collective learning* – referring to a number of approaches which state that in certain specific contexts a "collective space" can be created or can occur, implying certain particular conditions for the learning taking place.

The collective has appeared on two previous occasions in this book. The first was in connection with Oskar Negt's concept of experience (chapter 8), which in Henning Salling Olesen's definition says that

> "Experience is ... a collective process because when we experience as individuals we also do so through a socially structured consciousness." (Olesen 1989, p. 8).

Salling Olesen's presentation later states that it can be said that

> "the concept of experience is active, it creates coherence, it is critical and it is creative; it is also collective. The societalized individual cannot experience individually." (Olesen 1989, p. 68).

The second occasion when collectivity was mentioned was in the previous section on the concept of "the learning organisation", where, according to Peter Senge's definition, it states that

"... new and expansive patterns of thinking are nurtured, where collective aspiration is set free, and where people are continually learning how to learn together." (Senge 1990, p. 3).

It may be added at this point that the Danish book on this subject mentioned earlier is called

"The learning organisation – the capacity to create collective change" (van Hauen et al. 1995).

In this book there is generous reference made to concepts such as "collective behaviour", "collective learning" and "collective denial", but there does not seem to be any idea of the word collective having any meaning other than something which a number of people do together. It is unclear whether the individuals in collective learning learn the same or just learn together, and neither is it clear whether collective learning has special qualities that differ from individual learning. Collective learning is described as being "jointly owned" (p. 48), and collective learning is also called "team learning", and is contrasted with "individual learning in groups", while at the same time it is stressed that there are "differences in the team"; the group does not need to be homogenous (p. 138-139).

In contrast to these ambiguities, Salling Olesen's statements point back to the entire tradition of collectivity that has been central to traditional worker culture, also being a very important element in the basis of the workers' movement. Negt and Kluge thus refer to "collective societal experience" (Negt & Kluge 1993, p. 9), and in a summary of a long list of studies into worker consciousness, Danish psychologist Vilhelm Borg refers again and again to "the collective consciousness of the working class" and similar expressions – e.g. in the following summing up of a Norwegian study (Lysgaard 1967):

"The development of the worker collective occurs through a problem-interpreting process and an organising process. – As the workers talk together and exchange viewpoints and experiences, they interpret the particular common situation. A collective consciousness develops... which is neither a kind of 'average' of the opinions or ideas of the individual workers, nor does it need to exist as manifest ideas of the majority of the workers. – One of the most important functions of the worker collective is to preserve and elaborate this collective consciousness, which comes to act as a guide to the worker collective's organising process. The organising process contributes to the other aspect of development of the collective consciousness." (Borg 1971, p. 69).

If there is to be any meaning in operating with a concept of collective learning as something specific as distinct from the rather imprecise concept of "social learning" dealt with in chapter 7, that meaning must be that a group of people in specific circumstances can learn the same – which contradicts the basic assumption I made in chapter 2, that all learning occurs in the meeting between new impulses and previously established psychological structures, which are individual and different, meaning that the learning results will also be individual and different. And in my opinion it is not enough to state, as Salling Olesen does, that consciousness is socially structured – for although there is always a social element in the interaction processes that form part of learning, there are also always individual elements – learning is never purely and simply a social process.

However, in special circumstances there does seem to occur a phenomenon that distinguishes itself as something that could justifiably be called "collective learning". As far as I can tell, there are three conditions that must be met:

– Firstly, the collective in question must be in a common situation.
– Secondly, the participants in the sphere the learning is concerned with must have extensive common presuppositions.
– Thirdly, the situation must be of such a common emotionally-obsessed nature that there exists a clear basis for everyone to mobilise the neces-

sary psychological energy for transcendent (accommodative) learning and to be prepared for the common nature of the situation.

These conditions do not appear to have been systematically researched in connection with the formation of the collective consciousness in workers, but Borg states, with reference to the German Michael Vester, that opportunities for transcendence in collective learning are facilitated by long strikes and so on (Borg 1971, p. 99, cf. Vester 1969).

On the other hand, certain corresponding phenomena are to a great extent dealt with in connection with a right-wing authoritarian collectivity where there is no collective learning (positive connotation) but there is *mass psychology* (negative connotation). We see this first and foremost in Austrian psychoanalyst Wilhelm Reich's work on "The Mass Psychology of Fascism" (Reich 1969), in which an authoritarian style of upbringing and the ego-weakness that accompanies it are identified as the psychological basis for the collective support for Nazism. This problem was thoroughly considered at a later point by Theodor Adorno et al. in their work on "the authoritarian personality" (Adorno et al. 1950 – cf. chapter 7), and in a subsequent article, with direct reference to Freud's "Group Psychology and the Analysis of the Ego", Adorno focuses on a form of *collective narcissism* as the definitive psychological basis for Nazism (Adorno 1972, Freud 1959). In these contexts the three conditions mentioned above seem to have been largely present – and Thomas Leithäuser has also stressed that authoritarianism must be perceived as a social phenomenon rather than an individual one (Leithäuser 1998). In religious contexts there may well be corresponding factors in play as well.

Collective learning is thus not an unquestionably positive phenomenon, as it figures in the collective struggle of the working class. It can imply both a common consciousness and a common removal of personal responsibility. In a more modest example from earlier in this chapter, I wrote of high school teachers' tendencies to collectively repress the significance of grading (above in this chapter) – and there may be other current examples in connection with big musical or sports events, where the feelings of community that get repressed in our society's individualised everyday life are given a legitimate opportunity to flourish for a short while. The individualised society of today does not provide for collective learning, but for that very reason, there may be certain covert needs that push forward and are released on particular occasions.

Summary

The factors that have been dealt with in this chapter concerning the external conditions for learning can be summarised as follows:

1. The learning situation, regarded here as being the space in which learning takes place, will always influence the learning result. All learning is therefore "situated learning". At the same time, learning in one learning space is both influenced by, and influences, learning in the other spaces in which the person in question is involved.

2. At all times in everyday life there occurs informal learning that is often so-called "tacit learning", i.e. learning which is not immediately recognised, nor which can be expressed verbally. It may be possible later for parts of this learning to be set in speech, though other parts do not allow for this possibility.

3. In apprenticeship, trainee periods and other similar contexts, there may be practice learning through "legitimate peripheral participation", in which the learner gradually acquires the insights and norms of the community of practice. By these means it may be possible to avoid some of the problems of motivation and isolation that are present in institutional school learning, but at the same time there is a risk that the learning will be conformist in nature, with a weak theoretical foundation.

4. The majority of societally organised learning must necessarily take place in schools and other educational institutions, which will always be somewhat different from the world outside. This learning will therefore be of an institutional nature; it will be learning on the school's conditions and for the school's sake, and as a rule there will need to be an accom-

modative transcendence before it can be applied outside the world of the institution.

5. Learning that takes place at work will as a rule be immediately applicable to work, but will also take place on work terms, i.e. those of the employers, and can therefore easily lack a broad view and a subjective perspective.

6. Where a group is in a common situation that is emotionally laden and perceived as having an important common significance, and where the participants have extensive common presuppositions concerning the context, there may occur a collective learning that can be transcending, yet remove personal responsibility.

11. Learning, Motivation and Life Ages

Motivational psychology

The previous chapter was concerned with certain external conditions for learning in the form of the various spaces of learning. In this chapter I will look at the internal or subjective conditions of learning. Where does the energy or motive for learning come from, under which conditions is it mobilised, how does it relate to the external conditions, and what part does that play in learning?

In chapter 4 I established that learning is basically libidinal, i.e. that man is biologically equipped with a capacity for learning and a desire to realise this capacity, also that in the pre-school years there appears a particular resistance potential that can mobilise extra energy when the life fulfilment potential is constrained or blocked.

These matters have traditionally been dealt with in greater detail in *motivational psychology*. This has typically been concerned with analysing man's various motives and needs that have been listed and categorised as, for example, organic, emotional, social and cognitive motives etc. In the most common model these categories are in a hierarchy in which the basic organic motives on the lowest level, such as hunger, thirst etc., must be more or less covered before the motives on the next level can apply, right up to self-actualisation on the uppermost level, which becomes important only when all the other motives have been fulfilled to a reasonable extent (Maslow 1954).

I have already addressed this motivational approach in my earlier work, for I do not believe that motives can be distinguished, categorised and ranked in this way. This creates a pattern in which the categories form in practice the basis for dealing with motivation, instead of it being based in the complex and subjectively or objectively substantiated nature of motivation. Although man naturally has certain biologically-rooted motives, they are always developed socially and societally by means of the individual's interaction with the environment, and it is not possible to insist on a particular structure of normality and look on other motivational structures as deviant. It is also remarkable to what extent the categories that develop appear as a generalisation of the typical motivational structure in "white, American, heterosexual, middle-class males" – not least the so-called "achievement motive" which has been so central to motivational psychology in the USA (McClelland et al. 1953, cf. Illeris 1978).

Biographical research and life-span psychology

In my opinion, the most consistent responses to traditional motivational psychology are found in biographical research and life-span psychology, two relatively new fields of research that both insist on viewing and dealing with human motivations as a total entity that must be understood in the close context of the life course and the current life situation.

Biographical research thus focuses on the individual's unique life course as it occurs in a constant interaction with the societal conditions and the individual's own interpretation and acquisition of both the process and the objective framework:

> "Modern everyday life is not to be generalized. – Life history develops in interweaving subjective and objective dimensions. The dynamic of the interweave stems not least from the subjective interpretation and appropriation of everyday life as it is lived, structured by societal forces that cannot immediately be perceived, neither by groups nor individuals." (Weber 1998, p. 10 and 11-12).

> "It is... not that the individual person is controlled by external, societal structures, yet neither is it that the subject can freely construct his or her own life history. – Life history is understood... as a subject-object-dialectic, in which the subject manifests itself. The individual acting and learning subject should thus by no means be taken at face value – it is rather a dynamic structure of contradictions, in whose dynamic the learning process is embedded." (Andersen et al. 1998, p. 6).

In biographical research there are various approaches with regard to methodology and interpretations. Thus Kirsten Weber states that her interpretation is related to critical consciousness theory, as developed by Alfred Lorenzer and Thomas Leithäuser in particular (cf. chapters 7 and 6 respectively), which uses in-depth hermeneutical interpretation of thematic group discussions as a method (Weber 1998, p. 19). This contrasts with the biographical approach developed by Germans Fritz Schütze and Peter Alheit in particular (cf. chapters 5 and 9), which emphasises the use and systematic interpretation of the narrative biographical interview, i.e. an interview in which the interviewee is encouraged to tell his or her own life history, with minimal involvement from the interviewer (Alheit 1995, Olesen 1996, Dausien 1998). In a major life history research project carried out recently in Denmark, there was an attempt to combine these two approaches, with particular focus on the significance of work and social gender respectively (Andersen et al. 1998).

A third approach can be found in a large Finnish biographical project on education and learning, led by sociologist Ari Antikainen, using the following procedure:

"We collected our data by means of biographical and thematic interviews. In the first interviews the interviewees told their life stories orally. As needed, each interviewee was also asked more specific questions about education, self-definition, and areas of knowledge important in his or her life. An interview typically lasted three to four hours. We then picked out a list of significant learning experiences from each life story and presented it to the interviewee for approval or revision. – At the beginning of the second interview we considered the substances, forms and social context of these significant learning experiences in greater detail. Assuming that education can also destroy identity, we asked, finally, for the interviewee's most negative education-oriented experience. The second interview usually lasted about as long as the first." (Antikainen 1998, p. 14).

Thus, this is a procedure in which the interviewee takes the initiative to begin with, and then after a provisional analysis, there is a second round in which the initiative lies with the interviewer. The interpretation is not in-depth psychological in nature, but more concretely oriented towards circumstances, events and contexts of the process, with regard to a sociological elaboration in respect of the significance of gender, age, generation, urbanisation etc., and in the drawing on general assumptions about development in the significance of education for ordinary people over a period spanning three generations.

Biographical research thus takes an individual person's unique life story and its integration of societal conditions as the central starting point for understanding educational motivation, and from this it can be seen what can be generalised into more ordinary patterns and how this may be done.

In life-span psychology the focus is not on the individual person as such, but primarily on the identification and demarcation of various life ages and their characteristics – and from this it becomes quite clear that people in different life ages generally have essentially different motivational structures and different perspectives on learning and education.

Life-span psychology really began in the 1930s as an extension of child and developmental psychology into that of adult life (Bühler 1933, 1968). Already at this point there were considerations of different phase divisions for the life course, and more recently there have been many attempts to divide life up into a number of life ages based on various criteria, including Erikson's eight-stage staircase model, Kolb's three-stage conical model and Fjord Jensen's four-stage displaced double life arch model, all of which were discussed in detail and illustrated in chapter 9.

There is a widespread conception in life-span psychology that the various life ages typically have attached to them various orientations or "tasks", which partially determine the learning motivation; also that the life ages are separated by periods of major or minor crisis, in which the prevailing orientation is brought to an end and replaced by a new one.

I do not want to go into detail here about the various concrete phase or stage divisions. It seems obvious to me that although there may be differences in determining the exact transition points and other phase distinctions – Fjord Jensen operates with different transition points for social and interpretive life ages respectively within the same individual – nevertheless there is broad agreement on four main phases of interest with respect to learning, viz. childhood, youth, adulthood and mature adulthood. (I use here Giddens' term (1993) "mature adulthood" – in place of "old age" – because the latter concept easily brings to mind ideas of weakness. In many cases there is in fact a fifth phase after mature adulthood, in which there *is* a weakening of the cognitive functions and thus of the capacity for learning. Naturally, this may be important and interesting to work on – what is the nature of this weakness, what slips out and what is retained, how can the person relate to that, etc. – but that is beyond the perspective of this book).

In my view, these four phases, in relation to learning, can today be characterised as follows:

Childhood lasts from birth to the onset of puberty, which occurs these days around the age of 11-13 (previously it was at a later point). In terms of learning, childhood centres on the child developing and capturing its world.

Youth lasts from puberty until the preconditions for a more or less stable adulthood are established, typically through relatively permanent relationships with partners and work, or perhaps a consciousness of not wanting to enter into such relationships. It is a characteristic of present-day society that the period of youth is longer than it has ever previously been, and has a very fluid transition to adulthood; it is quite within the bounds of normality for it to finish anywhere between the ages of about 20 and 35. The end of it will often be incomplete, with a degree of connection to the youth phase being carried over into adulthood. In terms of learning, youth centres on the development of a personal identity – although postmodernists claim that this is not possible in our existing society (cf. chapter 6).

Adulthood lasts from the end of the youth period until the *life turn* – a concept which has been fully discussed in Danish by Fjord Jensen (1993), implying that the end of life has been perceived on the distant horizon, and the person is beginning to accept this and relate to it. The actual moment of the life turn and thus the transition from the first part of adulthood to mature adulthood is extremely fluid within the period stretching between the ages of about 45 to 65. There are also considerable differences between the genders in the nature of this transition. In terms of learning, the main orientation in adulthood is broadly towards the management of the life course and its challenges, typically centring on family and work, and more broadly, on interests, lifestyle and attitudes.

Mature adulthood lasts until death, or in terms of learning, perhaps only until mental weakness begins to take hold to a considerable extent, cf. above. In learning terms, mature adulthood – if energy and other circumstances permit it – is typically oriented towards bringing about richness and harmony in life.

In the following four sections I will look more closely at learning motivation and opportunities for learning in these four life ages, drawing on material from biographical research and life-span psychology as well as from sources and experiences that more directly concern the individual life ages. Then in conclusion I will try to point out certain trends that run through the life ages and link them together to a degree.

Children want to capture their world

The overall characteristic of children's learning is that in line with their development they are absorbed in capturing the world by which they see themselves surrounded and of which they are a part. In child psychology there are comprehensive descriptions of the many different facets and stages in this capturing process, including, for example, Freud's division into phases, Erikson's development ages and Piaget's stages theory. Here I will only point out certain overriding factors that determine some of the general conditions for the process.

In learning terms, it is naturally important that the cognitive learning capacity develops gradually throughout childhood – this is what Piaget's stages theory is about. When Bruner asserted that any subject can be taught in some intellectually honest form to any child at any stage of development (Bruner 1960, cf. chapter 9), this does not mean that children of any age can learn anything – but the reverse: that teaching must be appropriate to the children's age and presuppositions.

In addition, it is an important factor that children basically expect to be guided by their parents and other adults as to what and how they should learn. As babies their only connection with the surrounding world is through the mother and other adults, and the first "capture" involves establishing the separation between themselves and the surrounding world. The child is from the start subject to the control of adults and can only gradually free itself from it – Alfred Lorenzer in particular has in my view produced an important description of this process (esp. Lorenzer 1972, cf. chapter 7).

In childcare institutions and in the early years at school, children are still obliged to unfold and develop within a framework set by adults. They must of necessity accept this as a basic condition, even though naturally they can resist when they feel that they are being restricted or they are unable to understand what is going on – and this resistance is also a highly significant factor in development and learning (cf. my treatment of the concept of resistance in chapters 4 and 6). However, children are typically ready to accept explanations that tell them that learning something may be good or important for them later even if they cannot grasp it right now.

Nevertheless, the development of our late-modern society has brought about certain trends for change that apply to some of these basic factors affecting learning in childhood. These have been clearly identified by Thomas Ziehe (Ziehe & Stubenrauch 1982), but also appear in many other places.

In general, cultural liberation gives children plenty of opportunities for activities, relations and impulses which previously lay beyond their reach, while at the same time, the disintegration of traditions and norms weakens or removes a number of fixed points and structures from which children could previously take their bearings. Like young people and adults, children today perceive a number of potential choices from an early age – of which some are real and many others are only apparent – while previously there was a much higher degree of certainty, for good or ill.

The mass media play a special role here. More than parents or other adults, they give children the opportunity to experience – or often almost force on to them – a mass of impulses, including things like catastrophes, violence and sex; experiences to which they have not previously had access, and which can have strong emotional influences on them, as well as introducing these things in advance of the formation of personal experience, making it more complicated for them to later acquire their own experiences in these spheres.

Another important factor is that developments in some spheres of society can happen so fast that adults have difficulty keeping up, while children can leap, so to speak, straight into the development at its present stage, which in some areas makes them able to overtake adults. This typically occurs in the field of information technology, where teachers and parents often find that some of the children know more than they do themselves.

A sphere of learning that is of particular significance in childhood is gender socialisation. Many theories have been put forward on how this development occurs in an interaction between the given biological factors and the current societal factors. Here I will very briefly reproduce the main points of a conception developed by American psychoanalytically-oriented sociologist Nancy Chodorow (1978) and further elaborated by Harriet Bjerrum Nielsen of Denmark and Monica Rudberg of Sweden, partly by comparison with a large empirical project carried out in the USA in the 1960s, which was headed by psychologist Margaret Mahler (Mahler et al. 1975, Nielsen & Rudberg 1989, 1994).

The basis for this conception is that the first process of separation and individuation is almost always played out between the child and its mother or another woman. This means that a boy's gender identity is fundamentally built on an experience of difference, and a girl's on an experience of similarity. When in the course of the second year of life the boy starts to experience separation from his mother, they are both more prepared for this separation because of the gender difference: being a big boy means being separated from mother. A mother's relationship with a girl, however, centres on similarity, making the separation process more reluctant and ambivalent.

When the boy later discovers the difference between the genders, he can come back to his mother and experience a form of intimacy with someone of the opposite gender. The girl, on the other hand, has an earlier orientation towards confidentiality and intimacy; when she discovers the gender difference in relation to her father, she sees a new way to autonomy via an intimate relationship based on difference.

This fundamental difference has a great influence on children throughout the rest of their childhood. Both genders tend to practise gender roles. This takes place best among playmates of the same gender, so during this period children are usually divided by gender. Sexuality is not absent, but it is miscommunicated. Boys have to show off, for they believe that the way to intimacy is through autonomy. Girls become absorbed in their appearance and their friendships, for they believe that the way to autonomy is through intimacy.

Thus, the two genders take distinctly different paths in their childhood development, and for both genders, some of these factors are sharpened through late-modern society's limitless and overwhelming stream of indirectly mediated influences, both epistemic and emotional.

From a learning perspective, it is important to remember that childhood as a life age is basically influenced by the huge acquisition process of integrating and relating to the whole of the complex material, social and societal environment. This requires a broad spectrum of protracted constructive processes which the child is disposed to carry out in a way that is fundamentally unlimited and uncensored. The child is obliged to learn what can be learnt from the environment it is confronted with in order to be able to function adequately, and in this process it has to trust in the available adults and their support.

Childhood is typically a period of primarily gentle, gradual and stable assimilative learning processes, even though these processes have tended to become more complex and contradictory. Examples of the processes that are gone through are motor and linguistic development, acquisition of symbol management (reading, writing, arithmetic), and knowledge of the surrounding world and its rules, structures and means of function.

It is not so strange that Piaget, who performed exhaustive studies of some of these processes, gained a perception of the assimilative processes as central to learning (cf. chapter 4), for in the years of childhood and in the cognitive sphere, the assimilative processes *are* indeed extremely comprehensive. It is also these factors school is based on, both traditionally and in its own self-comprehension – and it is part of the reason why school is organised the way it is.

In connection with these assimilative processes, there also occur a number of accommodations, which are typically of the limited and correctional nature that Piaget paid attention to – directed towards getting the acquisition process back on track again when it has gone astray. However, in other spheres there are large and decisive accommodations in childhood learning – particularly in the spheres connected to identity development, including the development of gender roles (corresponding to Piaget's conception of the decisive role of accommodations in the individuation process, cf. chapter 2). These factors are elaborated and strengthened in the next life age, that of youth.

Young people want to construct their own identities

Youth has not always been perceived as existing as a life age in its own right. Historically the concept of youth developed together with capitalism and industrialisation:

> "The adolescent was invented at the same time as the steam-engine. The practical architect of the latter was Watt in 1765, of the former Rousseau in 1762." (Musgrove 1965, p. 33).

1762 was the year when French philosopher Jean-Jacques Rousseau published his famous book "Emile", putting child-centred pedagogy on the agenda. A need was at that time growing in the bourgeoisie for an extended schooling or period of upbringing in which the next generation could acquire the knowledge they would need, as well as suitable behaviour – and at the same time Rousseau argued for a child's right to be a child until that point.

In the beginning, youth was limited to a few years, but gradually it became a longer period and the notion of youth increasingly spread beyond the middle classes:

> "The definition of the adolescent implied a theory of the rate of progress towards maturity. This rate was to be retarded (or allowed to find its hypothetically 'natural' level) in order to insert between childhood and adulthood a discrete and distinctive phase of human growth and development." (Musgrove 1965, p. 51).

The period of youth has thus from the start been linked with a particular need for socially necessary learning and personal development. In Charlotte Bühler's first work on life-span psychology in 1933, she placed youth in an age interval from the age of about 15 to about 25, as the last half of the human period of growing up (Bühler 1933). And with Erik Erikson's book, mentioned earlier, "Identity, Youth and Crises", the conception of youth took the direction typical for the interpretation today, which is that youth is primarily a period for a more or less crisis-determined development of a personal identity or self-comprehension (Erikson 1968).

Historically, the development of the concept of youth has thus occurred in relation to the emphasis which, in the middle classes, was placed on the independent individual from the 1700s onwards. However, with the development of late-modernity, recent decades have seen a further expansion of the youthful period, so today it may often extend to the age of about 20 or more. In addition, youth has become very much idealised – and commercialised – as the age of freedom, no responsibilities, and happiness, while at the same time, the personal and societal problems that are attached to youth seem to be steadily increasing.

The essence of this development, particularly as seen from a learning perspective, is that the demands on the formation of identity have undergone an explosive growth in line with cultural liberation – it is definitely not by chance that in Danish we often talk of "identity work", which young people have to do, as well as get through their education, form relationships with a partner and find their place in society.

Previously there was family affiliation, a gender role, class attachment and usually also an attachment to a particular profession, as well as a mass of given values and norms that the young person was expected to take on, perhaps through a somewhat rebellious process; now all this is disintegrating or becoming redundant, and the young person must find his or her own way through his or her own choices. It is not only about education, career, partner and home; also lifestyle and personal identity must be chosen. Development in these areas has been overwhelming, and young people and society currently have to struggle with new, untried processes, the conditions of which change almost from day to day – new educational opportunities, new consumer opportunities, new communications systems and new lifestyle offers make themselves felt in an almost chaotic confusion, everything seems possible, and yet young people perceive countless limitations, for many opportunities are completely inaccessible for the vast majority – only very few can become actors or sporting heroes, even though many secretly wish for it and do what they can in the hope of achieving it.

According to Piaget at least, man is cognitively fully developed from puberty, i.e. man has reached the formal operational stage and is equipped to think logically and deductively. In terms of learning, the first part of the youth period is still subject to compulsory education, and later it is virtually a requirement to go through some youth education, and as a rule, also some further education of a more vocational nature. However, although this would appear to be education with a specific subject content, all learning in the youth period from the age of about 12 or 13 onwards is very much oriented towards the formation of identity and can only be understood in this light.

This contradictory relationship leads to a number of problems, for the school and education system developed primarily to deal with subject learning, while matters of identity in its broadest sense are what young people are concerned about. Therefore young people react more or less reluctantly to the academic subject requirements, which for the most part are forced upon them, and which they find outdated, while the representatives of the system attempt to keep the pupils' concentration on the academic work, which they themselves are trained in, are committed to, and are under an obligation to uphold.

Upper secondary school (gymnasium) can be seen as a typical battlefield for this conflict. An increasing number of young people go on to attend upper secondary school, for academic education is more and more becoming a sine qua non if you want to get on in life. However, upper secondary school subjects and their content, and the teachers' qualifications and ways of thinking, are firmly rooted in a time that no longer exists. Pupils go on to upper secondary school because it is their only option, and because here they can meet other young people with the same needs and problems, while the subjects, teaching and marks are for many a kind of necessary evil, which do not seem to be of much use to anyone. The teachers try to maintain in themselves and in others an understanding that, despite everything, what is happening is both meaningful and important, and there are fervent hopes that pupils will "take responsibility for their own learning". However, who wants to take responsibility for something they do not feel they have any great influence on?

One of the most striking effects of these factors is the dramatic drop in applications to technical and scientific courses. Even though these courses bring employment opportunities with high status in society, high priority and good salaries, most young people go in other directions, typically towards humanistic, social, pedagogical and societal subjects, for these provide far better opportunities for establishing an interaction between the academic content and the formation of identity.

The identity process is for most young people today far more important and far more urgent than career orientation, and in one way it is also a precondition for the choice of career, or part of it. So from the perspective of young people, there is good reason for the many searching activities, shifts and years out that the system views as expensive delays in the education of young people.

The most important things for young people to learn today are to be able to orient themselves, to be able to make choices that can be answered for, to keep up with everything, not to waste their lives on the wrong thing, to be able to decline in the many situations where a choice has to be made. Society and employers also demand maturity, independence, responsibility etc. – and as far as academic qualifications are concerned, there is always something to be got out of it if you do what you are interested in. Yet no-one can say which academic qualifications will be relevant in five or ten years' time, so everyone must be prepared to go on to further education throughout most of life. The best security for the future is not to learn a subject on what are perceived as traditional premises, but to be ready to change and take hold of what is relevant in many different situations. Uncertainty cannot be countered by stability, but only by being open, flexible and constantly oriented to learning (cf. Simonsen 2000).

Youth is also the period in which to learn how to deal with gender and sexual relations. Gender socialisation in childhood typically ends as described in the previous section with the two genders developing orientations and approaches very different in nature, and when they meet again in puberty, they each therefore have their own basis: the boys' way to intimacy comes through achievement and sexuality, and the girls' way to sexuality comes through confidentiality and intimacy. For both genders these opposing orientations are linked with the personal identity process – and here as in education it is the formation of identity that is given priority: young people today are often more absorbed in reflecting themselves in their partners than they are in the partners themselves. Typically, then, things start with great dreams of the ideal partnership, but the reality turns out to be a rocky road with turbulent ups and downs or obstructions, vulnerability and hurt over many years with unsettled relationships.

There is so much to be learnt in the period of youth: academically, emotionally, socially, societally – and most of all, in terms of identity. Whereas childhood is a time for constructive assimilative learning, youth is a period for major accommodations in which, one by one, profound changes and reconstructions are made to the knowledge structures and the emotional patterns with regard to identity in a broad sense and to educational and social relationships etc. And the reflexivity that is so characteristic of late modernity (cf. chapter 5), where it is always the individual's relationship to him- or herself that is the focal point of learning, unfolds without doubt most dramatically in the years of youth as an essential yet enormously taxing tool for the identity process.

Adults pursue their life goals

The beginning of the adult period may typically be marked by external events such as starting a family or finishing education. There are no decisively new cognitive opportunities; what happens in terms of learning and consciousness is that the person takes on the management of, and responsibility for, his or her own life, with this normally occurring gradually as a long process throughout the years of youth and into adulthood. All models in life-span psychology include a phase called *adulthood*, perhaps with a distinction between a first and second adulthood. This phase is typically characterised by the following:

- the person has moved from his or her childhood home and has taken responsibility for his or her own life project
- basic education is completed, perhaps including the gaining of a specific professional competence
- the person is in a family situation or similar with a partner, and very often with children
- the person is aiming for, and in many cases gains, a more or less permanent position in the labour market
- there may be changes in the family situation and/or the work situation.

In general this life phase has traditionally been marked by a kind of ambition that implies a striving to realise more or less clear life aims relating to family, career, interests or something else – but in late modernity this representation is also on its way to being overlaid by the continual societal changes, the unpredictability of the future, the conditioning of the market mechanism and the unending succession of apparent choices.

Many factors that were in earlier times, for good or ill, already marked out for the individual, have now become things to be decided on again and again. It is no longer possible to make your choice of life course once and for all when young, and then expect to spend the rest of your life accomplishing it. Whereas once a large number of factors were given, based on gender, for example, or class affiliations, all now appears to be redundant. The fact that this is only how it appears can be seen from statistics showing that the large majority of people, now just as previously, live their lives in the way that their gender and social background has prepared them for. However, this does not influence the perception that now this is something people choose themselves, something for which they are responsible, and thus have only themselves to blame if it turns out to be unsatisfactory.

Just a generation ago, there were still relatively firm learning and consciousness patterns that were taken as given based on gender, class and degree of urbanisation during upbringing. There was, as a typical basis for the general conception, the authoritative patriarchal middle class man, a pillar of society and an idealised norm – this could, and still can be, indirectly seen in a great deal of law, history, sociology and psychology. There was also his wife with her solicitous, modest and ambivalent function of housewife. There was a working class with a close-knit worker culture and consciousness, based on the experience of being the oppressed who carried out the toil of society, there were the women with their double burden of family and work and its attendant ambivalence, and there were also the industrious and often narrow-minded independent lower middle classes and country dwellers. There was a merging of societal position, learning, education and forms of consciousness, which were limited and often repressive, but which also created a pattern the individual could follow (Simonsen & Illeris 1989).

Just some fifteen years ago, Danish life-mode researchers Thomas Højrup and Lone Rahbek Christensen were able to mark out and differentiate by gender three main life modes – the self-employed life mode, the wage-worker life mode and the career-oriented life mode – as guidelines for the structuring of life and consciousness that applied to most of the population (Højrup 1983a, 1983b, Rahbek Christensen 1987). However, a large-scale survey of trade union members in the 1990s shows that the traditional working class today covers four very different patterns of attitude (Jørgensen et al. 1992), that late-modern sociologists weaken concepts of class (e.g. Giddens 1993), and that postmodernists question the very concept of identity (e.g. Usher 2000).

With these developments, learning in adulthood has taken on a completely new perspective. With the earlier, firmer structures, the individual could use his or her years of youth to develop an identity, or at least a sort of draft identity, that would be of help in governing future learning. In career terms, school and education would have provided for the acquisition of a groundwork that was regarded as feasible for the rest of that person's life, so that whatever was needed later could generally be gained through practice learning at work and maybe a few additional courses. In life also, it was necessary to keep up with any developments, but this did not go too fast for people to manage to get the requisite learning as they went along. Thus, for the vast majority of people, learning in adulthood was fairly manageable and predominantly assimilative in nature, with its most characteristic aspect probably being the development of a system of defence mechanisms that could screen out any new impulses that were too insistent, thus ensuring stability and self-respect.

Becoming an adult formally in our society means coming of age and so taking responsibility for one's own life and actions. This happens legally (in Denmark) on one's eighteenth birthday, but from a psychological perspective it is actually a process, as has been mentioned earlier in the text, and it is characteristic that this process has become longer and longer, to such an extent that today it is most often accomplished well into a person's twenties or perhaps never. Late-modern society's promotion of youth makes it difficult to let it go.

In the field of education, the prolongation of this process goes hand in hand with the continual extension of the average time spent in education, and the steady increase of the scope of adult education. It is not so very long ago that the majority of Denmark's population received only seven years' schooling, but today there are nine years of compulsory education and a clear state target that everyone should have at least twelve years' education; and a majority go on to a further course of education of a longer or shorter length before the end of the preliminary period of education. In addition to this, an increasing number of people take part in adult education courses, and young people's expectations are for recurrent or lifelong education.

However, it is basically characteristic that adults learn what they want, and have very little inclination to acquire something they do not want, i.e. something they do not perceive as meaningful for their own life goals, of which they are aware in varying degrees of clarity. A rule of thumb for understanding adults' learning would state that

- adults learn what they *want* to learn and what is meaningful for them to learn
- adults draw on the resources they already have in their learning
- adults take as much responsibility for their learning as they want to take (if they are allowed to).

As a consequence of this, rather than having various more or less unconnected motives as the foundation for their educational and learning activities, adults have more coherent *strategies* relating to goals that are normally fairly clear and known to the individual (Ahrenkiel & Illeris 2000). This approach to education is, however, far from always in accordance with the way adult education is organised, and neither does it accord with much of the participants' own expectations. For in the ordinary popular conception and throughout the many years of schooling, everyone more or less takes on board the traditional view that education and learning are the responsibility of schools and teachers. Teachers have to teach pupils what has to be learnt.

In the previous section I looked at how the conflict between the respective interests of the system and the participants dominates youth education today, creating major problems. In adult education these problems are basically different because adult education is nearly always voluntary in principle. Of course it is very often the case that someone needs to take a particular course to achieve a particular goal, but that person was also the one to choose the goal – in contrast to youth education, where there is no realistic alternative if there is to be any hope of a life on a level with what is normal in the eyes of society. However, there are also cases where employers, or in Denmark very often the unemployment authorities, compel adults into education courses against their will, although it is a common experience that they will learn very little from this; it is a reluctant process which is more like storage than learning (Ahrenkiel et al. 1999, Illeris 2001).

However, the academic content is the least problematic aspect of adult education today. With the pace of change and need for reorganisation in the late-modern period, the phrase lifelong learning primarily implies a need to be constantly prepared for reorganisation. This can be hard enough for young people, but for those who first got caught up in this development as adults, the challenge of reorganisation is even harder. The stability, self-assurance and professional pride that were crucial qualifications for many a few years ago, now seem like burdensome encumbrances. Where before there was stability, there now has to be flexibility, and if there is to be any hope of survival in the job market, the defence mechanisms of stability must very quickly be replaced with service-mindedness and readiness for change – regardless of whether the defence developed in the form of middle-class values or a limited wageworker consciousness.

Societal demands that adults must learn on a far greater scale and in a totally different way than previously are inescapable on every level. It is primarily a demand for a mental reorganisation and personal development, but there may also be technical or academic demands, e.g. typically in connection with information technology developments. In other words, these are demands for profound accommodative processes of a reflexive nature – and that is not something adults are accustomed to.

It is clear enough, however, that the normal situation in adult education is that the adults themselves have chosen, or more or less had to accept, the course in question – the choice can be predominantly libidinal or influenced more by necessity; it is usually both in some kind of combination. On this basis it could be expected that the adults would themselves take responsibility for the learning the course is providing. However, ordinary conceptions and experiences of education often get in the way of this. Even though the institutions, the teachers and the participants might say and believe otherwise, everyone in the education situation obstinately expects that the responsibility will lie with the teacher. It is, after all, the teacher who knows what has got to be learnt.

The situation is paradoxical, for while the adult participants behave like pupils, they have a very hard time accepting the lack of authority the traditional pupil role entails. They get bored and become resistant in a more or less conscious way – but nevertheless they will not themselves take on the responsibility, for that is actually far more demanding. The conflict can only be resolved by effectively making a conscious break with the prevailing roles as pupils and teachers at school. And as a rule it is the teacher who has to take the initiative and insist on it. It is normally only when the participants realise that they truly can take responsibility and use the teacher as a support for their own learning that the picture alters, and after that the way is clear for the learning to become goal-directed, effective, transcendent and libidinal, as is characteristic of a learning process actually chosen by the individual (Illeris 1998).

However, there is much to suggest that the conditions described here stand in the way of complete changes. The "new youth" of late modernity, who have in recent years turned youth education upside down, are well on their way to making their entry into adult education as the "new adults". Birgitte Simonsen has the following to say about this development:

> "In a few years' time, these young people will really come into adult education, and then we will need all the flexibility we can get. In the field of adult education we in Denmark have an extremely well-founded tradition for heterogeneity, which makes us hopeful. If, on the other hand, current trends towards homogeneity in large inflexible systems get the upper hand, major problems should be anticipated." (Simonsen 1998, p. 213).

Mature adults seek richness and harmony

"The age of maturity", "the third age" or "second adulthood" are all terms for the phase of life that for most people in modern society lies between the so-called life turn and actual old age, and can well last a period of twenty years or more.

The life turn is a psychological phenomenon concerning the perception and acknowledgement that the remaining time in your life is not unlimited. It is, however, most often external events that bring about and mark the life turn – typical examples are the children leaving home, losing a job, taking early retirement or being given reduced hours; it can also be a divorce or the death of a near one, and for women the menopause may play a part in the situation (cf. Fjord Jensen 1993).

In contrast to the first age of adulthood, the mature age is characteristically not dominated by the same form of purposefulness – the goals being reached for do not have the same existential nature as having a family, raising children, or work and career. As far as they are able – and the mature age is for many today a period with a certain personal and financial ability – people spend their time on things they perceive as quality activities, such as cultural or social activities, helping others, their partner, if they have one, their children, grandchildren, or disadvantaged groups they are involved with.

In this context there may often be important learning activities, both formal education and less formal processes of development and change, characterised by being something absolutely chosen by the person himself, because it is something he wants to do, something he considers important for himself or for other people. It can also be that the person needs to prove to himself and to others that there are things he is well capable of, that he simply has not had the opportunity to do previously.

Learning in mature adulthood can thus be characterised by a personal libidinal motivation, without that aura of necessity or external incentive which often forms the basis for learning in earlier adulthood. This could apply to things you would like to study, things you would like to understand, or experience, or learn and use in specific contexts.

However, it must be remembered that this only applies to relatively privileged mature adults. Many people have more than enough to do just getting by practically and financially, and have neither the opportunity nor the reserves to look towards the self-actualisation or learning in which those in more favourable positions increasingly get involved. The new wave of learning and education for mature adults is for the time being a middle-class phenomenon mainly.

Cognitively there may be a trend towards learning beginning to go more slowly if it concerns new areas the person is not very committed to, but this does not normally apply when it concerns things he or she is interested in, and for which he or she has good presuppositions and experiences. The usual popular notion that elderly people are worse at learning things can thus be seen to relate only to the fact that they can be *slower* in learning something *new* – which people are often not particularly interested in acquiring. People are satisfied with their own interests and experiences, and if the new matter is not connected to that, it can make it more difficult to mobilise psychological energy.

Naturally, dementia and other illnesses are another matter – but that subject is beyond the perspective of this book.

Lifelong learning

In the previous sections I have looked at some typical current background attitudes to learning in various life ages. It is important to stress that these are current attitudes, for life ages are only rooted in biology to a certain extent. The details of the various life ages are to a great extent determined by history and society, and can alter rapidly. It has become clear, for example, how late modernity has influenced learning today, particularly in childhood and youth, but also increasingly in adulthood.

The Finnish life process survey mentioned earlier (Antikainen et al. 1996, Antikainen 1998, Antikainen & Kauppila 2000) can further throw these attitudes into relief. Certain clear differences were found between the attitudes of three generations to education and learning: the oldest generation's life histories take the form of survival accounts, in which education figures as a limited benefit which provided the opportunity for a learning that could positively contribute to their struggles in life. In the middle generation, the life histories of the men in particular take the form of career accounts, and education and learning play a part as a means to career development. In the young generation the life histories are characterised by reflexivity and individuality, and education is perceived as a consumer item to be made use of when there is a need for it or an interest in it. It is clear that the very different perspectives on education imply correspondingly large differences in the nature of the learning that takes place.

Thus, very different frames of reference for society and consciousness determine the learning conditions in the various life ages, and these frames of reference change rapidly in step with developments in society and consciousness. Nevertheless, there are also a number of important common links running through the life ages which are more general and which to a certain extent run across changing circumstances. From the descriptions previously given, three closely linked long lines of this kind can be pointed out:

Firstly, a gradual *liberation* occurs throughout the life ages for the individual in relation to the societal determination of learning. Whereas learning in childhood is framed in an interaction between biological maturing and external societally-determined influences, in youth it is characterised to a great extent by young people's fight to have a say in things and, partly through this, construct their identity. In first adulthood people move towards learning what they themselves think is important, but to a great extent this is determined by their societal conditions. It is only in mature adulthood that societal determinations move into the background for those people who have the opportunities and the resources to liberate themselves.

In close interaction with this gradual liberation of learning from its societal bondage, there also typically occurs an *individuation,* i.e. learning increasingly directs itself towards the development of an individual person and is determined by personal needs and interests. Again it is a development which first takes off properly in the period of youth, but which only has a full impact in mature adulthood.

Finally, there also occurs a gradual development of a *responsibility* for learning, that is closely connected with the two other developments and so follows the same pattern.

In our society, it seems very clear that it should be both a condition and a goal for society to strive to organise itself on the lines of these developments and to support them. However, the earlier sections on social learning (chapter 7) and collective learning (chapter 10) may also serve as a reminder that learning is not only an individual process, and that education can also have other perspectives than supporting personal development and the provision of qualifications for individuals, as our late-modern market society so clearly puts in central position.

Man is and always will be a social being, the individual cannot develop and fulfil his or her potential without others, and so there will also always be a counter-movement towards the notion of the common good before the individual (see e.g. Wenger 1998) – it can be seen that there are many truly free learning initiatives in mature adulthood that may be both social in nature and have a social perspective.

Summary

The conditions concerning the internal psychological prerequisites for learning can be summarised as follows in continuation of what has already been described:

1. The motivation or the internal psychological motives behind learning evolve through the individual's unique life process in interaction with societal conditions and the individual's own interpretation of the pro-

cess and of the interaction. For the main life stages, the following factors may be emphasised:

2. Up to puberty, children are primarily occupied in capturing their surrounding world. In this process they are disposed towards leaning on adults for support, but they are also very much influenced by things beyond the immediate circle of adults, and particularly by the mass media.

3. Youth today typically stretches from the onset of puberty into the twenties and perhaps even into the thirties. In terms of learning, the period is dominated by the identity process, and other learning is often strongly related to this. This can easily lead to conflicts with the education process, which is organised in such a way as to place emphasis on academic teaching and qualifications.

4. In the period of adulthood up to the life turn, learning is usually goal-directed on the basis of the individual's own aims and strategies, which are typically based on a weighted interaction between desire and necessity. Adults often have trouble stepping out of the accustomed pupil role, while at the same time they also expect to manage their own learning. The new adult generation that is on its way may be expected to keep itself more in conscious control of its learning activities.

5. Mature adults – from the life turn to old age – increasingly turn towards educational processes of libidinal cultural and social activities of their own choosing, that may contribute to richness and harmony in their lives.

6. In spite of great differences in individual life processes, the development in learning orientation throughout the life ages seems to be characterised by a gradual liberation from societal ties, individuation in learning interest, and increased personal responsibility for learning.

12. Overview

Summary of the developed learning theory

In this final chapter I shall summarise the understanding of learning that has been developed through this book, and examine the positions of the various theoretical contributions in the tension field of learning as presented in chapter 1. I shall end up with some concluding considerations and perspectives as to the position and message of the book.

The following summary cuts across the previous chapters, and thus it will not follow the line of progression that the presentation has been based on. However, I try briefly to retain the most important aspects of the conclusions I have reached.

The learning conception presented is basically based on the idea that human ability to learn is an integrated part of the human life and survival potential and as such is libidinous in nature at the outset. However, during the pre-school years a resistance potential is split off as a separate potential which can be activated when the life potential meets serious obstacles.

As to the *process* of learning, I see it as an entity which unites a cognitive, an emotional and a social dimension into one whole. It combines a direct or mediated interaction between the individual and its material and social environment with an internal psychological process of acquisition. Thus, learning always includes both an individual and a social element, the latter always reflecting current societal conditions, so that the learning result has the character of an individual phenomenon which is always socially and societally marked.

The main categories of the interaction processes which make up the "raw material" or input of the learning processes may be characterised as perception, transmission, experience, imitation, activity or participation, respectively. However, these categories should not be regarded as separate, but rather as characteristics which can be combined in the single learning event, each of them being more or less present or prominent in a pattern unique to the specific situation.

The interaction starts with the "mother-child-dyad" between the baby and its primary care person. Already in this interaction the mother or other primary care person is the carrier of current societal markings and structures, and at the same time the interaction always takes place in a societally-structured space. Later the interactions will gradually take on the form of a direct or mediated relation to societal totality.

Through the internal psychological processes of acquisition, cognitive structures of knowledge and abilities and psychodynamic patterns of emotions, motivations and attitudes are developed in an integrated way. This integration means that cognitive structures are always emotionally obsessed, and emotional patterns include cognitive features. Together the cognitive and the psychodynamic are conducive of the development of personality.

The internal psychological processes can be of a predominantly cumulative (mechanical), assimilative (additive) or accommodative (transcendent) character. Through cumulative processes new structures and patterns are established, while new elements are added to already existing structures and patterns through assimilative processes. Through accommodative processes existing structures and patterns are dissociated and reconstructed so that new assimilative constructions can take place. Accommodative processes are activated when the individual meets impulses or situations which it cannot manage on the basis of existing structures and patterns. While memory and applicability of the learning results of cumulative and assimilative processes to some degree presuppose a subjective connection to the original learning situation, in principle the results of accommodative processes are freely accessible.

Furthermore, the learning results can be predominantly convergent (unambiguous) or divergent (ambiguous), assimilative construction can be more or less expanding (constructive) or consolidating (restrictive), and accommodative reconstruction can be more or less offensive or defensive.

A special form of accommodation is reflection, which typically comprehends material from different structures and takes place without any direct input of new stimuli from the environment. The basis of reflection is a more or less conscious experience of a subjectively important challenge or contradiction. Self-reflection or reflexivity is a special kind of reflection that may lead to increased self-consciousness and therefore is an important instant of personality. In late modern society, biographicity is developed as a junction of reflexivity and personality.

Learning processes can vary from limited events in a specific area of learning to broad and comprehensive developments comprising the whole personality and identity. They can be of a predominantly cognitive, emotional or social and societal character, but always include all of these dimensions to some extent, and they may also be integrated with biologically conditioned maturing or ageing processes. Learning typically takes place in phases or stages that change between "plateaus" with a relatively level and predominantly assimilative development, and steps or "jumps" of a predominantly accommodative nature.

Very special and demanding situations, often with a crisis-like character, can lead to deep and comprehensive transformative learning processes that include simultaneous changes in all the three learning dimensions and have to do with the very identity of the learner. Such processes of transformation may also be viewed as a complex of interwoven accommodations.

Some learning processes involve active resistance or defensive rejection, blocking or distortion. Typically impulses which are at odds with existing structures and patterns and therefore potentially might provoke accommodative processes may be distorted so that the discrepancy is rejected and the distorted impulse, accordingly, can be managed by assimilation.

As a whole, the totality of these interaction processes and internal processes of acquisition and elaboration form a lifelong process of experience. Learning takes on this character to the extent that it is related to a subjectively relevant social context in which the learner is actively involved and relates impulses to previous experience and future perspectives. Learning of this kind will typically concern problems which are subjectively important and are dealt with in relation to relevant possibilities of forward-pointing action on the basis of already established experiential patterns.

Both the general character of the learning situation – as for instance everyday life, school, practice, working life or collectivity – and its specific content and emotional appeal will always leave a mark on the learning that takes place. Correspondingly, the situation of the learner both as to general features such as age, gender and societal position and more specifically in relation to interests, background and preconditions in the situation, will also always mark the learning.

Positions in the tension field

In figure 1 in chapter 1, I presented the tension field between the cognitive, the emotional and the social dimensions inside which learning takes place. It was my basic assumption that these dimensions are always represented in learning processes and that a comprehensive learning theory consequently must include all three dimensions and how they are related to each other.

In the intervening chapters I have, accordingly, involved a number of theories about, or of relevance for, learning. I will now try to take a general view of these theoretical positions by approximately fitting them into the tension field. This may simultaneously contribute to an understanding of the character of the tension field.

Developmental psychological contributions
The upper line of the tension fields connects the cognitive and the emotional poles, and along this line most of what is normally labelled *developmental psychology* is situated as it usually comprises both the cognitive and the emotional or psychodynamic dimensions of individual development, whereas societal conditions are usually only briefly considered.

At the cognitive pole, I have placed *Piaget* as an important and typical representative of the cognitive position. Close to this pole I shall also place *Kolb*, whose theory and model also clearly relate to the cognitive dimension of learning. I also place *Nissen* here although his considerations of the specific demand of psychological energy in connection with accommodative processes place him one step further out of the line towards the psychodynamic pole.

I have placed *Freud* at the psychodynamic pole as the most important and typical representative. In this corner I shall also place *Rogers*, who clearly emphasises that his concern is the development of the self and only learning relating to this is of interest to him. However, it must be observed that Rogers conceives of the self as both a cognitive and a psychodynamic structure, and therefore his position is not close to the emotional pole but one step in the direction towards the cognitive pole. Right in the middle between these two poles is the position of *Furth,* who is deliberately trying to find an equal balance between Piaget and Freud.

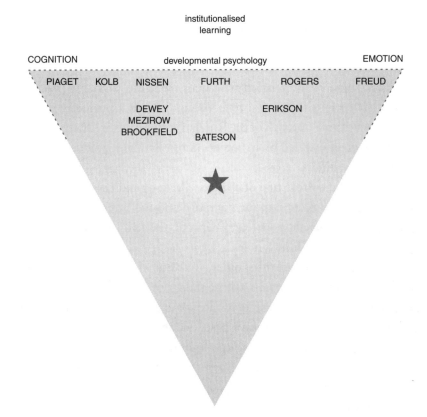

Figure 12: Developmental psychology oriented positions

In addition, some other contributing positions are mainly relating to the developmental psychological understanding although they are not positioned right up to the upper borderline of the field because they to some extent involve societal conditions. In direction of the cognitive pole I place *Dewey* and together with him *Mezirow* and *Brookfield* who, as I see it, have transferred the position of Dewey into adult education. In direction of the psychodynamic pole I place *Erikson,* and finally *Bateson* who with his many-sided contributions must be placed rather close to the centre of the field.

Outside the field, above the upper borderline, I place *institutionalised learning* (or school learning or scholastic learning) as a sort of learning space which has typically related its understanding of learning to developmental psychology.

The positions in the upper developmental psychological part of the tension field are thus as shown in figure 12 on the previous page.

Activity theoretical contributions

The left sideline of the tension field goes from the cognitive pole down towards the social and societal pole. Along this line I primarily place the activity theoretical approach of the Russian cultural historical school which is precisely characterised by its intention of relating cognitive learning to its societal conditions.

At this line I therefore first of all place *Vygotsky* and *Leontjev*, the former somewhat in the direction of the cognitive and the latter somewhat in the direction of the societal pole – and between the two I place *Engeström* as their contemporary Finnish heir.

Furthermore, there are three other contributors to be placed in the area along this line. Firstly *Bandura*, whose theory of "social learning" I find so cognitively oriented that, in spite of the fact that he launched this concept, I place him close to the cognitive pole. Secondly *Bruner*, who started his career right up in the cognitive corner but through a remarkable development over several decades has moved down along this sideline, so that I now find it correct to place him close to the societal pole. Finally, there is *Hacker* (and along with him I could also mention *Volpert*), who must also be close to the societal pole.

One certain position is that of *Holzkamp* (and also *Holzkamp-Osterkamp*) who while being closely attached to the cultural historical tradition, in his later years deliberately tried to reach out towards the psychodynamic domain and therefore must be placed a step towards the centre of the field. And, also in this area, there are *Argyris* and *Schön,* who are a little difficult to fit in. With their single and double loop model, they have an apparently individual psychological approach which should place them in the upper part of the field, but on the other hand they relate themselves to the domain of organisational learning which is a social area. Moreover, they primarily deal with the content side of learning but do not avoid emotional references. Thus, they must be placed close to the centre of the field, but somewhat in the direction of the cognitive pole.

Outside the left sideline between the cognitive and the societal poles are the positions of such approaches as *practice learning* and *the learning organisation,* which relate to the cognitive and social dimensions of learning without, strictly speaking, being learning theories.

The positions in the left side of the tension field are thus as shown in figure 13:

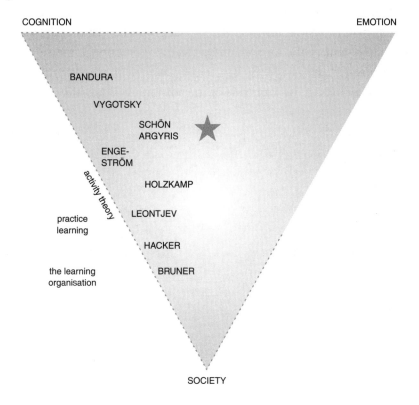

Figure 13: Activity theory oriented positions

Socialisation theory contributions
The right sideline of the tension field goes from the emotional pole down towards the social-societal pole. Along this line, the main contribution is

the critical theory of the Frankfurt School and its extension in the various more or less socialisation theoretical approaches of the Hanover School.

Nearest to the emotional or psychodynamic pole I place *Lorenzer*, nearest to the social-societal pole it must be *Negt*, and in between the two is the position of *Becker-Schmidt*. In addition, there are two more contributors from the Hanover School that I have involved, namely *Ziehe* – whose position must be a little up towards the developmental psychological area, and *Leithäuser*, who, at least in his earlier works about everyday consciousness, includes elements that reach out towards the cognitive pole.

Outside the right sideline I place the concept of *collective learning* which, without being a proper learning theoretical position, relates to the Frankfurt School and to the interaction between the emotional and the social dimensions.

The positions in the right side of the tension fields are, thus, as shown in figure 14:

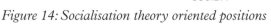

COGNITION

EMOTION

ZIEHE

LORENZER

LEITHÄUSER

BECKER-
SCHMIDT

socialisation theory

NEGT

collective
learning

SOCIETY

Figure 14: Socialisation theory oriented positions

Socially and societally oriented contributions

Finally, there are a number of positions which are clearly or predominantly socially or societally oriented and only in a general way relate to the psychological dimensions of learning. As the extreme example of this group of positions I have, at the outset, chosen to place *Marx* with his famous formulation in his sixth thesis on Feuerbach.

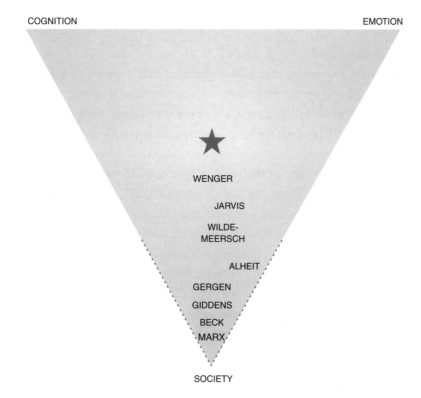

Figure 15: Societally and socially oriented positions

Close to this pole are also the positions of such modern sociologists as *Beck* and *Giddens*, and next to them I place *Gergen* as a representative of the social constructionist approach, which is essentially of a psychological nature but very much directed towards the social interaction processes. Another step towards the centre of the field, and still halfway between the two sidelines, I place *Wildemeersch* with his special interest in social movements, and after him *Jarvis* who tries to cover broadly and in a balanced way but still with a mainly sociological orientation. Close to the centre of the field is the position of *Wenger* whose concept of communities of practice tends to combine the social and the individual as seen from the social perspective. Finally, and a little out to the socialisation theoretical side, I place *Alheit* as a representative of the biographical approach.

The central, lower part of the tension field thus includes the positions as shown in figure 15 on the previous page.

Exceptions and totality

Finally, there are two positions that I have referred to in this book but not included in the figure, as they relate to other dimensions and are therefore impossible to place satisfactorily. These are the system theory position, as represented by *Luhmann,* and the postmodernist position, as represented by *Usher.*

Generally, the figure of the tension field with all positions filled is as shown in figure 16. It should here be mentioned that the learning approach presented in this book is positioned close to the centre of the figure, as its crucial point is that the whole tension field must be taken into account in any dealing with learning in theory or practice.

Considering the figure, it is rather striking that almost all of the theorists who have been mentioned are men. This is not due to any conscious selection on my part; for some reason or other it appears to be predominantly men who have taken an interest in the kind of learning theory I have dealt with here. The only women theorists in the triangle are Regina Becker-Schmidt, who has dealt explicitly with women's learning, and Ute Holzkamp-Osterkamp, who has been mentioned in connection with Klaus Holzkamp and has dealt primarily with motivation. In addition, the position of Jean Lave has been discussed thoroughly in the book, but her position is in "practice learning", placed outside the triangle, as it is not, strictly speaking, considered a learning theoretical position, but a field of learning.

Historically, this male dominance may, of course, be explained as a consequence of the fact that research and theorising in general have been male dominated. But this explanation only goes so far; by the 1930s, female researchers such as Charlotte Bühler in Europe and Hilda Taba in

America occupied important positions in fields of considerable relevance for learning such as developmental and educational psychology. And today in the field there are, no doubt, at least as many women as men.

However, the kind of research and theorising carried out by the female researchers already mentioned immediately provides an idea of the gender difference that exists in the field of learning theory: evidently female learning researchers tend to relate more directly to personal development, emotional conditions and learning in practice, whereas more abstract and structural approaches, such as those primarily dealt with in this book, seem to be a predominantly male interest.

Figure 16: Positions in the learning theoretical tension field

So the consideration of the gender issue inevitably leads to the conclusion that I, myself, and consequently also my book, are involved in a sort of gender division in interests and approaches – and there may be a basis and a need for some kind of parallel presentation of the same area or tension field as seen from a feminine point of view. However, I shall not be the one who is called upon to make this presentation, nor able to do it, and I hope that the masculine presentation I have made will in fact also be of interest to female readers, even though they may find it overly abstract and theoretical.

Conclusion and perspective

I have tried to show how the understanding of learning that I have presented has drawn on contributions from many different positions which together cover the whole of the tension field between the cognitive, the emotional and the social poles. However, this does not mean that the conception is merely a juxtaposition of a number of different contributions with their various scientific and theoretical bases and attitudes.

On the contrary, the understanding is built up from the fundamentally constructivist position which was developed by Piaget – who is generally acknowledged to be one of the founders of constructivism. I consider the linkage to the Freudian theory universe as relatively unproblematic in this connection. It has been made with a close reference to Furth's pointing-out of fundamental similarities between the theory constructions of Freud and Piaget, which makes it possible to see Freud's theories in a constructionist perspective. From this point of view, Freud's conception of human drives becomes a parallel to Piaget's conception of the function of equilibration between assimilative and accommodative processes – as a connecting link between the biologically and genetically developed fundamentals of the human species and the individual human being's construction of him- or herself as a subject, i.e. as a societal individual.

When learning, furthermore, is conceived of as an integration of the internal psychological processes that Piaget and Freud have dealt with and the social interaction processes between the individual and its environment, it also becomes possible in this frame of understanding to include sociality as a constructive force, such as it is conceived of in social constructionism. The contradiction between constructivism and social constructionism, which Gergen has paid much attention to, in my understanding takes on the character of an integrated interaction between two types of construction processes which are both essential to and necessary for learning.

Parallel to the close connections of internal psychological processes to the biological and genetic basis of the human species, the social processes have a basic connection to the societally developed environment. In the social processes, societally developed individuals are involved in situations which are framed by existing societal structures. In our modern society – and to a rising extent in societies the world over – this means the structures of capitalist, industrial society such as most fundamentally described by Marx and later further developed into the highly technological, global information and market society of today.

Thus, fundamentally learning is a process mediating between man as a biologically and genetically developed species and the societal structures developed by man. Learning develops knowledge, abilities, emotions and sociality which are important elements of the conditions and raw material of society. But societal circumstances also develop into independent structures with a character of given frames that set the conditions of both the knowledge, the abilities, the emotions and the sociality that can be displayed.

In this perspective, learning is an important mediating connection in a most topical question about whether human knowledge, abilities, emotions and sociality are able to match and cope with current societal structures which the very same human qualities have been the incentives of developing – or whether societal development has taken over the last bit of power from the human basis that has created it and, via conditions such as pollution, rape of resources, development of chemical and genetically manipulated substances and goods and the escalation of social imbalances, it is about to destroy its own existence.

Learning, in this connection, is not just a neutral process. Learning may contribute both to the strengthening of human forces and of blind societal developments – and societally institutionalised learning efforts in education and other places are, consequently, not just value-neutral technical-economic matters.

References

Adorno, Theodor W. (1972 [1951]): Freudian Theory and the Pattern of Fascist Propaganda. In Theodor W. Adorno: *Soziologische Schriften I, Gesammelte Schriften, Band 8*. Frankfurt a.M.: Suhrkamp.

Adorno, Theodor W. – Frenkel-Brunswik, Else – Levinson, Daniel J. – Sanford, R. Nevitt (1950): *The authoritarian personality*. New York: Harper & Brothers.

Ahrenkiel, Annegrethe – Illeris, Knud – Nielsen, Lizzie Mærsk – Simonsen, Birgitte (1999): *Voksenuddannelse mellem trang og tvang*. København: Roskilde University Press.

Ahrenkiel, Annegrethe – Illeris, Knud (2000): Adult education between emancipation and control. In Knud Illeris (ed.): *Adult Education in the Perspective of the Learners*. Copenhagen: Roskilde University Press.

Alheit, Peter (1994): The Biographical Question as a Challenge to Adult Education. *International Review of Education*, 40.

Alheit, Peter (1995): Biographical Learning. In Peter Alheit et al (eds.): *The Biographical Approach in European Adult Education*. Vienna: ESREA/Verband Wiener Volksbildung.

Allport, Gordon W. (1967): *Pattern and Growth in Personality*. New York: Holt, Rinehart and Winston.

Andersen, Anders Siig – Olesen, Henning Salling – Sommer, Finn M. – Weber, Kirsten (1993): *En oplevelse for livet*. Roskilde: The Adult Education Research Group, Roskilde University.

Andersen, Anders Siig – Andersen, Linda – Hansen, Leif – Larsen, Kirsten – Olesen, Henning Salling – Sommer, Finn M. – Ulriksen, Lars – Weber, Kirsten (1998): *Voksenliv og voksenlæring. Voksne mænd og kvinders uddannelsesdeltagelse og læreprocesser i livshistorisk belysning*. Roskilde: The Adult Education Research Group, Roskilde University.

Andersen, Vibeke – Illeris, Knud – Kjærsgaard, Christian – Larsen, Kirsten – Olesen, Henning Salling – Ulriksen, Lars (1994): *Qualifica-*

tions and living people. Roskilde: The Adult Education Research Group, Roskilde University.

Andersen, Vibeke – Illeris, Knud – Kjærsgaard, Christian – Larsen, Kirsten – Olesen, Henning Salling – Ulriksen, Lars (1996): *General Qualification.* Roskilde: The Adult Education Research Group, Roskilde University.

Antikainen, Ari (1998): In Search of the Meaning and Practices of Life-Long Learning. In Knud Illeris (ed.): *Adult Education in a Transforming Society.* Copenhagen: Roskilde University Press.

Antikainen, Ari – Houtsonen, Jarmo – Kauppila, Juha – Turunen, A. (1996): *Living in a Learning Society: Life-Histories, Identities and Education.* London: Falmer Press.

Antikainen, Ari – Kauppila, Juha (2000): The story of a learner: Educational generations and the future of liberal adult education in Finland. In Knud Illeris (ed.): *Adult Education in the Perspective of the Learners.* Copenhagen: Roskilde University Press.

Argyris, Chris (1992): *On Organizational Learning.* Cambridge, Mass.: Blackwell Publishers.

Argyris, Chris – Schön, Donald A. (1978): *Organizational Learning: A Theory of Action and Perspective.* Reading, Mass.: Addison-Wesley.

Argyris, Chris – Schön, Donald A. (1996): *Organizational Learning II – Theory, Method, and Practice.* Reading, Mass.: Addison-Wesley.

Ausubel, David P. (1968): *Educational Psychology: A Cognitive View.* New York: Holt, Rinehart and Winston.

Bandura, Albert (1977): *Social Learning Theory.* Englewood Cliffs: Prentice-Hall.

Bandura, Albert – Walters, Richard H. (1963): *Social Learning and Personality Development.* New York: Holt, Rinehart and Winston.

Bateson, Gregory (1972): *Steps to an ecology of mind.* San Francisco: Chandler.

Bauer, Mette – Borg, Karin (1986[1976]): *Den skjulte læreplan.* Copenhagen: Unge Pædagoger.

Beck, Ulrich (1992 [1986]): *Risk Society: Towards a New Modernity.* London: SAGE.

Becker-Schmidt, Regina (1987): Dynamik sozialen Lernens. Geschlecterdifferenz und Konflikte aus der Perspektive von Frauen. In Regina Becker-Schmidt & Gudrun-Axeli Knapp: *Geschlechtertrennung – Geschlechterdifferenz – Suchbewegungen sozialen Lernens*. Bonn: J.H.W. Dietz Nachf.

Berliner, Peter – Berthelsen, Jens (1989): Passiv aggression. *Nordisk psykologi*, 4, p. 301-315.

Berlyne, Daniel E. (1960): *Conflict, Arousal and Curiosity*. New York: McGraw-Hill.

Bernstein, Basil (1971): *Class, Codes and Control*. London: Routledge & Kegan Paul.

Bjerg, Jens (1972): *Pædagogisk udviklingsarbejde i folkeskolen*. Roskilde: Roskilde University.

Bjerg, Jens et al (1976): *Pædagogisk udviklingsarbejde – principper og vilkår belyst ved Brovst-projektet 1970-74*. Copenhagen: Munksgaard.

Borg, Vilhelm (1971): *Industriarbejde og arbejderbevidsthed*. Copenhagen: Røde Hane.

Bourdieu, Pierre (1998 [1994]): *Practical Reason: On the Theory of Action*. Cambridge: Polity Press.

Bourdieu, Pierre – Passeron, Jean-Claude (1977 [1970]): *Reproduction in Education, Society and Culture*. London: SAGE.

Bowles, Samuel – Gintis, Herbert (1976): *Schooling in Capitalist America*. New York: Basic Books.

Brookfield, Stephen D. (1986): *Understanding and Facilitating Adult Learning*. Milton Keynes: Open University Press.

Brookfield, Stephen D. (1987): *Developing Critical Thinkers*. Milton Keynes: Open University Press.

Brookfield, Stephen D. (1990): Using Critical Incidents to Explore Learners' Assumptions. In Jack Mezirow et al: *Fostering Critical Reflection in Adulthood*. San Francisco: Jossey-Bass.

Brostrøm, Stig (1977): *Struktureret pædagogik*. Copenhagen: Pædagogisk Landsforbund.

Bruner, Jerome S. (1960): *The Process of Education*. Cambridge, Mass.: Harvard University Press.

Bruner, Jerome S. (1966): *Toward a Theory of Instruction*. Cambridge, Mass.: Harvard University Press.

Bruner, Jerome S. (1996): *The Culture of Education*. Cambridge, Mass.: Harvard University Press.

Brückner, Peter (1972): *Zur Sozialpsychologie des Kapitalismus*. Frankfurt a.M.: Europäische Verlagsanstalt.

Burr, Vivian (1995): *An Introduction to Social Constructionism*. London: Routledge.

Bühler, Charlotte (1933): *Der menschlische Lebenslauf als psychologisches Problem*. Leipzig: Hirzel.

Bühler, Charlotte (1968): The General Structure of the Human Life Cycle. In Charlotte Bühler & Fred Massarik (eds.): *The Course of Human Life*. New York: Springer.

Chodorow, Nancy (1978): *The Reproduction of Mothering: Psychoanalysis and the psychology of gender*. Berkeley: University of California Press.

Christensen, Lone Rahbek (1987): *Hver vore veje*. Copenhagen: Etnologisk Forum.

Christiansen, Frederik Voetmann (1999): Exemplarity and educational planning. In Henning Salling Olesen & Jens Højgaard Jensen (eds.): *Project Studies*. Copenhagen: Roskilde University Press.

Christie, Nils (1971): *Hvis skolen ikke fantes*. Oslo/Copenhagen: Christian Ejlers.

Cole, Michael – Scribner, Sylvia (1978): Introduction. In Lev S. Vygotsky: *Mind in Society: The Development of Higher Psychological Processes*. Cambridge, Mass.: Harvard University Press.

Coleman, James S. – Campbell, Ernest Q. – Hobson, Carol J. – McPartland, James – Mood, Alexander M. – Weinfeld, Frederic D. – York, Robert L. (1966): *Equality of Educational Opportunity*. Washington: National Center for Educational Statistics.

Danish Ministry of Education (1995): *Act on the Folkeskole – The Danish Primary and Lower Secondary School*. Copenhagen: Danish Ministry of Education.

Dausien, Bettina (1998): Biographische Konstruktionen in Widersprüchen. In Kirsten Weber (ed.): *Life History, Gender and Experience*. Roskilde: The Adult Education Research Group, Roskilde University.

Dewey, John (1902): *The Child and the Curriculum*. Chicago: Chicago University Press.

Dewey, John (1916): *Democracy and Education*. New York: Macmillan.

Dewey, John (1938): *Experience and Education*. New York: Collier Books.

Donaldson, Margaret (1986): *Children's minds*. London: Fontana, 2. edition.

Dreyfus, Hubert – Dreyfus, Stuart (1986): *Mind over Machine*. New York: Free Press.

Duncker, Karl (1935): *Zur Psychologie des produktiven Denkens*. Berlin: Springer.

Elkjaer, Bente (1999): In Search of a Social Learning Theory. In Mark Easterby-Smith, John Burgoyne & Luis Araujo (eds.): *Organizational Learning and the Learning Organization*. London: SAGE.

Engeström, Yrjö (1987): *Learning by expanding: An activity-theoretical approach to developmental research*. Helsinki: Orienta-Kunsultit.

Engeström, Yrjö (1993): Developmental studies of work as a testbench of activity theory: The case of primary care medical practice. In Seth Chaikling & Jean Lave (eds.): *Understanding practice – Perspectives on activity and context*. New York: Cambridge University Press.

Engeström, Yrjö (1996a): Developmental work research as educational research. *Nordisk Pedagogik*, 3, p. 131-143.

Engeström, Yrjö (1996b): Development as breaking away and opening up: A challenge to Vygotsky and Piaget. *Swiss Journal of Psychology*, 2-3, p. 126-132.

Erikson, Erik H. (1950): *Childhood and Society*. New York: Norton.

Erikson, Erik H. (1968): *Identity, Youth and Crisis*. New York: Norton.

Erikson, Erik H. (1982): *Life Circle Completed*. New York: Norton.

Eskola, Antti (1971): *Socialpsykologi*. Stockholm: Almqvist & Wiksell.

Festinger, Leon (1957): *A Theory of Cognitive Dissonance*. Stanford: Stanford University Press.

Flavell, John H. (1963): *The Developmental Psychology of Jean Piaget*. New York: Van Nostrand.

Freire, Paulo (1970 [1968]): *Pedagogy of the oppressed*. New York: Seabury.

Freud, Anna (1942 [1936]): *The ego and the mechanisms of defence*. London: Hogarth Press.

Freud, Sigmund (1959 [1921]): *Group Psychology and the Analysis of the Ego*. London: Pelican Freud Library.

Freud, Sigmund (1962 [1927]): *The Future of an Illusion*. London: Hogarth Press.

Freud, Sigmund – Breuer, Joseph (1956 [1895]): *Studies on Hysteria*. London: Pelican Freud Library.

Furth, Hans G. (1981): *Piaget and Knowledge: Theoretical Foundations*. Chicago: University of Chicago Press, 2. edition.

Furth, Hans G. (1987): *Knowledge As Desire*. New York: Columbia University Press.

Gagné, Robert M. (1970): *The Conditions of Learning*. New York: Holt, Rinehart and Winston, 2. edition.

Gergen, Kenneth J. (1994): *Realities and Relationships*. Cambridge, Mass.: Harvard University Press.

Giddens, Anthony (1990): *The Consequences of Modernity*. Stanford: Stanford University Press.

Giddens, Anthony (1991): *Modernity and Self-Identity*. Cambridge: Polity Press.

Giddens, Anthony (1993): *Sociology*. Cambridge: Polity Press, 2. edition.

Goldberg, Arnold (ed.) (1978): *The Psychology of the Self*. New York: International Universities Press.

Gottschalch, Wilfried – Neumann-Schönwetter, Marina – Soukup, Gunther (1971): *Sozialisationsforschung*. Frankfurt a.M.: Fischer.

Greenfield, Patricia – Lave, Jean (1982): Cognitive Aspects of Informal Education. In Daniel A. Wagner & Harold W. Stevenson (eds.):

Cultural Perspectives on Child Development. San Francisco: Freeman and Company.

Greenspan, Stanley I. (1979): Intelligence and Adaptation: An Integration of Psychoanalytic and Piagetian Developmental Psychology. *Psychological Issues,* Monograph 47/48. New York: International Universities Press.

Griffin, Peg – Cole, Michael (1984): Current activity for the future: The Zo-ped. In Barbara Rogoff & James V. Wertsch (eds.): *Children's learning in the 'zone of proximal development'.* San Francisco: Jossey-Bass.

Guilford, John P. (1967): *The Nature of Human Intelligence.* New York: McGraw-Hill.

Gutt, Armin – Salffner, Ruth (1971): *Sozialisation und Sprache.* Frankfurt a.M.: Europäische Verlagsanstalt.

Habermas, Jürgen (1971): *Thesen zur Theorie der Sozialisation.* Frankfurt a.M.: Limit-Druck.

Habermas, Jürgen (1984/87 [1981]): *The theory of communicative action.* Cambridge: Polity Press.

Habermas, Jürgen (1987 [1981]): Lifeworld and system. In Jürgen Habermas: *The Theory of Communicative Action.* Cambridge: Polity Press.

Habermas, Jürgen (1988 [1963]): *Theory and Practice.* Cambridge: Polity Press.

Habermas, Jürgen (1989a [1968]): *Knowledge and human interest.* Cambridge: Polity Press.

Habermas, Jürgen (1989b [1962]): *The structural transformation of the public sphere.* Cambridge: Polity Press.

Hacker, Winfried (1986): *Arbeitspsychologie.* Berlin: VEB Deutscher Verlag der Wissenschaften.

Hacker, Winfried (1998): *Allgemeine Arbeitspsychologie.* Bern: Verlag Hans Huber.

Hansen, Erik Jørgen (1995): *En generation blev voksen.* Copenhagen: Socialforskningsinstituttet.

Hansen, Finn Thorbjørn (1997): *Kunsten at navigere i kaos – om dannelse og identitet i en multikulturel verden.* Vejle: Kroghs Forlag.

Hansen, Kirsten Grønbæk (1998): Er læring mere end situeret praksis? *Dansk pædagogisk tidsskrift,* 2, p. 6-16.

Hauen, Finn van – Strandgaard, Vagn – Kastberg, Bjarne (1995): *Den lærende organisation – om evnen til at skabe kollektiv forandring.* Copenhagen: Industriens Forlag.

Hedegaard, Mariane (1998): Udvikling, lære- og undervisningsvirksomhed eksemplificeret ved en drengs udvikling af motiver. In Niels Jørgen Bisgaard (ed.): *Pædagogiske teorier.* Copenhagen: Billesø & Baltzer.

Hedegaard, Mariane – Hansen, Vagn Rabøl (1992): *En virksom pædagogik: kritik og alternativ praksis.* Århus: Århus Universitetsforlag.

Hegel, Georg Wilhelm Friedrich (1967 [1807]): *The Phenomenology of Mind.* New York: Harper.

Hermansen, Mads (1996): *Læringens univers.* Århus: Klim.

Holzkamp, Klaus (1972): *Kritische Psychologie – Vorbereitende Arbeiten.* Frankfurt a.M.: Fischer.

Holzkamp, Klaus (1983): *Grundlegung der Psychologie.* Frankfurt a.M.: Campus.

Holzkamp, Klaus (1995): *Lernen – Subjektwissenschaftliche Grundlegung.* Frankfurt a.M.: Campus.

Holzkamp-Osterkamp, Ute (1978): Erkenntnis, Emotionalität, Handlungsfähigkeit. *Forum Kritische Psychologie.* 3. Argument Sonderband AS 28. Berlin: Argument-Verlag.

Horkheimer, Max – Adorno, Theodor W. (1944): *Dialectic of Enlightenment.* New York: Social Studies Association.

Højrup, Thomas (1983a): *Det glemte folk – livsformer og centraldirigering.* Hørsholm: Statens Byggeforskningsinstitut.

Højrup, Thomas (1983b): *The concept of Life-mode.* Lund: Ethnologia Scandinavica.

Illeris, Knud (1974): *Problemorientering og deltagerstyring. Oplæg til en alternativ didaktik.* Copenhagen: Munksgaard.

Illeris, Knud (1978): *Motivation i skolen – manipulation eller solidaritet.* Copenhagen: Munksgaard.

Illeris, Knud (1981): *Modkvalificeringens pædagogik.* Copenhagen: Unge Pædagoger.

Illeris, Knud (1984): Erfaringer med erfaringspædagogikken. *Unge Pædagoger,* 2, p. 22-33.

Illeris, Knud (1986): The Use of Projects in University Education as Inspiration for Project Management. In Eric Gabriel (ed): *New Approaches in Project Management.* Zürich: Internet.

Illeris, Knud (1995): *Læring, udvikling og kvalificering.* Roskilde: The Adult Education Research Group, Roskilde University.

Illeris, Knud (1997): The organization of studies at Roskilde University: the concept, practice and problems of project organization. In Roskilde University: *Principles of Education and Research.* Roskilde: Roskilde University.

Illeris, Knud (1998): Adult Learning and Responsibility. In Knud Illeris (ed.):*Adult Education in a Transforming Society.* Copenhagen: Roskilde University Press.

Illeris, Knud (1999): Project work in university studies: Background and current issues. In Henning Salling Olesen & Jens Højgaard Jensen (eds.): *Project Studies.* Copenhagen: Roskilde University Press.

Illeris, Knud (2001): *Adult Education as Mass Education.* Paper for the ESREA Conference: Wider Benefits of Learning. Lisbon 13.-16. September.

Illeris, Knud – Andersen, Vibeke – Kjærsgaard, Christian – Larsen, Kirsten – Olesen, Henning Salling – Ulriksen, Lars (1995): *Almenkvalificering.* Roskilde: The Adult Education research Group, Roskilde University.

Israel, Joachim (1969): *Socialpsykologi.* Stockholm: Svenska Bokförlaget.

Jackson, Philip W. (1990 [1968]): *Life in Classrooms.* New York: Teachers College, Columbia University.

Jacobsen, Bo – Schnack, Karsten – Wahlgren, Bjarne (1980): *Erfaring og undervisning.* Copenhagen: Gyldendal.

James, William (1890): *The Principles of Psychology*. New York: Holt, Rinehart and Winston.

Jansen, Theo – Finger, Mathias – Wildemeersch, Danny (1998): Lifelong Learning for Responsibility: Exploring the Significance of Aesthetic Ratnality for Adult Education. In John Holford – Peter Jarvis – Colin Griffin (eds.): *International Perspectives on Lifelong Learning*. London: Kogan Page.

Jarvis, Peter (1987): *Adult Learning in the Social Context*. New York: Croom Helm.

Jarvis, Peter (1992): *Paradoxes of Learning: on becoming an individual in society*. San Francisco: Jossey-Bass.

Jencks, Christopher – Smith, Marshall – Acland, Henry – Bane, Mary Jo – Cohen, David – Gintis, Herbert – Heyns, Barbara – Michelson, Stephan (1972): *Inequality: A Reassessment of the Effect of Family and Schooling in America*. New York: Basic Books.

Jensen, Johan Fjord (1993): *Livsbuen – Voksenpsykologi og livsaldre*. Copenhagen: Gyldendal.

Joas, Hans (1996 [1992]): *The Creativity of Action*. Cambridge: Polity Press.

Jørgensen, Henning – Lassen, Morten – Lind, Jens – Madsen, Morten (1992): *Medlemmer og meninger*. Aalborg: CARMA, Aalborg University.

Kjærsgaard, Christian (1996): *Kvalifikationskrav og uddannelsesmotivation*. Roskilde: The Adult Education Research Group, Roskilde University.

Knudsen, Herman (1980): *Disciplinering til lønarbejde*. Aalborg: Aalborg Universitetsforlag.

Kohut, Heinz (1977): *The restauration of the self*. New York: International Universities Press.

Kolb, David A. (1984): *Experiential Learning*. Englewood Cliffs: Prentice-Hall.

Krech, David – Crutchfield, Richard S. – Ballachey, Egerton L. (1962): *Individual in society*. New York: McGraw-Hill.

Krovoza, Alfred (1976): *Produktion und Sozialisation*. Frankfurt a.M.: Europäische Verlagsanstalt.

Kupferberg, Feiwel (1996): *Kreativt kaos i projektarbejdet*. Aalborg: Aalborg Universitetsforlag.

Kvale, Steinar (1980): *Spillet om karakterer i gymnasiet*. Copenhagen: Munksgaard.

Lave, Jean – Wenger, Etienne (1991): *Situated Learning: Legitimate Peripheral Participation*. New York: Cambridge University Press.

Leithäuser, Thomas (1976): *Formen des Alltagsbewusstseins*. Frankfurt a.M.: Campus.

Leithäuser, Thomas (1998): The Problem of Authoritarianism: Approaches to the Further Development of a Traditional Concept. In Knud Illeris (ed.): *Adult Education in a Transforming Society*. Copenhagen: Roskilde University Press.

Leithäuser, Thomas – Volmerg, Birgit (1977): Die Entwicklung einer empirischen Forschungsperspektive aus der Theorie des Alltagsbewusstseins. In Thomas Leithäuser et al (eds.): *Entwurf zu einer Empirie des Alltagsbewusstseins*. Frankfurt a.M.: Suhrkamp.

Leontyev, Aleksei N. (1981 [1959]): *Problems of the Development of the Mind*. Moscow: Progress. (Collected manuscripts from the 1930s).

Lipset, David (1980): *Gregory Bateson: The Legacy of a Scientist*. Englewood Cliffs: Prentice-Hall.

Lorenzer, Alfred (1972): *Zur Begründung einer materialistischen Sozialisationstheorie*. Frankfurt a.M.: Suhrkamp.

Luhmann, Niklas (1995 [1984]): *Social Systems*. Stanford: Stanford University Press.

Luria, Aleksander R. (1976 [1974]): *Cognitive Development*. Cambridge, Mass.: Harvard University Press. (Based on an empirical investigation in the 1930s).

Lysgaard, Sverre (1967): *Arbeiderkollektivet*. Oslo: Universitetsforlaget.

Lyotard, Jean-Francois (1984 [1979]): *The Postmodern Condition: A Report on Knowledge*. Manchester: Manchester University Press.

Mahler, Margaret S: – Pine, Fred – Bergman, Anni (1975): *The Psychological Birth of the Human Infant*. New York: Basic Books.

Mager, Robert F. (1961): On the Sequencing of Instructional Content. *Psychological Reports*, 9, p. 405-413. Southern University Press.

Marcuse, Herbert (1955): *Eros and civilization*. Boston: Beacon.

Marcuse, Herbert (1964): *One dimensional man*. London: Routledge & Kegan Paul.

Marx, Karl (1969): Theses on Feuerbach. In Karl Marx & Friedrich Engels: *Selected Works, Volume 1*. Moscow: Progress. (Written in 1845 and first published 1888 by Friedrich Engels).

Maslow, Abraham (1954): *Motivation and Personality*. New York: Harper & Row.

McClelland, David C. – Atkinson, John W. – Clark, Russell A. – Lowell, Edgar L. (1953): *The Achievement Motive*. New York: Appleton-Century-Croft.

Mezirow, Jack (1985): A Critical Theory of Self-Directed Learning. In Stephen D. Brookfield (ed.): *Self-Directed Learning: From Theory to Practice*. San Francisco: Jossey-Bass.

Mezirow, Jack (1990): How Critical Reflection Triggers Transformative Learning. In Jack Mezirow et al: *Fostering Critical Reflection in Adulthood*. San Francisco: Jossey-Bass.

Mezirow, Jack (1991): *Transformative Dimensions of Adult Learning*. San Francisco: Jossey-Bass.

Morsing, Mette (1995): Organisatorisk læring af anden orden – fra en struktur til en proces-orienteret teori om læring. *Virksomhedens strategi og ledelse*, 5, p. 1-28.

Mortimore, Peter – Sammons, Pamela – Stoll, Louise – Lewis, David – Ecob, Russell (1988): *School Matters. The Junior Years*. Wells: Open Books.

Musgrove, Frank (1965): *Youth and the Social Order*. Bloomington: Indiana University Press.

Negt, Oskar (1971 [1968]): *Soziologische Phantasie und exemplarisches Lernen*. Frankfurt a.M.: Europäische Verlagsanstalt.

Negt, Oskar (1976): Schule als Erfahrungsprozess. *Ästhetik und Kommunikation,* 22/23, p. 36-55.

Negt, Oskar – Kluge, Alexander (1993 [1972]): *Public sphere and experience.* Minneapolis, Minn.: University of Minnesota Press.

Nielsen, Harriet Bjerrum – Rudberg, Monica (1989): *Historien om jenter og gutter.* Oslo: Universitetsforlaget.

Nielsen, Harriet Bjerrum – Rudberg, Monica (1994): *Psychological Gender and Modernity.* Oslo: Scandinavian University Press.

Nielsen, Klaus – Kvale, Steinar (eds.)(1997): Apprenticeship: Learning as Social Practice. *Nordisk Pedagogik/Journal of Nordic Educational Research,* 3, Special issue.

Nielsen, Klaus – Kvale, Steinar (eds.)(1999): *Mesterlære – Læring som social praksis.* Copenhagen: Reitzel.

Nissen, Thomas (1970): *Indlæring og pædagogik.* Copenhagen: Munksgaard.

Olesen, Henning Salling (1981): Eksemplariske læreprocesser og arbejderuddannelse. *Unge Pædagoger,* 2, p. 13-26.

Olesen, Henning Salling (1989 [1985]): *Adult Education and Everyday Life.* Roskilde: The Adult Education Research Group, Roskilde University.

Olesen, Henning Salling (1996): Experience, Life History and Biography. In Henning Salling Olesen & Palle Rasmussen (eds.): *Theoretical Issues in Adult Education.* Copenhagen: Roskilde University Press.

Olesen, Henning Salling – Jensen, Jens Højgaard (1999): *Project Studies – a late modern university reform?* Copenhagen: Roskilde University Press.

Olsen, Ole Andkjær – Køppe, Simo (1981): *Freuds psykoanalyse.* Copenhagen: Gyldendal.

Piaget, Jean (1946): *La formation du symbole chez l'enfant.* Neuchâtel: Delachaux et Nestlé.

Piaget, Jean (1951 [1945]): *Play, Dreams and Imitation in Childhood.* New York: Norton.

Piaget, Jean (1968): *Le structuralisme*. Paris: Presse Universitaire de France.

Piaget, Jean (1980): Recent studies in genetic epistemology. *Cahiers de la fondation des archives Jean Piaget,* nr.1.

Polanyi, Michael (1966): *The tacit dimension*. New York: Doubleday.

Reich, Wilhelm (1969 [1933]): *The Mass Psychology of Fascism*. New York: Farrar, Straus & Giroux.

Rogers, Carl R. (1951): *Client-Centered Therapy*. Boston: Houghton-Mifflin.

Rogers, Carl R. (1959): A Theory of Therapy, Personality, and Interpersonal Relationships, as Developed in the Client-Centered Framework. In Sigmund Koch (ed.): *Psychology: A Study of a Science, Vol. III.* New York: McGraw-Hill.

Rogers, Carl R. (1961): *On Becoming a Person*. Boston: Houghton-Mifflin.

Rogers, Carl R. (1969): *Freedom to Learn*. Columbus, Ohio: Charles E. Merrill.

Roskilde University (1997): *Principles of Education and Research*. Roskilde: Roskilde University.

Rutter, Michael – Maughan, Barbara – Mortimore, Peter – Ouston, Janet (1979): *Fifteen Thousand Hours*. London: Open Books.

Schuller, Tom (1997): *Modelling the Lifecourse: Age, Time and Education*. Bremen: Universität Bremen, Ph.D. Thesis.

Schuller, Tom (1998): Age and Generation in Life Course Modelling. In Kirsten Weber (ed.): *Life History, Gender and Experience*. Roskilde: The Adult Education Research Group, Roskilde University.

Schulze, Gerhard (1992): *Die Erlebnisgesellschaft*. Frankfurt a.M.: Campus.

Schön, Donald A. (1983): *The Reflective Practitioner: How Professionals Think in Action*. New York: Basic Books.

Schön, Donald A. (1987): *Educating the Reflective Practitioner*. San Francisco: Jossey-Bass.

Senge, Peter M. (1990): *The Fifth Discipline: The Art and Practice of the Learning Organization*. New York: Doubleday.

Simonsen, Birgitte (1976): *Dansk uddannelsespolitik og planlægning*. Roskilde: RUC-forlag.

Simonsen, Birgitte (1998): Individualisering og demokrati i ungdoms- og voksenuddannelserne. In Knud Illeris, Birgitte Simonsen & Annegrethe Ahrenkiel: *Udspil om læring og didaktik*. Copenhagen: Roskilde University Press.

Simonsen, Birgitte (2000): New young people, new forms of consciousness, new educational methods. In Knud Illeris (ed.): *Adult Education in the Perspective of the Learners*. Copenhagen: Roskilde University Press.

Simonsen, Birgitte – Illeris, Knud (1989): *De skæve køn*. Copenhagen: Unge Pædagoger.

Torvinen, Liisa (1996): Developing orientation in business education. *Nordisk Pedagogik*, 3, p. 144-154.

Usher, Robin (1993): Experiential Learning or Learning from Experience: Does it Make a Difference? In David Boud et al (eds.): *Using Experience for Learning*. Buckingham: Open University.

Usher, Robin (1998): Adult Education and Lifelong Learning in Postmodernity. In Knud Illeris (ed.): *Adult Education in a Transforming Society*. Copenhagen: Roskilde University Press.

Usher, Robin (2000): Impossible identities, unstable boundaries: Managing experience differently. In Knud Illeris (ed.): *Adult Education in the Perspective of the Learners*. Copenhagen: Roskilde University Press.

Usher, Robin – Kosmidou, Chrysoula (1992): Experiential Learning and the Autonomous Subject. In Danny Wildemeersch & Theo Jansen (eds.): *Adult Education, Experiential Learning and Social Change*. Haag: VUGA.

Usher, Robin – Bryant, Ian – Johnston, Rennie (1997): *Adult education and the postmodern challenge*. London: Routledge.

Vester, Michael (1969): Solidarisierung als historische Möglichkeit. *Heidelberger Blätter,* 14-16.

Volmerg, Birgit (1990): Arbeit als erlebte Wirklichkeit. *Psychosozial,* 43, p. 80-91.

Volmerg, Ute (1976): Zur Verhältnis von Produktion und Sozialisation am Beispiel industrieller Lohnarbeit. In Thomas Leithäuser & Walter R. Heinz (eds.): *Produktion, Arbeit, Sozialisation.* Frankfurt a.M.: Suhrkamp.

Volpert, Walter (1975): *Lohnarbeitspsychologie – Berufliche Sozialisation: Emanzipation zur Anpassung.* Frankfurt a.M.: Fischer.

Volpert, Walter (1987): Psychische Regulation von Arbeitstätigkeiten. I Joseph Rutenfranz & Uwe Kleinbeck (eds.): *Arbeitspsychologie,* volume 1. Göttingen: Verlag für Psychologie.

Vygotsky, Lev S. (1978): *Mind in Society: The Development of Higher Psychological Processes.* Cambridge, Mass.: Harvard University Press.

Vygotsky, Lev S. (1986 [1934]): *Thought and Language.* Cambridge, Mass.: MIT Press.

Wackerhausen, Steen (1997): The scholastic paradigm and apprenticeship. *Nordisk Pedagogik,* 3, p. 195-203.

Wartofsky, Marx W. (1979): *Models: Representation and scientific understanding.* Dordrecht: Reidel.

Webb, Thomas W. (1997): Transaktionspædagogik og Dewey. *Dansk pædagogisk tidsskrift,* 1, p. 24-31.

Webb, Thomas W. – Nielsen, Jørgen Lerche (1996): Experiential Pedagogy. In Henning Salling Olesen & Palle Rasmussen (eds.): *Theoretical Issues in Adult Education.* København: Roskilde University Press.

Weber, Kirsten (1995): *Ambivalens og erfaring: Mod et kønsdifferentieret læringsbegreb.* Roskilde: The Adult Education Research Group, Roskilde University.

Weber, Kirsten (1998): Towards a New Understanding of Adult Learning. In Kirsten Weber (ed.): *Life History, Gender and Experience.* Roskilde: The Adult Education Research Group, Roskilde University.

Wenger, Etienne (1998): *Communities of Practice: Learning, Meaning, and Identity.* Cambridge, Mass.: Cambridge University Press.

Wildemeersch, Danny (1991): Learning from regularity, irregularity and responsibility. *International Journal of Lifelong Education,* 2, p. 151-158.

Wildemeersch, Danny (1992): Ambiguities of experiential learning and critical pedagogy. In Danny Wildemeersch & Theo Jansen (eds.): *Adult education, experiential learning and social change – the postmodern challenge.* Haag: VUGA.

Wildemeersch, Danny (1998): Social learning as social change – social change as social learning. In Knud Illeris (ed.): *Adult Education in a Transforming Society.* Copenhagen: Roskilde University Press.

Wildemeersch, Danny (1999): Paradoxes of Social Learning. In Henning Salling Olesen & Jens Højgaard Jensen (eds.): *Project Studies.* Copenhagen: Roskilde University Press.

Wildemeersch, Danny (2000): Lifelong Learning and the Significance of the Interpretive Professional. In Knud Illeris (ed.): *Adult Education in the Perspective of the Learners.* Copenhagen: Roskilde University Press.

Wolff, Peter H. (1960): The Developmental Psychologies of Jean Piaget and Psychoanalysis. *Psychological Issues,* Monograph 5. New York: International Universities Press.

Ziehe, Thomas (1978): Subjektiv betydning og erfaring. *Kontext,* 35, p. 82-98.

Ziehe, Thomas (1980): Skoleforsøget Glocksee. *Kontext,* 40, p. 48-64.

Ziehe, Thomas (1985): Vorwärts in die 50er Jahre? In Dieter Baacke & Wilhelm Heitmeyer (eds.): *Neue Widersprüche. Jugendliche in den 80er Jahren.* Munich: Juventa.

Ziehe, Thomas (1991): Om prisen på selv-relationel viden – Afmystificeringseffekter for pædagogik, skole og identitetsdannelse. In Jens Christian Jacobsen (ed.): *Refleksive læreprocesser.* Copenhagen: Politisk revy.

Ziehe, Thomas (1998): Adieu til halvfjerdserne! In Jens Bjerg (ed.):
Pædagogik – en grundbog til et fag. Copenhagen: Reitzel.

Ziehe, Thomas – Stubenrauch, Herbert (1982): *Plädoyer für
ungewöhnliches Lernen.* Reinbek: Rowohlt.

Ølgaard, Bent: Gregory Bateson: En præsentation. *Udkast,* 3, p. 245-
273.

The Author

Knud Illeris is a Professor of Educational Research at Roskilde University, founded in 1972 as an alternative to the traditional University of Copenhagen. For almost 30 years the author has been a well-known, trendsetting and sometimes also controversial figure in Danish and Scandinavian educational research, debate and development. His professional background is in psychology and he is a very productive researcher and author on topics such as learning and qualification theory, motivation, curriculum design and development, youth psychology, and vocational youth and adult education. Since 2001 he has been the Research Director of Learning Lab Denmark's consortium for research in Workplace Learning.

Index of Names

A

Adorno, Theodor W. 127, 200
Alheit, Peter 96, 164, 205, 236
Allport, Gordon W. 93
Antikainen, Ari 205, 224
Argyris, Chris 162-164, 171, 193-194, 232
Ausubel, David P. 31, 123, 150

B

Bandura, Albert 122, 232
Bateson, Gregory 45, 48, 52-58, 60, 138, 162, 193-194, 231
Bauer, Mette 187-188
Beck, Ulrich 46, 92, 235
Becker-Schmidt, Regina 129, 132-135, 139, 147, 154-155, 164, 234, 236
Berliner, Peter 103
Berlyne, Daniel E. 83
Berthelsen, Jens 103
Bjerg, Jens 34-35, 161, 163, 168, 171
Borg, Karin 187-188
Borg, Vilhelm 198
Bourdieu, Pierre 185-186, 189
Breuer, Joseph 164-165
Brookfield, Stephen 47, 109-111, 231
Brückner, Peter 123, 128
Bruner, Jerome S. 63-64, 123, 156, 160, 208, 232
Bühler, Charlotte 206, 213, 236

C

Chodorow, Nancy 210
Christensen, Lone Rahbek 218
Christie, Nils 185
Cole, Michael 54-55, 137

D

Dewey, John 38, 51, 147-153, 159, 231
Dreyfus, Hubert 120, 165-166, 171, 173, 181-182
Dreyfus, Stuart 120, 165-166, 171, 173, 181-182
Duncker, Karl 47
Dupont, Søren 10

E

Engeström, Yrjö 11, 47-48, 52-60, 138, 140, 173, 192-193, 232
Erikson, Erik H. 166-168, 172, 206, 208, 213, 231

F

Feuerbach, Ludwig 19, 235
Flavell, John H. 27, 33
Freire, Paulo 28, 59, 123, 154
Freud, Anna 104
Freud, Sigmund 18-19, 27, 65-68, 73, 75-83, 104-105, 108, 139, 147, 164-166, 171, 200, 208, 230-231, 238
Furth, Hans G. 27, 31, 64-69, 72-83, 105, 166, 231, 238

G

Gagné, Robert M. 63-64
Gergen, Kenneth J. 125, 235, 239
Giddens, Anthony 27, 46, 92, 186, 207, 218, 235
Greenfield, Patricia 178-179
Greenspan, Stanley I. 65
Griffin, Peg 54
Guilford, John P. 42

H

Habermas, Jürgen 128

Hacker, Winfried 191, 232

Hansen, Kirsten Grønbæk 51, 113, 165, 185, 190

Hanson, Finn Thorbjørn 113

Hegel, Georg Wilhelm Friedrich 150

Hermansen, Mads 50, 53, 121

Holzkamp, Klaus 138-140, 232, 236

Holzkamp-Osterkamp, Ute 70-72, 74, 138, 236

Horkheimer, Max 127

Højrup, Thomas 218

J

Jackson, Philip W. 187

Jarvis, Peter 99, 123-124, 235

Jensen, Johan Fjord 166, 168-171, 206-207, 222

K

Kant, Immanuel 150

Kjærsgaard, Christian 196

Kolb, David A. 37-42, 77, 124, 135, 145, 159, 163, 169-172, 206, 230

Krovoza, Alfred 128

Kupferberg, Feiwel 58

Kvale, Steinar 177, 180, 188-189

Køppe, Simo 78-79

L

Lave, Jean 140, 176-180, 184, 236

Leithäuser, Thomas 11, 104-107, 109-112, 128, 139, 147, 200, 205, 234

Leontjev, Aleksei N. 48-49, 138, 165, 192, 232

Lewin, Kurt 38, 159, 163

Lorenzer, Alfred 67, 123, 128-132, 139, 147, 205, 209, 234

Luhmann, Niklas 46, 93, 236

Luria, Aleksander R. 48, 165

Lyotard, Jean-Francois 111

M

Mager, Robert F 100

Mahler, Margaret 210

Marcuse, Herbert 127

Marx, Karl 19, 56, 235, 239

Maslow, Abraham 93, 203

Mezirow, Jack 40, 46-47, 58-59, 94, 109-112, 162, 164, 231

Morsing, Mette 195, 197

Mortimore, Peter 187

N

Negt, Oskar 128, 147, 150-155, 164, 197-198, 234

Nielsen, Birger Steen 10

Nielsen, Harriet Bjerrum 210

Nissen, Thomas 32-33, 36, 42, 47, 94, 161, 163-164, 230

O

Olesen, Henning Salling 151-152, 197-199, 205

Olsen, Ole Andkjær 78-79

P

Passeron, Jean-Claude 185

Piaget, Jean 17-19, 23, 27-33, 36-38, 41-42, 46-47, 49, 53, 64-80, 82, 94, 105, 112, 117, 122, 125, 129-131, 138, 145, 150, 159, 161-162, 164, 166, 168, 170-172, 194, 208, 211-212, 214, 230-231, 238

Polanyi, Michael 178

R

Reich, Wilhelm 200
Rogers, Carl R. 35-36, 59, 64, 93-94, 164, 230
Rousseau, Jean-Jacques 212
Rudberg, Monica 210

S

Schön, Donald A. 40, 47, 159, 163, 166, 182, 193-194, 232
Schuller, Tom 160, 169, 171-172
Senge, Peter 195, 198
Simonsen, Birgitte 10, 185, 215, 218, 222

T

Taba, Hilda 236

U

Ulriksen, Lars 10
Usher, Robin 11, 111-113, 125, 168, 218, 236

V

Vester, Michael 200
Volmerg, Birgit 105, 107

Volmerg, Ute 196
Volpert, Walter 191, 232
Vygotsky, Lev S. 17-18, 23, 28, 48, 50-51, 54-57, 122, 137, 164, 232

W

Wackerhausen, Steen 189
Wartofsky, Marx 56-57
Watt, James 212
Webb, Thomas W. 40, 147, 149-150, 155
Weber, Kirsten 10, 134, 204-205
Wenger, Etienne 11, 27, 121, 132, 140-142, 155, 159, 176-177, 179-180, 184, 225, 236
Wildemeersch, Danny 11, 132, 135-137, 140, 155, 235
Wolff, Peter H. 65

Z

Ziehe, Thomas 46, 78, 91-92, 113, 128, 147, 153, 209, 234

Ø

Ølgaard, Bent 53-54

Index of Subjects

A

accommodation 30-31, 33, 37, 42, 47, 53, 57-60, 69, 71, 74-77, 79-80, 82-83, 85, 94-95, 105, 108, 145, 194, 228

achievement motive 204

acquisition 9, 16, 18, 20, 22, 25, 34, 40, 55, 59, 63-65, 68, 90, 99, 117, 124, 132, 170, 176, 178, 181, 204, 211, 227-229

acquisition process 9, 16, 20, 25, 99, 211, 227

action perspective 156

activity 48-51, 56-57, 70, 76, 94, 120-121, 124, 137-138, 143, 146, 156, 176, 184, 192, 227, 232-233

adaptability 89

adaptation 29-30, 43, 48, 58, 60, 69, 163

adjustment 14, 29, 43, 70, 98, 122, 163, 168, 178, 187

adult education 58, 109-111, 124, 132, 135, 187, 219-222, 231

adult learning 124

adulthood 109-110, 169, 207-208, 212, 216, 218, 222-226

aesthetic 127, 136

affective 48, 63-64, 67, 69-72, 74, 77, 80-81, 84-85, 113, 131

afterthought 46-47

age 29, 66, 68-69, 72, 77, 161, 169, 206-209, 211-214, 219, 222, 226, 229

ageing 16-17, 24, 172, 174, 229

aggression 78, 81, 83, 102-103, 114

alienation 82, 127

ambivalence 132-135, 144, 146, 218

analytical thinking 88

anger 81

angst 107

animal experiments 32

apprenticeship 175, 177, 179-181, 183-184, 201

artificial intelligence 181-182

assessment 47, 60, 188

assimilation 29-33, 37, 42, 53, 57, 59, 69, 72, 75-77, 79-80, 82, 84-85, 105, 145, 194, 229

assumption 129, 199, 230

attention 36, 64, 71, 123, 128, 153, 164, 182, 187, 191-192, 195, 211, 239

authoritarian 54, 127, 180, 200

autonomy 66, 210-211

B

banking education 28

behaviouristic 27, 122, 138

biographicity 93, 96, 98, 229

biography 96, 164

blocking 102, 104-105, 114, 184, 229

C

capacity 17, 65-68, 74, 83-84, 88-89, 120, 148, 173, 195, 198, 203, 207-208

capitalist 19, 150, 183-184, 188, 192, 239

capitalistic 106, 149, 151-152, 183, 185

career 156, 171, 179, 188, 190, 213, 215, 217-218, 222, 224, 232

catharsis 164-165

challenge 98, 103, 108, 160, 220

change of perspective 88

chaos 113

childhood 59, 81, 109, 166, 169-171, 207-212, 215-217, 224

choice 18, 27, 34, 52, 112, 121, 136, 215, 217, 221

cognitive 17-18, 20, 22-23, 25, 27-31, 33-37, 40, 43, 46, 59, 61, 63-65, 67-75, 77, 80-82, 84-85, 87, 89, 91, 95, 97, 105, 113, 117-118, 124, 130, 145-146, 153, 157, 161, 166, 168-169, 175, 203, 207-208, 211, 216, 228-234, 238

cognitive dimension 22-23, 27, 37, 43, 117, 146

cognitive dissonance 46

collective 48, 57, 108, 151, 163, 175-176, 188, 195-202, 225, 234

D

death drive 76-79

defence 85, 100, 103-104, 108-109, 111, 113-114, 117, 134, 184, 219-220

defensive accommodation 82, 85

delearning 173

dementia 223

democracy 91, 102

democratic 102, 152, 155

desire 45, 65, 67, 75, 83, 195, 203, 226

development process 37, 44, 130-131

development theory 76-77, 80

developmental psychology 63-64, 132, 206, 231

dialectic 78, 127, 143, 150-151

differentiation 28, 34, 42, 70

dimension 18-20, 22-23, 25, 27, 37, 40-41, 43, 57, 74, 77, 117-119, 140, 142, 145-146, 178, 227

disciplining 186, 188

disposition 66

dissociation 30, 35, 44

distorting assimilation 105

distortion 104-105, 114, 152, 229

divergent 42-44, 72, 228

diversity 30, 39, 42, 71, 106-107

division 64-65, 67, 106, 111, 138, 208, 238

double bind 53-54, 56-57, 193

double loop 162, 164, 171, 193, 232

drive 67-68, 75-79, 89, 104

dynamic 28, 68, 74, 77-78, 85, 159, 194, 204

E

educational planning 13, 22

ego 67, 78, 94, 200

elaboration 15, 32, 47, 95, 98, 122, 138, 140, 159, 177, 192, 206, 229

emancipatory 109, 128

emotional dimension 20, 22-23, 74, 117, 146

emotions 18, 20-21, 63, 65-66, 68, 70-74, 85, 118, 138, 175, 178, 239

emotionally obsessed 81, 118, 228

empathy 101

energy 18, 20, 36, 47, 60, 74-75, 78-81, 83-84, 88, 97, 105, 108, 114, 118, 134, 200, 203, 208, 223, 230

engagement 142

equilibrium 29, 42, 75, 166

error 101

everyday consciousness 104-105, 107-109, 111-112, 114-115, 117, 128, 134, 178, 234

everyday learning 175, 178

everyday life 13, 38, 83, 102, 106-107, 110, 133, 178, 200-201, 204, 229 exemplary 154-155

exemplarity 154, 156

existential 81, 135, 166, 168, 222

expansive learning 48

expectation 110

experiential learning 37, 145, 157, 159

experiential pedagogy 147, 150, 152-153, 155-156

experimentation 38, 41

expertise 165, 171, 181-182

extension 30, 34, 41-42, 51, 59, 105, 123, 127, 130, 132, 136, 143, 147, 194, 206, 219, 234

extensionality 186

F

family 96, 133, 171, 187, 208, 213, 216-218, 222

feedback 53

flexibility 14, 35, 89, 95, 113, 220, 222

Frankfurt School 23, 105, 126-129, 132, 139, 147, 150, 164, 234

free school 152

further education 188, 214

G

gender identity 210

gender role 59, 213

gender theory 132

general qualification 88

genetic 17, 87, 239

goal-directed 24, 49, 51, 70, 90, 120-121, 124, 126, 136, 139, 178-179, 184, 221, 226

grading 13, 21, 185, 188, 200

group 19, 89, 122-123, 128, 136, 198-200, 202, 205, 235

growth 148, 152, 170-172, 212-213

H

habits of expectation 110

Hanover School 126, 128, 139, 152, 164, 234

harmonisation 104

harmony 138, 195, 222, 226

history 27, 71, 94, 129, 137, 139, 163, 204-205, 218, 224

homogeneity 222

humanism 148

humanistic 35, 64, 93, 128, 215

hurt 115, 216

hysteria 165

I

id 67

ideal 51, 93, 111, 128, 149, 156, 161, 216

identification 137, 206

identity 46, 59-60, 68, 87, 90, 92, 95, 97, 109, 113, 131, 136, 141-142, 144, 166, 168, 188, 196, 205, 207, 210, 212-216, 218, 224, 226, 229

identity confusion 168

identity development 196

identity formation 68, 168, 213-216

ideological 164, 185

imagination 88, 90, 131, 164

imitation 66, 120, 124, 143, 179, 181, 227

impoverishment 108, 137

imprint 76, 119

impulse 105, 107, 229

independence 14, 69, 81, 95, 101, 188, 215

indignation 103

individualistic 93, 111, 136, 149

individuality 89, 91, 97, 136, 224

individuation 30-31, 210, 212, 225-226

industrial sociology 192
informal learning 178-179, 183, 201
initiative 14, 148, 206, 221
insight 15, 56, 73, 180
institutional reflexivity 92
institutionalised learning 14, 24, 45, 88, 184, 232, 239
instrumental 128, 180, 188, 193
integration 118, 171, 181, 206, 228, 238
intellectual 33, 64, 69, 88-89, 92, 97
intelligence 17, 42, 69, 130, 165, 181-182
intention 9, 41, 51, 232
interaction process 9, 15-16, 20, 22, 25, 99, 154, 225
internalisation 19, 67
interplay 20, 77, 150
interpretation 43, 53, 57, 66, 78, 89, 98, 100, 110, 118, 127, 130, 204-206, 213, 225
intimacy 210-211, 216
intuitive 67
involvement 94, 121, 143, 152, 205
isolation 104, 154, 201

K
know-how 181
knowing-in-action 182
knowledge-constitutive interest 128

L
late modern 93, 229
learning by addition 29
learning by expanding 48, 52, 54, 57
learning dimension 18-19, 23, 27, 37, 43, 77, 117, 140, 142, 146, 178
learning in practice 175, 183, 191, 236-237

learning jumps 159, 163-165, 172-173
learning model 37, 41, 122, 159
learning process 19-20, 24, 32-34, 36, 38, 41, 52, 55, 84, 123, 126, 142, 160, 204, 208, 227, 239
learning psychology 14, 16, 18, 21, 32, 45, 63, 99, 163
learning result 16, 20, 73, 175, 201, 227
learning space 103, 191, 193, 197, 232
learning theory 9-10, 27, 29, 31, 37, 48, 52-54, 57-58, 64, 112-114, 124, 127, 132, 138, 140-143, 145, 161, 177, 192-195, 227, 230, 236-237
learning to learn 45, 60, 195, 198
legitimate peripheral participation 177, 179-180, 201
legitimising 92, 185
leisure time 106, 187
levelling 104
libidinal 45, 65, 67, 75, 78, 84, 188, 203, 221, 223, 226
libido 83
life course 80, 92, 95, 136, 160, 164, 166, 169, 171-172, 174, 204, 206, 208, 217
life fulfilment 67, 74-77, 80-81, 83-85, 88, 97, 101-102, 108, 144, 203
life mode 218
life phase 217
life situation 204
life span 166, 168, 204, 206, 208, 213, 216
life turn 170, 207, 222, 226
lifelong learning 220, 223
lifestyle 95, 208, 213-214
lifeworld 128
limitation 63, 81, 132, 144, 154
logic 30, 38, 76-77, 129-130

M

management 67, 128, 146, 181, 193, 195-197, 211, 216

market society 136, 138, 225, 239

marxist 19, 123, 127, 129, 152, 196

mass psychology 197, 200

mass-communication 107

materialism 129, 165

maths 73, 100, 102, 190

maturation 16-17, 24, 129, 172

maturity 66, 212, 215, 222

meaning 9, 15, 18, 45-46, 56, 59, 67, 75, 91, 106, 109-110, 113, 125-126, 141-142, 144, 147, 173, 176, 198-199

mechanical learning 32

mechanisms of defence 104, 108, 113, 220

media-transmitted 143

memory 15, 228

meta-cognition 47

meta-learning 45, 47, 57-58, 60, 74

mirroring 46, 49, 94-95, 97

misdevelopment 166

misknowledge 100

mislearning 99-101, 114

model 37-38, 41-42, 52, 54, 68, 120, 122, 135-136, 141-142, 159-163, 165-174, 181-182, 193-194, 203, 206, 230, 232

moderate 180

modernisation 92, 185

modernity 90-93, 113, 128, 186, 216-217, 221, 224

motivation 36, 44, 58-59, 61, 69-70, 73, 79, 83, 88, 90, 96-97, 108, 196-197, 201-203, 206, 223, 225, 236

motivational dimension 25

motivational psychology 83, 203-204

motivational qualifications 89

motor 17-18, 34, 187, 211

N

narcissism 200

need 20, 36, 45, 75, 79, 106, 108, 115, 126, 180, 187, 189-190, 198-199, 201, 212-213, 220, 222, 224, 238

O

object 13, 48-50, 66-67, 75, 131, 150, 192

object reflection 48-50, 192

objective 48, 124, 126-127, 134, 204

obligation 58, 136, 149, 186-187, 214

observation 38, 41, 45, 71, 89, 179

obsessed 66, 73, 81, 118, 190, 228

obsession 73, 84

offensive 82, 85, 108, 228

offensive accommodation 82

old age 169, 207, 222, 226

on-the-job training 183

openness 35, 89, 113, 115, 144

operational 29, 214

oppression 68, 133

organisation development 142, 192, 194

organisational learning 48, 162, 191, 194, 197, 232

organisational psychology 47-8, 162

organism 52, 70-71, 76

P

paradigm 122, 189

parents 81, 186, 208-210

participant direction 156

participation 91, 121, 142-144, 146, 177, 179-180, 183, 190, 196, 201, 227 passive 35, 103, 120, 154

pedagogical 50, 58, 79, 92, 103, 113, 123, 137, 147, 152, 155-156, 158, 161, 187, 215

pedagogy 32, 40, 59, 99, 123, 147, 149-- 150, 152-153, 155-156, 179, 212

perception 36, 40, 44, 56-57, 70, 73, 75, 83, 88-89, 94, 96-98, 102, 119- 120, 129, 143, 145-147, 177, 211, 217, 227

personal development 57, 64, 82, 87- 91, 95-98, 102, 173, 213, 225, 237

personality 35, 63-65, 67, 77, 80, 87- 88, 90, 93-95, 97, 112, 125, 127, 130-131, 192, 197, 200, 228-229

personality psychology 63, 87

perversity 80

phase 161, 165-166, 168, 206-207, 212, 216-217, 222

phobia 105, 114

phylogenesis 52

planning 13, 22

pleasure principle 66-68, 83

post-modern 111-113, 115, 117

post-modernity 113

postmodernist 111, 168, 236

power 50-51, 69-70, 108, 127, 135, 142, 149, 176, 184, 186, 188, 195, 239

power relationships 195

practice learning 142, 175, 179, 182- 184, 190-191, 201, 218, 233, 236- 237

practice shock 190

precondition 55, 66, 82, 103, 106, 184, 215

presupposition 197

problem orientation 156

problem situation 56, 60, 166, 181

problem solving 47, 50, 88, 136

professional competence 217

professional learning 171

professionalism 182

programmed learning 34

progressive 34, 80, 109, 147, 152, 173

project work 58, 154, 156, 158

projection 104

psychoanalysis 129, 139

psychoanalytical 18, 65, 94, 104, 127, 147, 152, 165

psychodynamic 18-19, 25, 37, 72, 83- 84, 87, 89, 228, 230-232, 234

psychological energy 18, 20, 47, 60, 74- 75, 79-80, 83, 108, 118, 200, 223, 230

psychological structure 107

psychosexual 66, 166

punishment 54

pupil role 221, 226

Q

qualification 16-17, 24, 88, 90-91, 121, 137, 171, 185, 196

qualification requirements 88, 91, 196

R

rationality 106, 128, 139

reaction 47, 76, 82, 105

readiness 30, 35

readiness for change 220

reality principle 66, 68, 83

reality testing 134, 164

reconstruction 30-31, 35-36, 43-44, 74, 77, 80, 82, 85, 228

reduction 104, 151

reflecting 107, 192, 216, 227

reflection 45-50, 58, 60, 74, 92, 95, 97, 110, 135, 138, 181-182, 192, 228

reflection-in-action 47, 182
reflexivity 46, 87, 90-98, 113, 115, 117,
    134, 136-137, 144, 216, 228-229
reflexivity of modernity 92
reflexivity of the body 92
regression 78, 104
regulation 81, 192
rejection 28, 99, 104-105, 114, 229
religion 56, 139
reorganisation 35, 44, 81, 191, 220-221
repression 81-82, 102, 104, 106-107,
    128, 147, 188
resistance 23, 80-83, 85, 88, 97, 100-
    104, 108, 114, 117, 128, 134, 144,
    184, 188, 203, 209, 227, 229
resistance potential 80-81, 83, 85, 88,
    97, 102, 108, 114, 128, 203, 227
response 45, 52, 70, 76, 82-83, 122,
    134, 180
responsibility 14, 89, 91, 101, 135-137,
    163, 183-184, 186, 202, 215-217,
    219-221, 225-226
restrictive 77, 79, 82, 84, 96, 102, 104,
    114, 228
restrictive assimilation 82
reconstruction 30-31, 35-36, 43-44, 74,
    77, 80, 82, 85, 228
rigidity 34
role 13, 17, 50, 59, 76, 87, 110, 120,
    124, 133, 143, 147, 154, 171, 175,
    180, 187-188, 196, 209, 212-213,
    221, 226
rote learning 34, 90
rule 71, 73, 88, 108, 176, 201-202, 214,
    219, 221

S
scheme 30, 32
scholastic 180, 189, 232

school learning 35, 139, 181, 184, 190,
    201, 232
school obligation 186
scientific concepts 50-51
self-actualization 93
self-comprehension 92, 95, 102, 190,
    193, 211, 213
self-confidence 89, 95
self-image 59
selfishness 136
self-perception 188
self-referential 93
self-reflection 46, 91, 93, 97, 228
self-regulation 144
sensibility 89, 95
sensitivity 35
service-mindedness 220
sets of assumptions 109-110, 115
sexuality 75, 211, 216
significant learning 35-36, 59, 64, 94,
    146, 164, 205
single loop 162, 193
situated learning 20, 140, 176-178,
    180-181, 201
skill 18, 179
skills learning 34, 90
sociability 89, 95
social constructionism 124-125, 140,
    144, 239
social dimension of learning 19, 57,
    117, 140, 142
social learning 117, 120, 122-123, 125,
    132-137, 140-141, 143-144, 154-
    155, 199, 225, 232
social psychology 19, 111, 123, 127-128
social responsibility 135-136
socialisation 16-17, 19, 24, 46, 67, 109,
    117, 123-124, 126-129, 131-132,
    135-136, 143-144, 180, 187, 191,

210, 215, 233-234, 236

socialisation theory 19, 46, 126-129, 233-234

socialist 155

sociality 154, 238-239

societal dimension 19, 25, 117, 119

sociological imagination 88, 164

sociology 127, 192, 218

solidarity 156

sorting 103, 185

spiral model 159-160

stabilisation 68, 77

stage 29, 37-38, 53, 78, 131, 135, 160, 165-168, 170-171, 174, 206, 208, 210, 214

storage 196, 220

structure 9, 19, 21, 23, 30, 41, 49, 63, 69, 71-72, 80, 91, 106-107, 110, 130, 132, 160, 166, 172, 193, 204, 231

student-centered 35, 64

subjective 58, 70, 131, 134, 139-140, 146, 151, 153, 157, 192, 196, 202-204

subjectivity 130, 139-140

subject-object-dialectic 204

subject-oriented 43

superego 67

survival 28, 43, 74, 78, 81, 83-84, 220, 224, 227

symbol formation 66-68

symbolic violence 186

system theoretical 52, 93

system theory 236

systematic 32, 34, 50, 68, 88, 112, 205

T

tacit learning 178, 201

teacher-directed 51

teacher-controlled 51, 54

team learning 198

tension field 19-20, 118, 123, 227, 230, 232-233, 236-238

the learning organisation 191, 194-195, 198, 233

the self 35, 46, 77, 94-95, 97, 111-112, 170-171, 230

thematisation 108, 110, 134

theme-horizon-schemes 107-108, 112, 115

theory of instruction 64

therapy 35, 90

third age 222

time structure 106-107

tolerance 87, 101, 134

tradition 18, 48, 50-51, 54, 94, 105, 121, 137-140, 146-147, 150, 152, 155, 175, 179, 184, 189, 192, 198, 222, 232

transcend 53, 56, 64, 134, 163, 173, 182

transcendent 10, 30, 44, 58, 72, 102, 108, 111, 114-115, 138, 163, 191, 194, 200, 221

transcendent learning 30, 102, 108, 111, 200

transfer potential 73

transformative learning 45, 57-61, 74, 94, 109, 164, 229

transitional learning 164

transmission 119-120, 124, 126, 137, 143, 227

U

uncertainty 13-14, 16, 113, 115

unconscious 68, 71, 110, 131

uneasiness 191

unemployment 220

upper secondary school 188, 214

V

vicarious learning 122
vocational 88-91, 156, 179, 181, 189, 214
vocational training 179, 189
vulnerability 113, 115

W

wage work 133, 185-186, 188-189, 195
work psychology 191
working life 24, 229

Y

youth 78, 91, 128, 153, 166, 168-169, 187, 207, 212-216, 218-221, 224-226
youth education 128, 214, 220-221

Z

zone of proximal development 50-51, 54-55, 57, 164